review
by

Chalmers Johnson

Curious
LIVES

Also by Richard Bach

Stranger to the Ground

Biplane

Nothing by Chance

Jonathan Livingston Seagull

A Gift of Wings

Illusions: The Adventures of a Reluctant Messiah

There's No Such Place as Far Away

The Bridge across Forever

One

Running from Safety

Out of My Mind

Messiah's Handbook

Curious
LIVES

Adventures from the Ferret Chronicles

Richard Bach

HAMPTON ROADS
PUBLISHING COMPANY, INC.

Cover design by Marjoram Productions
Cover star photograph © Comstock.com;
ferret and great ferret constellation © Anne Dunn Louque.

Hampton Roads Publishing Company, Inc.
1125 Stoney Ridge Road
Charlottesville, VA 22902

434-296-2772
fax: 434-296-5096
e-mail: hrpc@hrpub.com
www.hrpub.com

If you are unable to order this book from your local
bookseller, you may order directly from the publisher.
Call 1-800-766-8009, toll-free.

Library of Congress Cataloging-in-Publication Data

Bach, Richard.
    Curious lives : adventures from "The ferret chronicles" / Richard Bach.
        p. cm.
    Summary: A collection of five novels featuring ferret protagonists,
These are tales about courage, sacrifice, heroism, creativity, and finding what matters
most in life.
    ISBN 1-57174-457-6 (acid-free paper)
    1. Ferrets—Fiction. 2.
Fantasy fiction, American. I. Title.
    PS3552.A255C87 2005
    813'.54—dc22
                                        2005019754

10 9 8 7 6 5 4 3 2 1
Printed on acid-free paper in Canada

"I live for hard-bitten journalism that seeks to shatter the coziness of corporate military power"

— NIK NOVAK

Contents

Foreword

I TRAVELED THE KINGDOM of Oz when I was a kid, every book, and there were fourteen of them. In love with the characters, in love with the enchanted land of their adventures.

"Is it real, Mom? Is Oz real?"

She replied as mothers get to do, sometimes, one sentence that lasts a lifetime: "It's real in the writer's mind, Richard, and now it's real in yours."

That was the first day I met good-news bad-news: Oz exists! (You can't get there by train.)

As I didn't know just then how to ask what was on my mind, I spent the next half century framing my questions:

If Oz exists in our mind, then can no one destroy it, ever? *yes it can be*

Is the world in our mind, too, and not outside?

What if all we see about us are reflections of what we think is so? *it is*

What's reflected when we decide to change our thought?

Thanks to those early journeys deep into lands beyond maps, here I stand today, bored at last to stone with dramas about evil, films about war and malice and crime. I promised that if I had to watch one more prison scene, one more aggression, one more gigantic spectacular stupendous explosion on-screen, fiction or non, I'd walk out and rebuild the universe.

—Boom!—

What if something happened, I got to wondering as I walked away, and a culture grew up without evil, without crime or war? What would it do with all the energies that we squander on our destructions?

How would it feel to live in a world where we choose our highest right and not our darkest wrong, where we lift each other instead of always and ever putting each other down? *you get eloused*

How could such a civilization begin, and where would it go?

So were born The Ferret Chronicles, the story of a doomed civilization that returned to life upon the single act of one individual.

—*Richard Bach*

Book·1

Shamrock

The Ferrets and the Humans

Once there was a team of ferrets, exploring mysteries, who landed upon a small blue planet and discovered a hidden valley that opened onto the land of the humans. The ferrets found these creatures a promising species, of grace and charm, intelligence and curiosity, of warm humor and great courage.

Because of this, and because of the dangers and promises ahead for the young race, the ferrets gave to the humans four powers with which they could prevail over the challenges to come.

The first was the power of fire, the second was the power of the wheel, the third was the power of written language, the fourth was the power of courtesy and respect, one to another.

The humans were quick to learn, and cherished the gifts that the ferrets had brought. As the explorers prepared to depart, the humans begged them to stay and to share with humankind the delight of the brave new civilization that would rise.

The ferrets were touched, and promised to return. On the day of their departure, one human turned to them. "Of these powers, dear ferrets, which is the first among them, which would you have us guard above all others?"

"Well asked," replied the ferrets. "Without fire can you prosper, and without the wheel, and without the alphabet, for many have prospered on your planet and across the galaxies without these. The one power without which no civilization can long survive, however, is the last, the power of courtesy and respect for each other and for all life."

The humans murmured, understanding, and used their new letters to scribe the Courtesies on tablets of onyx, the words finished in purest silver. When the ferrets had departed, the new race learned swiftly, mastering the natures of fire and wheel and alphabet.

They pondered long, however, how best to protect the most precious of powers, and at last it was agreed to keep the Tablets of the Courtesies in the safest place their world could offer. From reverence, no copy was made, nor were its holy words read but by those who first had heard them from the ferrets.

And so it came to pass that the one essential of the Four Gifts was weighted in rare metals and precious jewels, locked within a giant chest of iron, and after a long voyage and with great ceremony, was given to the waves and buried, safe forever in the uttermost part of the sea.

How others deal with gifts we've given is not our decision, but theirs.

- Antonius Ferret, *Fables*

1

Sнамкоск Ferret set a cup of Mandalay blackberry tea on the side table, tilted a tiny pitcher to add a dash of honey (poured, not stirred) and curled herself in the comfort of her Cases Unsolved chair. The antique she had bought at a used-thing sale, whirl-dots for pattern, soft as woven sunlight.

As the fire warmed the hearth and her own sable-chocolate fur, the detective set a small disk of black felt upon the chair and reviewed the facts.

The patterns of cornstalks fallen in the fields were always finished and complete; they were ever the same, almost an insignia: two stars, one large, one small, joined by a sweeping curved pathway.

The patterns had always been discovered in the morning, having appeared sometime between dusk and dawn, under a full moon. There were no marks of tools or machinery of any kind. There was no reason for the designs, nor meaning in them.

Here she reached a paw to stroke her whiskers as she stared into the light of the fire, and corrected herself.

No apparent reason, she thought. Every mystery cloaks an inner reason, each one gives its meaning only when we have allowed ourselves a new point of view. There are no secrets, she had learned. Through observation, inquiry, through the kaleidoscope of intuition, we detect what has been facing us all along.

She sipped her tea in the office of her flat, watching the fire.

About her in the modest dark-paneled room stood her desk with notepads and pens, the old clock which had ticked in her home since she was a kit, her microscope, brass polished, focus knob worn from use. Here were her shelves of books: *Analysis from Zero, Principles of Deduction* and thirty volumes of *The Paws of Knowledge,* a set much lined and dog-eared. From a peg on the wall hung her crimson tam-o'-shanter and snow-color scarf of many pockets. By the door a letter-drop and a whimsical bell made from an old ship's telegraph, the pointer at *Engines Standby.* All peaceful stillness.

Within her was no such quiet. She watched the fire, yet behind her eyes flashed scene after instant scene—the patterns, the clues, connections between the known and the possible.

Miss Shamrock Ferret earned her living by imagining possibilities, and now the images tumbled like a runaway slide show. Scene after scene rose and fell, possibilities slanting at the wrong angle, near misses, pictures out of match with the portrait of a mystery.

Now she lifted the disk of felt, and holding it gently between her paws, she closed her eyes, opened a door of imagination.

How I love this job, she thought, breathing the scent of Mandalay. How I love *finding out!*

2

IT WAS DARK at the top of the mountain, and that is why they had come, nine kits and Miss Ginger Ferret, all warm scarves and hats, journeyed here to settle on moss and grass, tails curled about them, eyes wide in starlight.

"Turning way out in space," said their teacher, "there are millions of stars around us. And in all the sky, one of them is your own. You'll know your star when you see it. It will be the warmest, the most friendly of all, and when it whispers to you, reach up your paw and say hello."

A little voice in the night: "My own star, Miss Ginger?"

"Your very own. Always you'll remember this night. Even when tonight has drifted into long ago, when many things have changed, when you're flying free and when you're deep in tests and challenge, your star will be with you still. Your star."

Fluffy masks and whiskers turned upward, scanned from horizon to zenith.

"Which is *your* star, Miss Ginger?"

The teacher pointed southward. "See the Seven Kits, Jimkin, four in a straight line with the triangle on top? Mine is Corrista, the second brightest, sparkling blue."

Ginger remembered the night she had first seen her star, shining silent above the meadow not far from her home. How constant had it been, and how reassuring, that light in the sky! Since that hour, Corrista had twinkled as though it knew everything was going to turn out for the best, no matter whether Ginger cried sometimes, or doubted her destiny. And ever had her star been right.

One voice after another, the teacher heard from the young ferrets, saw paws reaching. "Hello . . ."

Ginger Ferret knelt by them each, looking into the heavens. "The blue one there, Mikela, is that your star?"

"Yes, Miss Ginger."

"It's called Veya, in the constellation of Erinaceus, the Hedgehog. See his paws, and his eye? So Veya is his nose. The story goes that the hedgehog once saved the life of a baby meadow vole in the night, when it slipped and fell into a stream above the rapids. Erinaceus splashed into the water, lifted out the baby, returned it to its parents' burrow and went upon his way, thinking nothing of it. But Mustella, the Great Ferret, was watching from above and saw what had happened. So it came to pass that at the end of his life on Earth, the hedgehog was lifted up into the stars, for all to see and remember to be kind to the smallest living thing."

While the galaxy wheeled slow motion overhead, Ginger Ferret told the kits the names of the stars they had chosen. With her paw she outlined their constellations, told the stories of how each had come to be in the sky. She told them the legend that ferrets themselves had left their home planet a hundred centuries ago and come to Earth from another sun and a different planet.

She showed them the Polecat star, around which all the others turned, and the twinkling outline of Mustella herself nearby, body shaped like a water dipper, its handle three stars curving, the brightest become the Great Ferret's eye.

"The legend says that Mustella is the only constellation in the sky that looks the same from Earth as it does from Ferra."

"Is that true, Miss Ginger, or is that a story like Erinaceus?"

"Most stories grow from what's true. Hedgehogs are kind to meadow voles, even today. But no one's quite sure where we come from."

The last of the kits waited patiently, listening, watching the others.

"Have you found your star, Shamrock?" asked her teacher.

The little one pointed. "Yes, ma'am. It's there, in the Great Ferret."

"The edge of the dipper, the brightest one?"

"No. In the middle of it."

A shock of heat went through the teacher, from her nose to her tail. Could this kit have chosen . . .

"Draw two lines, corner to corner, in the square. Right near where they come together. It's not very bright."

The teacher turned to the little ferret. "Of all the stars in the sky," she murmured, "that's who called to you, the one at Mustella's heart?"

"Yes, ma'am . . . is that all right? It's not very big . . ."

"Do you know the name of that star?"

"No, ma'am."

"Shamrock, that's Pherrine. The legend says that's the star of our home planet."

"Why is it a story, Miss Ginger? Why don't we *know*?"

The teacher smiled, wistful in the dark, some deep spark of her soul yearning for home. "What are you most curious about, Shamrock? Things that have already happened, or things that are going to happen?"

A silence while the little one thought it through. Her mother and father had asked her questions all her life, showed her how to observe, to imagine, to research, deduce: "Why is it so, Shamrock? Why did this happen as it did, and not some other way, or not at all?"

"I'm most curious about . . . *anything that's a mystery!*"

Ginger blinked. This one could widen the world.

A white-masked kit stood near, listening. "*I'm* most curious about what's going to happen!"

The teacher nodded. "You're like most of us, Hopper. What's already happened, our own history, isn't as exciting for us as creating new futures." She smiled. "Why not, Shamrock?"

"Because we can make any future come true," said the kit, "because the future isn't finished. The past is."

A voice in the dark: Jimkin. "But can't we change the past, too, Miss Ginger, if we really want to?"

"Philosopher ferrets say we can."

"I want to be a philosopher ferret," said Jimkin.

Whether such would be the path for one of her kits their teacher couldn't say. Every ferret is a magical creature, she knew, and now the night had split, skyrockets into nine new tomorrows. In each of the nine lived a kit with its own star to be a friend, for always and ever.

3

By THE TIME SHAMROCK arrived, the meeting hall of the village was filled with farmer ferrets. She had promised a solution to the mystery in their cornfields and no one wanted to be last to hear.

The hall went quiet as she walked to a stage framed in the inks of drying maize and the pastels of this season's pumpkins and squash. Centerstage stood a table lit by an overhead light.

She set a wicker cake-basket upon the table, unsnapped four brass latches but did not remove the cover, left it there under the light. Whispers through the crowd: What's in the box?

She lifted a paw-held microphone and the whispers subsided. "Thank you, gentleferrets," she began, the clear, firm voice of a skilled investigator. "The Case of the Midnight Patterns has been a wonderful challenge for us all." She paused, looking from face to face, a room of many-shaded furs and masks, of eyes watching as though she were the illusionist come to explain a magic.

"Help me test my answer," she said, "with some questions for you."

At once her listeners changed from observers to players in a game of wits with the unknown. *Help me test my answer* was to become quintessential Shamrock Ferret, her clients enlisted to become detectives themselves.

"Concerning the fields where the patterns have appeared," she asked, "has there always been a stream, larger than a brook but smaller than a river, within a thousand paws' distance?"

A murmur through the hall, a nodding of whiskers and masks, a chorus of assent. Yes, as a matter of fact, every field with a crop pattern did lie not far distant from a stream neither large nor small.

"Have the fields, as one faces north, always been to the left of the river, and never to the right?"

Thoughtful nods. Yes, that is so.

"Has a pattern ever appeared after a foggy or rainy night, or has the sky been clear, before a pattern is found?"

Silence of her clients reflecting upon the matter, then nodding, confirming with each other, and once again the voice of assent. The weather had been fine, every night a pattern was formed.

Shamrock nodded her thanks for their help. "Has this last season been an unusually prosperous one? Would anyone say that this has been a difficult year for farming?"

A sparkle of laughter through the crowd. By no means had this been a hard year for agriculture. Though they worked from dawn to dusk through the whole land of trim farms and tended fields nearby, the ferrets and their village had prospered.

"Does anyone recognize this?" She held up the disk of felt, the shape of a beret, half the size of her paw.

A word from the fourth row, surprise and shock. "Why, I found one of those! On my hilltop field, in the April pattern!"

"So there you have it," said Shamrock. "Thank you, gentleferrets, the case has been a worthy test. I appreciate the honor of your invitation to solve it. Your mystery designs, your crop patterns, are the work of *visiting Parisian artist mice.*"

Silence from the group, paws moving to stroke whiskers as they watched Shamrock.

If the detective had a favorite moment in the solution of a case, it was this one, laying the answer before her clients, watching disbelief melt in the heat of evidence.

"When the iron molecules within it have been magnetized," she explained, "a cornstalk will bend swiftly and permanently upon the application of only one substance: painters' flax-leaf oil. The artists prefer to work near the left bank of a stream, as they are accustomed to, of course, in Paris. Clear skies are required, and the light of a full moon, to inspire the lunatic in creative minds which would not otherwise consider such a lark. Of course, as would be expected in any large group of travelers, someone loses their hat."

"Why do they need our fields, Miss Shamrock, and cornstalks for their canvas? If the design comes to them in the full moon, why don't they . . . paint it at home?"

The detective nodded. "That's a good question. The designs do not come to the artists, though, the artists come to the designs. Your corn is their canvas. Your fine deep soil was altered many centuries ago, the iron oxide polarized by intense magnetic fields.

"The mice don't create the figures, but they sense where they are, and with their oil they free the cornstalks to flow the way paint flows, following electric brushstrokes long past."

A different voice from the audience. "How can the mice know to do this, Miss Shamrock, when it's never occurred to us that we have patterns in the ground?"

"These are artist mice," said the detective, "sensitive to the currents of worlds the rest of us cannot feel. Butterflies migrate around the earth for reasons they do not know, and in the same way these delicate creatures have been led to your fields, sensing only that art lies beneath."

"Then there must be other patterns, waiting!"

"Most likely, yes."

"But Miss Shamrock, what do the patterns mean?"

Here the young detective frowned. "You've asked me to solve the mystery of the crop pattern appearances," she replied, "how was the corn bent, who entered your fields, and why. What the patterns mean is a different mystery, one I haven't solved. Off the tip of my tail, a guess before evidence, I'd suspect the patterns are a message left here by the ancients, to remind us of something important."

"Remind us?"

"What do philosopher ferrets say? *We know all there is to know. There's nothing learned, but remembered.*"

Came a voice from the center of the meeting. "Have you other proof of your Parisian artist-mouse hypothesis? You've said the left bank, but how are you certain they were Parisian mice? It may sound a little far-fetched to others . . ."

It was still fresh in her mind, her vision, holding the miniature beret. Closing her eyes was like opening them in a different place, the home of the French cap and its owner, in the studio of the artist mice.

"*We invent nothing,*" their leader had exclaimed to the artists, their brushes and flax-leaf oil packed into battered valises. "*We discover! We liberate the art within!*"

In her mind she had traveled with them to the fields beyond the sleeping ferret village, had watched the mice brush the oils deftly, seen the cornstalks collapse under moonlight to follow the curving energies of forces laid down long ago.

But to others a different answer could still be true. So much to explain!

"Of course," she said. "How are we certain they are Parisian mice? If you wish to explore the left banks of the streams near any crop pattern, you will find underground entrances to the staging areas for the artists. When you do, you will find the pawprints of many individuals, and you may find something like this, as well . . ."

She held up a scrap of colored paper and read, "*Chemin de fer de Paris à Londres, tout ensemble.*"

She spoke to the last row in the hall. "This, gentleferrets, is a group-excursion railway ticket, purchased for the evening train, on the date of the appearance of our latest pattern."

"A coincidence?" someone asked. "Can we be certain?"

"What do the patterns have to do with our prosperity?" asked another. "Why did you need to know if this has been a good year for us?"

"Allow me to answer both questions at once," said Shamrock. "A coincidence? And, what does your prosperity have to do with the mystery?"

She tapped briskly on the cover of the wicker cake-basket center-stage, then lifted it and set it aside.

Blinking under the light and rising from a tiny lounge chair by a table set with fresh-baked bread and chunks of Camembert, stood a European field-mouse, brown-whiskered, dressed in a grand bow tie of flowing silks, a black felt beret to match the one the detective had displayed earlier.

Shamrock extended the microphone toward the creature.

"*Bonjour, mes amis,*" said the diminutive artist, his voice amplified in the speakers. "This is a good question, your prosperity."

The audience gasped. It would have been enough for Shamrock to have explained the mystery. She was not required to produce the principals.

"We are, how do you say . . . *la lune* . . . we are lunatic on certain evenings, when the moon is full. We are not malicious." After the astonishment, not a sound from the audience, staring from the mouse to Shamrock and back again.

The rodent looked to the detective, then back to the farmer ferrets. "We would not have appeared," he said, "nor have done our work, if to bend the corn would have brought you not wonder but hardship."

Then it was silent. Hearing no further questions, the little animal reached a paw toward the cheese, lifted a morsel.

"Hurray for the mice!" cried one of the farmers. "Shall we invite them to visit now as our guests, by first-class railway, to bring their paintings and show them in the square?"

The mouse set down its meal and swept the cap from its head in a flourishing bow to all, its nose nearly touching the floor of the case.

So ended the meeting in a round of cheers for the artists, and a cheer for Shamrock, too, along with payment for contract complete and mystery solved.

On the way home, the ferret train chuffing from the dark of a tunnel into daylight, Shamrock made a note from her own unquenched curiosity: *What do the patterns mean?*

4

Bᴜʀʀᴏᴡꜱ Fᴇʀʀᴇᴛ returned to the city not long after Shamrock, immersed the whole drive in thought, fascinated with the detective's solution to the Case of the Midnight Patterns.

He watched the highway curl and divide past the windscreen of his Austin-Furet, glanced at a road sign:

Please maintain
the speed
at which you feel safe
under these conditions

He touched the tape recorder in his scarf pocket.

"Not only has our young detective solved the mystery," he said, "but as with the Case of the Flying Delphin and the Case of the Too Many Blossoms, she did it in a few hours, a morning's investigation and an evening's analysis at most.

"Her tests must continue, of course, but it seems that we have a powerful candidate on our paws.

"Advise N and S," he said.

An afterthought: ". . . and ZZ."

He turned off the recorder. What would our civilization be, he thought, if we had no examples?

5

Fʀᴏᴍ ᴛʜᴇ ᴅᴀʏ ꜱʜᴇ was born, Shamrock Ferret was surrounded in questions.

"Look at the bubbles, Shamrock!" her mother would say, bathing her kit. "Why are they round instead of square? Why don't they sink in the water?

"Why does the sky change colors, little Shamrock? Where do stars go in the daytime? What do clouds weigh?"

"Hallo, Shamrock," her father would say, morningtimes. "Are you sure we're awake, and not dreaming breakfast? Why do we dream at all?"

Her parents ever were asking why, and little Shamrock loved to answer, making up explanations when she didn't know. Questions were feather-touch tensions, answers made the tensions go, left a warm place where they had been.

Psychometry, at first, was a game. "This scarf was worn by a very special ferret," her parents said. "Hold it in your paws, close your eyes, tell us what it was like to be this animal." And sure enough, there were visions in the dark, beginnings of a skill that would help their kit no matter which direction her curiosity might lead.

"Can you hold the box," they asked, "and tell us where it came from?

"Trust your imagination, Shamrock. If it feels like you're inventing a story, invent away! The stories you imagine are probably true."

Instead of leaving her powers behind as she grew, the kit developed them; practice made her what others called a *sensitive*. No one discouraged or ridiculed her interests; in the ferret way they encouraged them instead, delighting in her adventures as she did in others'.

Shamrock grew to excel not only in psychometry, but in logic, in analysis, deduction, cryptography, patterns. Grown-ups coming to visit would bring thousand-piece puzzles, watch while the kit assembled them in minutes, humming tunes to herself. They'd shake their heads and smile, bewildered. If it was a test of mind, Shamrock Ferret could solve it, often in several ways.

She painted one bedroom wall herself, from a photo of the famous storefront office: *Nutmeg & Bergamont*, an arc of gold letters on black glass, *Detectives*, a mirrored arc beneath.

In the research drawer of her little desk were news clippings of Nutmeg Ferret's cases, Shamrock's notes on how the celebrated investigator had solved them, step by step, how she might have solved them differently.

Nutmeg's Case of the Missing Star, of the Tilted Factory, of the

Secret Gift, every clue explained in a whirl of sparkling insight at the end, as breathtaking to the kit as were high-wire acrobatics to others.

Investigating her heroine, Shamrock found that Nutmeg Ferret had been a kit from a northcountry village, fur like smooth cinnamon, modest and soft-spoken. Her gift was to take the complicated apart, piece by piece, with questions so simple that they answered themselves.

"Now, why would this be?" In time, the power of her words had made it a household phrase to ferrets around the world. Puzzled, they'd echo the sleuth of the spice-color fur: *Now, why would this be?*

There's a reason I can't get enough of Nutmeg, wrote Shamrock to her diary: *The Case of My Favorite Detective*. It's that level, open gaze. Every magazine photo, television interview, I can see it. Nutmeg Ferret misses nothing. As soon as she notices, she understands. When I think of her, everything in the world makes sense.

Nutmeg's life is all purpose and adventure, thought Shamrock, and as though she were already the detective she yearned to be, the kit was happiest wondering, investigating, bringing the hidden to light. Alone in her room, she whispered, "I'll be like Nutmeg, someday."

Not long after, a strange thing—a salesferret had called: large, light-masked and a little unkempt, as though his fur had been brushed backward here and there, a bundle of brochures and a volume from *The Paws of Knowledge*.

He thanked her parents for their time, accepted a place on the sofa. "A world of research on one shelf!" he told them. "Everything your kit will want to know. Not quite, with a mind like hers, but she'll find Most Everything About Most Everything, as we like to say. With *The Paws of Knowledge*, why, there'll be no mystery she can't solve!"

At this her mum and dad had looked keenly at the salesferret. Chance turn of phrase, or had the big animal guessed their kit's passion for the unknown?

He handed his sample (*Volume 13: Megalith to Nudibranch*) to the youngster studying him. "Open it anywhere, Miss Shamrock."

As luck would have it, the page fell open to *Mysteries, Great, of the World*. Halfway down the text an outline began:

Aircraft, Unknown:

Alphabet, Ancient Ferrune:

Aqua-Bees:

Found only in Loch Stoat, near the palace at Mustelania, aqua-bees are said to nest underwater, rising to the surface and flying to pollinate undetermined flowers in or near the palace before returning. No study has been devised to learn the secrets of the aqua-bee without disturbing its home or habits, so little is known of these rare creatures. Local legend, however . . .

Little is known . . . no phrase could be more magnetic to Shamrock Ferret.

She clasped the volume to her, the book nearly half her height. "Oh, *please!*" she implored. "Mum, Dad, there's so much to learn! Did you know, at the palace there are *aqua-bees?*"

Her parents looked at each other, then to the salesferret. *The Paws of Knowledge* was thirty volumes of higher education, an investment far beyond the budget of their little household.

After their visitor had left, the kit's parents reminded, "You have the museum, not far away, you have the library . . ."

"But I can't jump from one to . . . Dad, I can't check out *thirty volumes!*"

"*Can't,*" said her father. "There's a strong word, Shamrock . . ."

She apologized, and found that she could check out three volumes at a time, of the ten-volume kit's edition of *Paws*, simple words and pictures.

She did not ask her parents how it was that the salesferret had known her name, why he had rubbed chalk to lighten his mask, nor did she tell them later that her investigation showed he had visited no other house on her block and, as far as she could tell, no other in her neighborhood.

What would Nutmeg Ferret have to say about this? Nutmeg would begin at the beginning, she thought: *Now, why would this be?* Yet for once the question did not resolve itself for Shamrock, the kit unwilling to see the simple answer.

Late one afternoon, carrying volumes Four through Six home

from the library, she saw from afar that a heavy wooden crate had been left upon her doorstep. Her parents did not leave packages untended on the step, so the kit knew that whoever had left it had not rung the doorbell.

Why would this be? Because they did not wish to be identified.

She ran the rest of the way home.

The crate had no return address, no delivery markings, though her scarf-pocket magnifying glass hinted that it had been wheeled there from a closed vehicle on a red paw-trolley. Two words, *Shamrock Ferret*, had been stenciled in black paint on the wood.

The screen door opened as she finished her search for clues. "Hallo," said her father, "what do we have here?"

He opened the crate for her, but his kit already knew. It was the adult edition, all thirty volumes: *The Paws of Knowledge*.

Neither family nor friends were surprised when it happened that Shamrock's pastime became her profession, when the young ferret opened an office at last, a small room in her flat at 7 Blessingthorpe Lane, near the edge of the city: *Shamrock Ferret, Detective.*

Looking back, her neighbors told the press that they had always known it would happen. The kit was the sweetest little thing, thoughtful, kind to everyone. Never had her family been rich, but my, that youngster was brilliant, always had a way of solving puzzles.

What her neighbors didn't know was that long before she had cracked the Case of the Midnight Patterns, before she had solved the Case of the Flying Delphin, even before she had opened her office, Shamrock Ferret was being watched.

6

THE MUSEUM OF Ancient Times had ever been a magnet for Shamrock. Old things fascinated, early tools and housewares and instruments in the Hall of Artifacts, boats and carriages in the Hall of Travel. Now the pattern in the cornfields was a constant engine within, driving her with its mystery—something old had caused those designs.

Today she entered the Hall of Paintings, just completed, high windows over sheer marble walls. Lost in thought, she walked with a crowd of visitors between scenes ordered by centuries. Here a ferret merchant ship, flags before the wind, bright sails on a sea of double-sky blue, laden with silks and spices. So fine the art that one could distinguish the masks and whiskers of the animals in the rigging, the helmsferret at the wheel.

Down the way, a work found in the catacombs of the Lost City, thought to be of Pheretima herself, at the palace.

The patterns were laid down centuries ago, thought Shamrock. To solve the puzzle of their meaning, do I have to solve the puzzle of our own origins, as well?

At the end of the hallway, a simple canvas. It showed a silvery blue vase of pale blossoms, set on the sill of an oval window overlooking a tapestry of polka dots.

Oldest Known Ferret Painting, said a plaque beneath the wooden frame. *Subject: Flowers.*

Shamrock slowed, stopped there, the crowd parting, flowing around her. How could art from long ago be so familiar? The flowers, painted in exquisite detail, were common enough, *Dodecatheon furetii*, the delicate Shooting Star of the parks and fields.

The detective stared at the painting. Somewhere she had seen this vase. Where?

Her powers of recall, often extraordinary, offered random guesses. In the show windows of Furry Home, they suggested. No. In a curio shop as you passed. The shop was . . . where? It was . . . don't tell us . . . it was . . . there are so many shop windows . . .

While she waited for her answer, Shamrock studied the painting, tilted her head to see the vase from a different angle.

At last the recall division of her mind reached its limits. We're sorry, we don't know where you saw it. Patience, please. It will come to us.

Shamrock sighed, shook her head. She left the museum and headed home, haunted by the feeling that she had been remembering her future, that the painting had a value to her that she could not place.

Had it been a coincidence, she chanced upon the old scene, this day, this hour, this moment? She shook her head. What had happened was no coincidence—coincidence is always an answer to questions we have asked.

What do the patterns mean?

When she opened her door, a card fell from the handle to the threshold. She stooped to retrieve it and read:

Burrows Ferret

Nutmeg & Bergamont, Detectives

7

"WOULD YOU CARE for tea, Miss Shamrock?"

"Please don't bother, Mr. Burrows."

"No bother, ma'am. I have it here." Burrows Ferret set the tea service upon her desk, poured a cup of Mandalay blackberry for the detective. From a pitcher of honey, a small dollop. Sprig of mint, twist of lime.

"Here you are, ma'am."

"Thank you!" Shamrock felt as if she should be the one serving tea to her new associate.

Sometimes butler, sometimes sleuth, Burrows had left his card not so long ago, yet at once had he become indispensable.

A large, dark-masked creature, fur the color of mahogany, he had a remarkable mind for detail, Shamrock found, a talent for deduction and rather considerable experience at detecting, having been employed at Nutmeg & Bergamont for quite some time before starting a brief practice on his own.

"I found that I don't work as well alone as I do with others, Miss Shamrock," he had said after she had read his understated résumé. "I've been following your cases and frankly am quite impressed with your skills. If you would do me the honor of testing me in your office, I suspect that you might find yourself considerably less burdened by detail."

Shamrock had watched him closely. Modest to the point of self-effacing, there was something about Burrows vaguely familiar, as determined and constant as a star above.

"Small cases are my specialty," he had told her. "The greater mysteries seem to be yours, if you will forgive my observation. I enjoy discussion and analysis. I have learned how to ask a question. It could be that we might make an excellent team."

So had Shamrock been impressed, these last weeks, so had she enjoyed his mind and manner, that today she asked a question of her own. Picking a card from her desktop, she offered it for his inspection. "Look at this, would you please, Mr. Burrows? Tell me what you think."

He studied it, turned it over. It was what it appeared to be, a business card. Yet the lettering startled him: *Burrows Ferret, Shamrock & Burrows, Detectives.*

"Miss Shamrock, this is scarcely necessary. I have yet to prove my value as your assistant, let alone your partner."

"Oh, Mr. Burrows, you're already proven! With your qualities, I'm surprised that you weren't a partner at Nutmeg and Bergamont."

"In point of fact, Miss Shamrock—"

"Please no more discussion, Mr. Burrows, over something so simple. The position is yours if you will have it. I feel the change is in our best interest. If you know a reason otherwise, I shall not insist."

"Thank you for your confidence, Miss Shamrock. I accept the honor and the responsibility."

To the young detective's relief, Burrows Ferret had taken over the media cases, freeing her from the routine of Interview, Analyze, Verify and Correct.

IAVC, staple of the detective business. In the rush to press, in their zeal to satisfy curiosity, newsferrets did not always confirm a story so much as they could, before setting it to print. The more interesting the story, in fact, and the more intriguing, the less likely it was to be true.

First, claimed the media, readers want to know. Second, all in good time, readers want to know the truth.

That a fascinating story may not be accurate was the bread and butter of detective ferrets, their names appearing often on the *Not Quite So* page of the daily papers.

There had been a story in the morning news, for instance, and a headline: *Stilton Ferret Risks Life to Save Kit's Doll from Avalanche.*

No sooner had the paper hit the streets than Burrows answered the telephone. "Shamrock and Burrows, at your service."

He listened. "I understand," he said. "Of course we can."

He penciled notes on his pad. "It will be done, Miss Yvette. Thank you for engaging us to resolve the issue."

Shamrock looked up from the Case of the Invisible Clock . . . how could a ferret vanish from his home in the city and reappear on the other side of the continent, no recollection of his disappearance or how he had traveled?

"Anything interesting, Mr. Burrows?"

"Yes, ma'am, as a matter of fact. That was MusTelCo's corporate office. Stockholders are calling: they saw the headline this morning. Is the world's richest ferret so reckless that he gambles his life and the future of his company to recover a stuffed animal?"

The shadow of a smile; in an instant she had analyzed the case. "Did Stilton Ferret Save Kit's Doll from Avalanche?"

"He did."

"Did Stilton Ferret Risk Life, doing it?"

"Stilton saw the kit drop her penguin in the snow when the warning sounded; he recovered the doll, returned it. The avalanche came downhill next day. I'll confirm this, of course, with the kit and her parents, and the ski patrol. Our correction will say that the penguin is safe, little Eliza is grateful and Stilton's life was at no time at risk."

She nodded. "Thank you, Mr. Burrows." Why would the world's biggest corporation, she wondered, call the world's smallest detective agency with such an important correction?

"My pleasure, Miss Shamrock."

He touched the flower on his desk, added water to its vase. Shamrock stiffened.

The museum! She had seen the old painting's vase in the museum!

But the museum was huge, city blocks under one roof. Where in the museum?

Somewhere, somewhere, said her recollection. Don't tell me, I'll get it. Same building, a different floor from the painting.

8

SHE RUSHED INTO the Museum of Ancient Times nearly at dusk, hurried down the Hall of Paintings till she stood breathless, waiting, before the scene that had so drawn her the day before.

The canvas waited, a cry without words, as though painting were pantomime. Then the young ferret sighed. So close. Something . . . she couldn't put her paw upon the answer.

Gradually faded the light in the windows above the prehistoric work as day turned through sunset. She stood and studied, the detective a living net beneath the art, await for its clue to fall.

Night darkened, nearly to the shade of the painting's polka-dot tapestry. Minutes more, and it was as though the painting had changed to match the sky.

Shamrock Ferret blinked, transfixed by the scene. The fur of her tail stood straight.

That isn't a tapestry behind the vase, she thought, it's night sky. Those are no polka dots, they're stars—that's *Mustella*, the constellation of the Great Ferret! This oval frame is no country window, *it's the viewport of a starship!*

Her paw flew to her magnifying glass, she stepped forward, leaned to the painting, focused the lens. There, barely discernible around the oval, amid the cracks of ancient color, lay the faintest spots of an automatic welding machine, bonding frame to bulkhead.

Ten millionth visitor to this art, Shamrock Ferret was first to understand. Painter unknown, a smile across the ages: the flowers are Shooting Stars, dear viewer, and the polka dots are home.

Centuries, it's been with us, thought Shamrock, every day the answer in plain sight.

And the vase, that vase . . .

Her recollection powers blinked awake. *Early Artifacts!* Sorry it took so long. Fourth floor. You see, there are actually a number of vases that have caught your interest, and we had to sort the ancient one from . . .

"Fourth floor!" said Shamrock aloud, rushed past late-going visitors, heading for Early Artifacts, impatient with the stately rise of the elevator, the gentle opening of its door.

Her paws slid to a stop on polished marble, in front of a glass enclosure. There stood the vase of the painting, unruffled by sudden discovery.

Barely a paw high, it gave instant scale to the painting downstairs. The viewport, then, must have been three paws high at most, and two wide, suggesting a craft smaller than legend. The ship to bring the first ferrets to Earth was not a giant among the stars, thought Shamrock, it had been the size of a ferryboat!

There was a sign by the glass case: *Replicas of the artifacts are available at the museum store. If you wish to borrow an original artifact, please return it at your earliest convenience.*

Back by dawn, she promised, lifting the vase and leaving her business card where it had stood: *Shamrock Ferret, Shamrock & Burrows, Detectives.*

By the time she trotted up the steps to her flat, she was deep in mystery. She had asked, coincidence had given her the painting for an answer.

"What do the patterns mean?" *We come from the stars!*

9

Is THERE STILL A WAY to save the world? thought Avedoi Merek. Is anyone left who wants to save it?

The philosopher ferret surveyed the remains of the city through what had once been the window of his study, now a jagged hole in the side of this modest villa, books and scrolls and disks tumbled about within, smoke and flames scattered to the horizon for Ferra's sunset.

We've defended ourselves nearly to death, he thought, and lacking miracles we're going to topple on over, defending to the last.

He sank into his thinking chair, its fabric torn by falling plasters.

What miracle, no assumptions beyond ferrets are intelligent, we're practical, curious, we love to laugh, we love adventure? What simple idea can save us now?

They ask me to speak to what's left of the world, as though . . .

He sighed, exhaling hope. What can I say, what can any creature say, to change the course of history after such a war as this?

It is

just,

too,

late.

10

SHAMROCK FERRET settled in her Cases Unsolved chair, smoothed her tail about her. She held the ferretmetal vase, lustrous silvery blue, in her paws and closed her eyes, remembering not to think, to allow its scenes to come to her unbidden.

Just let the story happen, whatever I need to learn from this vase. Just let it be . . .

It was a room, Shamrock saw, once a comfortable library, a grand view over housetops to a soaring metropolis.

Now glass was blown from every window, shambles for furnishings, one wall gone, the view beyond of flames splashed near and distant, a city shattered.

She so shrank from this sight, a meteor storm across a living planet, that her body shivered in her worn chair, she nearly opened her eyes to stop the scene from coming.

She did not. For curled at a splintered desk was a smallish ferret, not much larger than Shamrock herself, fur the color of sand and night.

His eyes were closed, but she knew his thought.

So desperate are they now, that they ask me to speak to the world, prisoner become savior. What words can save? I am one animal, I watch the end of civilization as I know it. It is just, too, late.

In her imagination, she stepped toward him, and at the sound, his eyes opened. "Who are . . ."

". . . you?" they asked together.

"My name is Shamrock," she said. "I'm from . . ." She stopped, not knowing how to tell him where she was from.

She was to him a flickering hologram; through her body could he see the fires on the horizon. And yet she lived. Was she some alien race, arrived past its chance to save the life of his world?

He nodded. "I'm the last of ferret civilization," he told her, "one of the last. You came to rescue us from ourselves. You found only Avedoi Merek, and the end."

Shamrock blinked, unbelieving. "Avedoi Merek? I found *Avedoi Merek*?"

He looked through the missing wall, turned back to Shamrock. "Ferra will go on. Our planet will barely notice we're gone. A small irritation vanished, the race of ferrets."

"Avedoi Merek! Sir, you're not the end, you're the—"

"Would it have been so difficult," said the other, unhearing, "just to have been kind to each other? Why must ferrets be the only animal cursed with this magnetism toward hatreds and putting-downs, we're-number-one, us-against-them?"

Shamrock gaped, astonished at the fires surrounding. "Meteors?"

The philosopher tilted his head, puzzled that the alien didn't guess.

"No meteors." He touched his chest. "The disaster wasn't out there, it was in here. One side thought, 'We're good, you're evil.'

The other side thought, 'No, you have it wrong: *we're* good, *you're* evil!'"

How could this remarkable animal joke in such a moment, she thought, fires still burning? Not funny. "*Evil ferrets?* What are you saying, sir?"

He didn't hear. "The war began, each side convinced we can harm others without harming ourselves and the ones we love. Can't be done. . . ." He shrugged. "Can't be done."

The philosopher roused himself. "Highest perspective, of course: it doesn't matter. We are indestructible light, all of us. Dying out of bodies is as much a dream as living in them. Change the dream to nightmare, though, it's no fun. We're the most fun-loving animal in the universe! Why would we choose this tragedy, to hurt each other, to hurt ourselves and our kits?"

The room swirled, Shamrock understanding at last. "War?" she whispered. "*Between ferrets?*"

Avedoi Merek nodded, studied her closely. "You're from another star, aren't you?" It was not her appearance he saw, but her attitude, her shock at what she had heard.

"No," he said. "You're not from another place, you're from another time. Our destruction wouldn't surprise if you were from the past. You're from the future."

"Yes," she said. "No. I'm dreaming. I'm imagining."

"Aren't we all. And the race of ferrets has imagined its own ending. Now we've decided to end dreams in war against each other." He looked to Shamrock, as though for hope. "Haven't we?"

"Sir, I can't believe . . ." She struggled to explain the obvious, frustrated that this brilliant animal could not understand: ferrets do not fight wars.

"*The Courtesies!*" she said. "Avedoi Merek, it was you who set them down! How could there be war . . . *what happened to the Courtesies?*"

The philosopher watched her for the longest time before he spoke.

"What courtesies?"

11

To any client who might have opened her door, Shamrock Ferret was asleep in her Cases Unsolved chair, nose tucked under her paw, a ball of warm sable encircling an ancient vase. Anyone entering would have stopped at the sight, held their breath and tiptoed away, closing the door silently behind.

The detective, however, was not asleep. Lured by the mystery of ferretkind's distant past, her breathing was quick and shallow as she watched events in this state that any other would call trance.

"*What Courtesies?*" she cried. "Avedoi Merek, you wrote them! *The Ferret Way!* Your book is so ancient that some say you never existed, your name's a code we all forgot!"

The philosopher smiled the faintest of smiles. "My dear strange visitor, have you come to the wrong address? *The Ferret Way* is a title and some notes, nothing more. An idea, a path that could have been, but for . . ."

He moved his paw toward the scene outside, the fires in the night. "Too late. It will never be written. Could-have-been is fiction, now."

Shamrock refused to surrender. "Aren't you baffled?" she said. "Don't you wonder how I can appear before you out of the air, your hallucination of the future who happens to know every line of a book unwritten, it's just notes in your mind? Has this . . ." she searched for the word ". . . war destroyed your curiosity? Have I found the wrong address? Is there *another* Avedoi Merek?"

"The future," said the animal, as though speaking that word for the first time. "If you're my future, then for all its . . ." He blinked at her. "The war is not the end of the world!"

Shamrock felt brittle tension cracking away. "In my time, sir, we've *forgotten* your war! My time, war's unimaginable. Because of you. *The Ferret Way*, it's so deep in our culture we're incapable of war. Don't you remember? *Who reads, loves, lives the Ferret Way becomes keeper of light, ennobling outer worlds from one within!*"

"You've set a civilization on a book I haven't written! I don't know those ideas myself. How can I find them out?"

"That's easy enough," said Shamrock, desperate. *"I'll tell you!"*

The animal at the desk stared at her, stunned in paradox. Then, for the first time since before the rockets had fallen over Ferra, Avedoi Merek laughed.

12

"YOU DON'T REMEMBER, sir?" Shamrock Ferret stood by a shattered window-wall that had once lifted seamless from rooftops far below, knowing she dreamed, unafraid of the height.

"'Not laws,' you said, sir, 'not rules: Here is a constitution of courtesies, should you choose to live by them. The courtesy you show to those you love, show the same to all, be you a civilization of one . . .'"

Avedoi Merek wrote on scorched paper in the ancient Ferrune, his own words echoing from a reader generations removed.

". . . or of millions," he whispered as Shamrock fell silent, watching. He wrote as though in trance himself.

". . . these courtesies to self and others will be your justice, lifting you beyond strife and destructions, now and forever."

He no longer cared about too late, about hopeless, no longer despaired what one animal could say to a shattered planet. Letters flew beneath his paws, listing the Courtesies without so much as slowing, one to the next:

Whatever harm I would do to another, I shall do first to myself.

As I respect and am kind to myself, so shall I respect and be kind to peers, to elders, to kits.

I claim for others the freedom to live as they wish, to think and believe as they will. I claim that freedom for myself.

I shall make each choice and live each day to my highest sense of right.

Shamrock stood fascinated, a silent witness. The Courtesies were so fundamental to her race that many insisted they were not declaration but ferret nature, genetic code. Now, word by word, she watched the ideas written.

Avedoi Merek looked up to her, his eyes alight. "Of course!" he murmured. "As we shift our energy from destructions, where can it go but to adventure instead? Instead of turning rockets on ourselves, we change their direction—into the stars, us aboard!"

She nodded, and the facts came together. We came to Earth from space. The painting, the vase she held this moment in her office, art it was but history more. And history had begun with one animal, with this gentle ferret before her.

"Is it true?" she asked. "We have a legend about you."

The philosopher smiled. A legend about one so humble as himself?

"In the archives," said Shamrock, "I found a story. It said that Avedoi Merek once was asked what he would do if he knew he was to be attacked by warriors."

"Oh? By warriors? What did I answer?"

"*'Die.'*"

He laughed. "Good for me. At last I learned to stop fighting."

"Is the story true?"

"No."

What's true, thought Shamrock, is the idea behind the story: when every noble, gentle creature refuses to fight, nobility and gentility will disappear before warriors. All that will remain, at the end, will be an angry few, gnashing their hatreds in the ruins of a silent planet.

"You're changing the world," she said. "Can you feel it, now, do you know it as you write?"

Preoccupied, the animal spoke just above a whisper. "I change nothing, Miss Shamrock. Ferrets change when we decide a new way of thinking will make us happier than an old one. No other way. We're too stubborn. I write to change myself."

It felt to Shamrock as if she were a spirit no longer required in this place. She had reminded one animal of what it knew, and now it wrote for others who might someday care.

She woke in her Cases Unsolved chair, reached at once to her notepad.

Her psychic voyage had offered a clue to one scene, about which the destiny of a civilization had turned. Not ferret nature, said the dream, not genetic code. Once, long ago, we changed our minds: end violence. In its place, no matter what: courtesy.

A sensitive's fable or a civilization's history?

13

"WOULD YOU CARE for tea, Miss Shamrock?"

"Why, yes, thank you, Mr. Burrows."

He brought the china, poured her Mandalay and a swirl of honey. "Difficult case?"

She nodded, and he left her to her deduction. So deep ran the Courtesies that Burrows saw in her nod how warm his kindness felt to her, how glad she was that he was there.

She sipped the tea, staring at a fringe of carpet.

"Mr. Burrows," she said.

He appeared at once. "Yes, Miss Shamrock?"

"I need your help."

"Of course."

The fluffy animal settled himself in the Cases Resolved chair nearby, turned to her and said not another word.

Shamrock thought for a long while, her partner silent. "I saw Avedoi Merek and the ferret war," she said at last. "I saw him write the Courtesies."

Burrows did not respond. "I need your help," to ferrets, means, "Please listen." No comments, no suggestions, no debate. Just listen.

"But seeing is not proof. How do I know it happened?"

Her partner listened.

"War between ferrets, Mr. Burrows? Not likely. We're smart enough, we don't need disaster to learn kindness."

Silence for minutes. "And yet, if there had been war, and ferrets overcame it, we need to know! If I could prove it was a choice, we made . . ."

Burrows listened.

"One does not war against friends," she said. "At some point we decided: all ferrets are friends. Us-and-Them changed to Us."

Long silence, her eyes closed. "If that deciding happened not slowly, over a million years, but in the minute I saw Avedoi Merek lift his pen . . . that's not dumb genetics, Mr. Burrows, that's one animal and an idea!"

Burrows nodded, Shamrock didn't see.

"And if that's true, the power of one animal and an idea," she said, "how many other walls are out there, painted invisible, holding us back, waiting for us to wake up?"

The clock ticked.

"Evidence, Mr. Burrows! Nothing I saw can I prove. Did I witness some golden deed that picked up history and set it on different tracks? Or was I imagining fiction?"

At last she turned to him, said her test in a word. "Evidence."

He listened.

"I'm done, Mr. Burrows. Thank you for your help."

The other animal reached a paw and brushed his whiskers. "An honor to listen, Miss Shamrock. You have a remarkable mind."

He rose and padded softly to his desk.

"Comments, Mr. Burrows? Where is my thinking weak?"

He lifted a cup of tea gone cool. "You're a sensitive, Miss Shamrock, your psychometry has proven itself so far. To the best of my knowledge, it has never been meaningless, is that true?"

"So far."

"Some will question the paradox, of course. If we travel to the past and give an author ideas he has not yet written, where did the ideas come from, us or him?"

"Him, of course. Multiple worlds."

"I'm afraid I haven't studied that branch of mystery, Miss Shamrock."

"I was telling him his own ideas. But as soon as he saw me, the world split away from the world in which he didn't see me. In one world, he writes the Courtesies alone, in the other, a vision reminds him. Not one past and future, Burrows, many pasts, many futures. No paradox."

"I must study, indeed," said her partner, his eyes twinkling. "I suppose there are worlds in which I study, and in which I don't. In which I put off studying . . ."

Shamrock nodded, solemn. "Every possible variation of every possible variable. Every decision separates the universe from what it would have been without it."

"I trust that we have now entered the universe in which Miss Shamrock Ferret solves the very mystery of our origins."

She looked to him, saw the twinkle in his eyes and laughed. "One of those universes, I hope!"

Shamrock reached to the ancient vase, touched it softly. She closed her eyes.

14

IT WAS A STAGE, she saw, a raised circular platform, brighter than the dim about. It stood before an auditorium of seats empty save for herself. Beyond the seats, a council chamber.

Inlaid, high on a wall of dark wood, a silver map of the planet Ferra. Beneath it, the harsh figure of a two-headed creature, a winged serpent, emerald green, thunderbolts in one claw, arrows in the other.

Beneath the serpent stood a wide, curving desk, places there for nine governors; in four of them sat ferrets of varying furs and masks but of one defeated countenance. Each wore a black scarf, and an emblem affixed, the emerald serpent.

As Shamrock looked about her in the empty place, Avedoi Merek entered and walked down the aisle of the auditorium, alone. The gentle animal stepped to the center of the platform, stood quietly in his white scarf, the emblem of the serpent pinned at his throat.

An unimposing figure, she thought, no chiseled features, no penetrating gaze, yet about him . . . it was as though, when he took the stage, some great magnet energized.

As the remains of ferret civilization watched, the philosopher faced a world's cameras and the surviving members of his nation's council.

"You will forgive me if I am not so eloquent or entertaining this evening," he said. "I have little to say, but perhaps I speak for most of us still alive."

He studied the remaining leaders, looked into the cameras beyond them to survivors on every corner of the globe.

"From this day forth," he said, and then he paused for the longest while, "I withdraw my consent from evil."

The words echoed from speakers in halls and homes and public spaces.

I withdraw my consent from evil. Any other time, the idea would have been a puzzle, a trick of words. Today, however, Avedoi Merek became the voice of a civilization's conscience, stark and straight, and today a race of animals listened.

"I withdraw my consent," he said, "from war." Soft-spoken, an impossibility all of a sudden required.

"I withdraw my consent from violence," said Merek. "From hatred. From malice."

He looked into the heart of every one of his race left alive.

"I withdraw my consent from these. In my actions. In my thought. In my choices."

He reached to the emerald serpent pinned at his throat, unfastened it, let it fall. "I withdraw my consent from evil. Forever."

Once there would have been a flicker of lights across the map of the continent, protest from those needing to argue definition and circumstance, to cry for patriotism. Now, after what had happened, the map was still.

An entire society with the freedom and the power to destroy itself listened, numbed at how close it had come to doing so.

"We have one chance to save ourselves and our future. There is one way, and it is so simple that it is impossible."

Watching, some ferrets fancied that they could see light around the face of this gentle creature, once chained and jailed, enemy of the state for speaking against a ferret war. The first hearts felt hope glimmer in darkness.

"May I ask?" he said. "Who has enjoyed our experiment with destruction? Who is happy for what has happened?" Two questions, and silence.

Enjoyed? the ferrets thought, smoke still rising from ruins about them. *Happy?*

Here the image faded, spiraled out of reach, and Shamrock blinked awake in her Cases Unsolved chair.

She shook herself, as much to shudder away the weight of the old time as to clear her mind of the image. She set the blue-metal vase gently on the table alongside her chair.

He had told her the truth, she thought. There had come the end of the world, and the one who rose against it was Avedoi Merek.

Have I stumbled into some different past, she thought, an ice-warped Ferra from might-have-been? She rubbed her eyes, stirred uneasily in the chair.

He called us to our highest right.

Different pasts, maybe. But could there have been a violent Before in the past we know today? She shivered. No history had hinted such a thing.

Ever have ferrets been creatures of warmth and courtesy. Always have we loved action and adventure, always we've been willing to overcome fear and to face peril along the paths that we've chosen.

Yet Shamrock trembled at what she had seen. That was no alternate past, it had been herself from today carried back to Avedoi Merek's demolished home, herself in the council chamber, her own heart singed, so near the arson of a civilization.

The vase stood silent on the table by her chair as if it were watching her, wondering why she had come to learn what no one else remembered.

Either ferret history is wrong, she thought, or my psychic powers have turned more dark and destructive than any creature's, ever.

She engaged the mystery, could not resolve it.

In all *The Paws of Knowledge,* in every ancient scroll and passage, not a word of war between ferrets. Ferrets can be mistaken, but they do not lie. Could it happen that somehow an entire culture *forgot* what once had been?

With a start she heard the clock chime dawn. She had agreed to return the vase to the museum at her earliest convenience. That was now. She lifted the ancient art and hurried to the museum.

It was light when she removed her business card and set the vase gently behind its glass, but she could not shake from her mind the gloom of the violence she had seen. Cities had been turned to fire, lives of peers and elders—lives of kits!—had been lost.

Ferrets don't ruin, she thought, her steps whispering on the early sidewalk, past shops asleep, undefended, no locks for their doors. We don't harm, we don't destroy. Even the suggestion—an unkind ferret—it makes one smile. Every ferret respects every other, lives always to its highest right. It is our way.

Were she any other creature, Shamrock Ferret would have shivered and put the whole strange scene from her mind, studied her next case and never looked back. But for this creature, the impossible was mystery, and mystery must always be resolved.

15

HER SOLUTION THAT week to the Case of the Invisible Clock provoked a flurry of attention in the press, stories for a few days that Burrows needed to correct.

His release to the newsferrets explained that contrary to speculation, Shamrock Ferret was not accomplished in sorcery, she was not a master illusionist, she did not possess a bionic brain.

"Miss Shamrock," he wrote, "is extraordinary in that she is a careful observer of ferrets and scenes, she has a retentive memory, she considers alternate possibilities and she applies established principles of deduction to her business, which is to detect that which is overlooked by others."

All of this was true. Shamrock noticed. And so she noticed, not long after Burrows had come to work with her, that she had been earning somewhat more attention from the press than she had before. She found the timing odd, discounted it.

MusTelCo, for instance, could have gone to any qualified detective to correct an erring headline, she thought. The giant company hadn't sent a card and a kit's stuffed penguin to thank Burrows for publicizing Shamrock Ferret, but for getting the corporation out of hot water. A little publicity is normal, she thought. When one deals with mysteries, one must not be surprised at the interest of inquiring minds.

Haunting her now was the much bigger puzzle that no one had hired her to solve: the Case of the Golden Deed. Did one ferret change history? If he did, how could she prove it?

Anyone watching Shamrock would have smiled, that afternoon. For an hour her fluffy body lay motionless, fast asleep in the bedroom above the office. Next instant blankets flying, lights aflare, the ferret diving from her hammock, fur awry, hooking a scarf as she bolted downstairs and out the door.

"Good afternoon, Miss Shamrock," said Burrows as the door slammed shut.

The mystery's not what happened before Avedoi Merek stood in the cameras of Ferra, thought Shamrock, running toward the museum, *it's what happened after!* The answer's still in the vase!

Panting from her run, she burst out of the fourth-floor elevator. Sometimes the best you can do is not-think. So many levels of the mind . . .

She had opened the glass door of the case before she realized that what she had come for was no longer there. The spot where the vase had stood was empty save for a business card:

Nutmeg Ferret
Nutmeg & Bergamont, Detectives

16

SHAMROCK BENT over the antiquities display and listened to the silence while it roared in her ears. No, she thought. Something is wrong. Coincidence helps us, coincidence does not block our way. How can it be that it's *gone?*

She returned to the elevator, rode in no hurry to the main floor, walked out the door and down the steps to the sidewalk, her puzzlement more real than the city around her.

If coincidence helps, she thought, how am I helped that the world's most famous detective has borrowed my vase at the very hour I need it myself? The question was a mini-case itself, and her inner observer stood apart, watched her solve it.

> Does Nutmeg Ferret know I want the vase?
> Assume yes.
> Has she taken the vase to help me?
> Assume yes.
> How am I helped, if I miss the vase?
> No answer.
> What do I learn from not having the vase?
> No answer.

Eyes down, watching the sidewalk, the detective sniffed in frustration. Her inner observer smiled.

> If I learn—something—why should Nutmeg Ferret, whom I have ever admired and never met, care?
> Because I matter to her.
> Why do I matter to her?
> Wrong question.
> Is it Nutmeg alone? What of the shadowy Bergamont?
> Wrong question.

Burrows would know the answer, she thought, but it would not be ethical for me to ask after his former employers. She set her jaw. There is nothing I cannot detect on my own, without help.

She swept her mind clean, started over.

> Why do I need the vase?

Because it is soaked in the images of centuries ago, and I can unlock those images when I hold it in my paws.

Good answer! she thought. Follow it, follow it!

Is what I need to know outside of me?
No.
Does empty matter contain knowledge that I do not?
No!
Why do I need the vase?
It helps me see what I already know.
Why do I need its help?

The mystery felt Shamrock closing on it highspeed. It leaped aside, darted for cover, not fast enough. Quick as a shadow the detective closed her paw, seized it in a flash, midair. It sighed, smiled at her: "Nice catch, Shamrock!"

Why do I need its help? Sometimes, unless you start over, you'll never start at all.

By the time she reached home, Shamrock Ferret was running again. She flew up the steps, threw open the door, her partner looking up startled from his desk.

She trembled excitement. "Thought-experiment, Mr. Burrows! Imagine a report in *Ferret Science* magazine. Two tests of the accuracy of psychometry: one with the sensitive holding an object, one with the sensitive holding a *substitute* for the same object! Which test is more accurate?"

She threw her hat and scarf toward the wall. Both missed their pegs, tumbled to the floor. She retrieved them, paced the office. Why do you take so long, Mr. Burrows?

"Why, they're the *same*, Miss Shamrock. Bless my whiskers, what an interesting experiment! The reason, you see, is that the information they seek—"

"—is not in the object, it's in the *sensitive!*"

She leaped headlong to her Cases Unsolved chair.

"Mr. Burrows, bring me something!"

"Of course, Miss Shamrock. What would you like?"

"Anything! Something I can hold."

A smile, and he offered MusTelCo's stuffed penguin.

She looked up to him, smiled back, glad for his calm. "Thank you. I suppose I might settle down a bit."

"There's nothing wrong with adventure, Miss Shamrock."

With this, Burrows, ever thoughtful, bade her good evening and departed in white scarf and tweed hat. Shamrock heard the purr of his Austin-Furet starting, easing away into the streets. Then she took the penguin in her paws, settled properly in her chair, relaxed and closed her eyes.

"I hold a vase," she whispered, "from an ancient time . . ."

The first image came clear: a ferret kit, all dusty sable, grasped a fluffy cloth penguin in its teeth, dragged it toward a playpen tunnel.

The detective opened her eyes. "Hm . . ."

Three deep breaths, she thought. Body relaxed. Mind relaxed. I am in the council chamber . . .

Flash of a penguin diving, then darkness swirling around her. Let go, she thought, let the image offer itself.

Then, no warning, instant clarity:

A penguin stood upon the lighted platform, facing the remains of the council under the scowl of the two-headed serpent. Shamrock murmured, and the penguin dissolved to the form of a ferret, the color of sand and night.

"Who has enjoyed our experiment with destruction? Who is happy for what has happened?" Avedoi Merek stood alone before a planet's cameras, asked the questions into silence.

"If we are not happy," the words slow, uninterrupted, "if our experiment has brought us not well-being but pain and loss and horror, must we, ever? repeat it."

Not a sound in the chamber, not one response light on the map of the planet. By his presence alone did this creature command the attention of survivors everywhere.

At once a cloud of penguins fluttered and soared, squawking, stark tuxedos in the air, turning and diving through the scene, shredding the moment.

"No," said Shamrock upon her chair, unsmiling, firm, tenacious to watch. "Let this continue! *Without interruption . . .*"

The penguins vanished, squawks echoing away.

"I am a simple animal," said Avedoi Merek, "of more questions than answers. One of my questions is this: What would happen, if we accept for everyone, that constitution which we already accept for ourselves? Not laws, not rules.

"Here is a constitution of *courtesies*, should we choose to live by them. The courtesy we show to those we love, show the same to all, be we a civilization of one or of millions:

"Whatever harm I would do to another, I shall do first to myself.

"As I respect and am kind to myself, so shall I respect and be kind to peers, to elders, to kits.

"I claim for others the freedom to live as they wish, to think and believe as they will. I claim that freedom for myself.

"I shall make each choice and live each day to my highest sense of right."

As though he were an alchemist alone in some dark workshop, Avedoi Merek transmuted pain and terror into resolution. His words were neither plea nor demand—one creature stood before the rest and made a personal decision, invited his race to join him if it wished.

Watching, eyes closed, Shamrock Ferret had changed from observer to witness. Whether any other walks with him, she thought, I will. In trance, she waited for him to continue the list of courtesies by which her culture lived to this day. *I take the name Ferret,* she murmured, *to declare always that I am not rival or enemy, but of one family . . .*

But the animal who stood before the council and the cameras of his world was silent.

At last, nearly a whisper: ". . . thank you." The ferret nodded to himself. He had forgotten nothing. "Thank you."

Then he turned and stepped from the platform, walked away. He glanced toward Shamrock, as though he felt her presence more than saw it.

A door opened to an outside hallway, the shadow of a penguin beyond. Avedoi Merek passed through, the door closed.

In her trance, Shamrock saw a few scattered lights begin to flicker upon the map of the planet, then more, and then yet more. Hundreds and hundreds of lights.

17

IT WAS TRUE, thought Shamrock. The answers we seek are not outside us, but within. Psychometry, like every other science, is a tool to find what we already know. Artifacts help because we believe they will help.

When Burrows arrived next morning, Shamrock was curled on the sofa, reviewing her notes of the evening past.

If ferrets had been violent creatures who chose to give up violence, she thought, the change in civilization more likely happened all at once, from one traumatic event, than from a few laying down arms before others.

Avedoi Merek had said so himself: "If some choice has brought us horror, must we, ever? repeat it."

That instant, thought Shamrock, that was the moment we changed.

Now: What possible proof could exist that what she had imagined was real? Where was her evidence?

The detective stayed up late, built a nest of heavy volumes, most of her *Paws of Knowledge* around her, massive butterflies circling her Cases Unsolved chair.

Then she was off to the library, a few of the volumes surrounding printed in the ancient Ferrune. What she found was a blank wall.

There is no mention in any record, anywhere, of any war, ever in history. No battles, no dates of combat, no victory or defeat, nothing but peace and harmony through the history of the race of ferret-kind, since the beginning.

But I saw it! I saw the ruins of cities, hope destroyed in rubble and fire. I saw Avedoi Merek speak to the world! How could I imagine that, from nothing, no precedent in all the records of my race?

18

"WOULD YOU CARE for tea, Miss Shamrock?"

"Yes, thank you, Mr. Burrows, I would."

The engine-telegraph doorbell rang, the handle moved from *Engines Standby* to *Ahead Full*, then back again.

"Come in, please," said Burrows.

There was no response, no sound from bell or door. He poured tea and honey, set the service down, crossed the room and opened the door.

"Bless my whiskers," he muttered. "There's no one here!"

He looked left and right onto the street outside, saw no one. Then he looked down, stooped to the threshold, lifted a sheet of metal foil, silvery blue. "Hello . . ."

The big ferret blinked at strange markings, shook his head, looked once more down the street. Then he closed the door, walked to Shamrock and set the foil before her. "I'm afraid I'm a little rusty on my ancient alphabets."

Shamrock frowned a question at him: Ancient alphabets?

Not printed, was the sheet, but rather illuminated in gold, fine-wrought vines curling around the margin, trumpet-flowers of royal purple encircling the page.

In the center, lettered by paw, shining Ferrune calligraphy:

[Ferrune calligraphy — three lines of decorative runic characters]

Shamrock was not rusty on her Ferrune, she loved the old characters.

> "In the moat, which is Loch Stoat," she read,
> A strange petal flowers.
> What is the pollen for?
> S.

As she held the foil, she closed her eyes, called images forth. Flash of a meteor through the night, a sunken ship, a blossom opening beneath the waves. And then, odd sight, an image of herself, as in a mirror, smiling.

That no one waited on her doorstep was not astonishing. Tips and clues from those who did not wish to be known were normal in her business. Ferrets are curious about others, modest about themselves—so thrived their television and tabloids. But why this peculiar message, and whose the initial at the bottom?

Why would someone want anonymously to offer a clue, and if clue it was, to which of her cases did it apply?

She set the foil down. "What do you make of it, Mr. Burrows?"

"It's ferretmetal, Miss Shamrock."

Indeed, she thought. And . . . ?

"Someone would like you to make a journey."

"To Loch Stoat."

"So it would seem."

"To do what?"

A long silence. "My guess, Miss Shamrock, is that you intend to find out."

Once he had joined Shamrock Ferret, the courtesy of ethics had broken Burrows' contact with Nutmeg and the firm for which he had worked. If they were behind this, he thought, whatever they had planned they had done it without his knowledge or consent.

19

HER RESEARCH changed at once, turned on Loch Stoat.

The earliest reference she found was written in Ferrune, a sonnet on the building of the palace upon its shores; the latest was a fantasy by kits' writer Budgeron Ferret. Fantasy, however, she thought, entering the Ebon Mask bookstore, is not meaningless.

She found a little chair in the kits' section of the bookstore, sat there and read Budgeron's book through before she bought it.

A serpent in Loch Stoat, indeed. But a very different sort of serpent, as Budgie and his friend Bvuhlgahri Bat had discovered, one with a gift that could change their time. Was it fiction, the writer's imagination overlapping her own, or could a serpent beneath the waters of the loch be a clue in the Case of the Golden Deed?

20

BURROWS DROVE the distance from London, the Austin-Furet purring happily at speeds only an expert driver could manage.

Shamrock held her breath, once, in the highlands, gripped the pawhold as the roadster drifted high power around a tighter turn than most.

"I'd hold on, too," he told her, "in any other machine. But the Furet and I, we've driven our share of rallies, a bit more challenging than the F3 to Scotland. Safety is control, Miss Shamrock, no matter speed, and control is something I've . . ." He glanced at her. "Would you care to slow a little, ma'am?"

The detective released her grip, relaxed her body from nose to tail. "As fast as you dare, Mr. Burrows."

Her partner laughed, admiring the young detective. The Furet took the next turn with a little less torque, and without the drift.

By afternoon the two ferrets motored slowly through the grounds of the palace at Mustelania. Bright flags flew in sunlight from the towers, kits and grown-ups picnicked and played on the broad lawns and parks. Groups joined together, tours through the vast basements of the palace itself, the largest library on earth.

Adjoining the palace to the east glittered the waters of Loch Stoat. Burrows navigated traffic till they arrived at the shore, then as others turned left to follow the highway north, he angled right onto a grassy lane, stopped by a waterfront restaurant.

"Hungry, Miss Shamrock?" he said. "Perhaps a late lunch before we're off to sea? I highly recommend the *crêpes flambées.*"

Odd, thought Shamrock. How is it that Burrows could be such a regular customer so far north?

The maître d' nodded to Burrows, led the partners to a place overlooking the water, and though the restaurant was not crowded, Shamrock remarked that they had been given the best table in the house.

"I must say you deserve it, Miss Shamrock," said Burrows. "It's not every day that one solves such a case as yours."

She laughed. "It's a long way from solved. So far, the Golden Deed is in my mind, I'm afraid. We've come all this way on the hope of a clue that seems to be eluding us."

She recited once again what she had memorized the instant she had seen the metal scroll: "'*In the moat, which is Loch Stoat, a strange petal flowers. What is the pollen for?*' Sixteen words, Mr. Burrows, sixty-six characters."

"Eighty-one characters, counting spaces, ma'am. The number of words plus the number of letters equals the total number of characters."

She shook her head. "A dead end, I'm afraid. Six *A*'s, no *B*'s, two *C*'s, no *D*'s, six *E*'s . . . I don't believe it's a letter puzzle. It doesn't seem to be a number puzzle."

The waiter arrived, a handsome animal, pale fur, black paws and mask, scarf the color of the loch. "A fine choice," he said of their order. He looked with strange intensity at Shamrock, and a curious smile. "Would you care for our Mandalay tea, ma'am?"

She looked to him, startled. "Yes," she said, "yes, please."

"And honey. Poured, not stirred?"

She nodded, wordless.

"Of course, Miss Shamrock," and he left toward the kitchen.

"Mr. Burrows," she said, "what was that about?"

Her partner smiled. "What was what about?"

"'Miss Shamrock,' when I've never been here before."

He shrugged. "Solve the cases you've solved, your picture in the magazines, ma'am, it's not amazing you're becoming known, here and there."

"My picture in the magazines."

Her partner shrugged. "*Who's in the News*, that sort of thing. There have been some mentions. Your cases are interesting, your ways. The up-and-coming detective, unique mind, that sort of thing. You may not choose to read about yourself, others do."

She shook off the implications, that is, the shattering change ahead should ever she shift from private animal to public.

Ferrets delight in their celebrities, their aristocracy of merit, its dukes and princesses chosen from every calling. If you excel at your craft, there is a good chance that curious ferrets will need to know why, to find what makes you different.

The kit Shamrock had been no exception, following Nutmeg Ferret's cases, eager to learn all she could of how her heroine's lightning mind worked, what she thought, how she lived.

Burrows watched sunlight on the loch, stretching blue and deep to mossy hills beyond, as silent at his place as though he were listening to his partner's hidden conversation.

Heaven help animals caught in the blaze of ferret curiosity, thought Shamrock, for they need the help of angels. Everyone lives to her or his own highest standard, erring from time to time, learning from errors; she was no different. Celebrity ferrets, though, are expected never to err.

No matter one's old calling, the new one, after a ferret catches the curiosity of others, is role model, example. For every animal, everywhere in the culture.

"Without the poetry," said Burrows, shattering her thoughts, "the scroll tells us this: Loch Stoat is protecting something that is odd and beautiful, which affects the world in ways we don't know. To solve your mystery, you've got to find out what that something is and what it does."

Shamrock frowned, shook her head. "Simpler than that, Mr. Burrows. If it's a clue to the Golden Deed, and I'm not sure it is, it's saying that what I need to know is in the loch. At the bottom of the loch, I suspect."

"And what is it that you need to know, Miss Shamrock?"

She smiled. The question was with her day and night. "Proof," she said. "Evidence. Without evidence, Shamrock Ferret's not solved anything, she's a psychic time traveler, telling stories."

"The proof's underwater?"

"I'll find it there, Mr. Burrows, or it's going to find me, on my way to the bottom."

Her partner startled at the words, as if she knew more than she was telling: *it will find me.*

She nodded, her highest right demanding a decision. "I'm going to be met," she said. "Whoever wrote that scroll expects me to come looking."

21

SHE LEARNS ALL she can, thought Burrows, she pours fact through experience, and then she leaps, trusting intuition. One must admire her courage. He nodded. Courage is the final test.

The *ScubaFerrets* boat arrowed toward the center of Loch Stoat, Shamrock listening to intuition, wishing the riddle might have been a little more specific about *where* in Loch Stoat its strange petal might flower.

Then without knowing why, she called, "Stop here, please!"

The captain smiled behind her sunglasses, reached her paw to the throttle. The boat slowed, stopped, reversed at idle power until Shamrock nodded. "That's fine, thank you, ma'am."

Then, engine off, the boat drifted on the rippled mirror of the lake.

"It's deep out here," said the captain, a ferret the color of charcoal, cap low over her eyes, scarf ruffled on the hint of a breeze. "There'd be a lot more to see near shore . . ."

"This will be fine, thank you."

Shamrock snapped the buckles of the diving harness about her, slipped on fins and weight belt and mask, tested her air supply. She fastened a reel of white line to her belt, lifted a sealed floodlight.

"Wait for me, please, Mr. Burrows," she said. "If I don't find an air supply down there, I'll be back before long. But I suspect . . ." She flashed him a look of delicious adventure. "If I'm not back by sunset, bring a light and follow my line."

"If you're not back, I'll be following sooner than that, Miss Shamrock."

High sun plunged spears of light into the water around the boat, the shafts gleaming near the surface, then fading away, no bottom in sight.

Shamrock stepped to the transom ladder, swung her paws free and dropped into the water. In that second she thought this might be a foolish idea, free-diving toward she didn't know what, expecting guidance to appear on its own.

She waved to Burrows, swept her fear aside. Not foolish. There is a case to be solved. Then she was gone, a sable form sinking through dark crystal.

"She won't see much, Mr. Burrows." The captain smiled at the detective's partner. "It's the deepest part of the loch. Why dive where there's nothing to see?"

22

SHAMROCK TURNED as she sank, watching, a thousand bubbles trapped like bright pearls in her fur. Everything beyond was featureless blue mystery.

No floor below, not a fish to be seen, even the boat above disappeared from view. But for the dim line uncoiling from the reel at her belt and her own silver breath trailing upward, the detective could have been floating in space.

Three hundred paws down, the surface was a hazy direction in the dim, nothing more.

Now what, she thought, wait? Ferrets of action do not wait. I've got enough air to go to the bottom, but not to explore. Touch down, a few minutes for a square search and it will be time to come up again, decompressing along the way.

She switched the floodlight on, dropped lower. Looking down, darkness, the beam fetching out twenty paws into gloom then swallowed up in nothing.

Down she sank, descending at a speed she reckoned would give her a few seconds' warning before she hit the bottom.

Now through her beam darted a single silver flash, smaller than a minnow, flying upward. Then another in its trail, glittering briefly in Shamrock's light. They showed no curiosity about her, did not stop or circle as fish might have circled about a diver. They're not so much fish, she thought, as insects on some mission. Underwater insects? she wondered. *Aqua-bees?*

Then there it was, the floor of the lake, all of a sudden surrounding her so far as her beam could penetrate.

A bottom not jagged rock but smooth as a platter, a cloud of silt rising up where her paws touched. Images fluttered as she touched, rapid-clicking, a deck of picture cards shuffled, and stopped on the last, an arching bow of color.

Her paws slid on the surface, which curved gently downward to her left. The farther she slid, the steeper the curve, till she kicked free and free-fell once more beside this boulder towering into the dark.

A second landing, and Shamrock stood upon what seemed to be a floor of matted grass.

She swept her light beneath the boulder. At the end of the sweep a sudden sparkle glinted back, reflected from midnight.

The great shape did not rest on the bottom, she noticed, but some ten paws above it, as though supported by rock. There was room underneath to stand, to walk for some distance.

The detective did not think as much as she watched, gathering information. She could not stay long.

The reflection glittered from her light as she approached, till it shimmered like quicksilver overhead, an air pocket beneath this sleeping giant.

A dim form touched her in the darkness, and she bolted back, spun the light upon it. The form was silent, unmoving. The form was a steel ladder.

An instant of eerie shock, sparks and high voltage in Shamrock's mind. This is no rock, she thought, it's a ship! Sunk to the bottom . . .

She unfastened the reel from her belt, tied the line to the lowest rung of the ladder. Time jerked into high gear, the detective juggling possibilities so swiftly that she barely followed:

something someone invited her, connect riddle connect Ferrune connect *petal flowers*, connect psychometry, connect Stilton Ferret connect Avedoi Merek ?! connect Burrows connect Loch Stoat—time— connect palace ?! connect Nutmeg & Bergamont connect aqua-bees ?! *what is the pollen for?* connect Budgeron Ferret connect why ship, why sunk, when sunk—*time!*—how sunk, where built, connect Courtesies ?! connect Ferret Way ?! connect war connect *Paws of Knowledge, Volume 13* connect Dad and Mum connect bubbles? connect Curious Patterns ?! connect Miss Ginger connect your very own star . . . years tucked inside seconds as the detective watched the blur. —Time—

TIME!

Shamrock touched her watch, unbelieving. In what had seemed no longer than a breath to her, the dive-limit marker had jumped beyond its redline. Too late, nearly, she must be on her way upward, she must decompress from the deep in stages, and without air to breathe, without time, she couldn't do it. Every second she stayed at this depth made it worse, made it less probable that she would survive unless she started upward minutes ago.

What is this ship?

She grasped the ladder in her paws, lifted herself from lakebed toward the quicksilver reflections, betting her life there would be a chamber above, an entrance to the ship.

Breaking the surface inside the chamber, Shamrock glistened like a sea otter on the rungs of the ladder, her light casting harsh shadows in this place that had been so long black. As her paws touched the ring-shaped floor of the air lock, she heard a distant click and the chamber was flooded in soft light.

All painted metal, the walls and ceiling were continuous curves, a simple place, unfurnished save for pawrails leading to the ladder and to the circle of water through which she had entered. To her left, an oval hatch, taller than Shamrock, closed.

At last we meet, she thought. Whoever had sent the message, the riddle in Ferrune, must wait not far away.

"Hallo?" she called.

There was no answer. No one came to meet her, nor had sign or notice been left for her. She shed her diving harness, fins and weight belt, set them by the floodlight at the ladder.

The locking wheel of the hatch was spun tight. Never had she seen a locked door, but seafarers needed them, she knew, for water-tight security in the bulkheads of their ships.

She touched the metal wall. Impressions flickered behind her eyes, these plates under construction. Visions of a shipyard, larger than any she knew, thousands of ferrets at work on scaffolds, hoisting tools she had never seen, joining one curving piece to another.

Now a muffled metal clank echoed in the chamber, solid metal rose to seal the watery entrance. Shamrock heard the sound of air escaping, she felt the pressure change in her ears.

It won't be long. She stood quietly, assessing nearly to overload.

Why the silence? Somewhere someone must have turned the chamber lights on, they must have operated the air lock. Yet why would there be an air lock in a sunken ship? Why should there be air at all?

She relaxed, smiled at herself. There is a reason, she thought. There is always a reason, and before long each step of my mystery will make perfect sense.

Shortly she heard the whine of gears meshed, noticed the hatch locking wheel turn by itself, motor-driven, a hiss of air as it lifted from its seal and slid aside.

This is not a shipwreck, it is a working vessel underwater. A submarine! She shrugged aside a wave of questions. Whatever is supposed to happen, she thought, is happening.

She stepped through the hatchway, followed the turn of the passage once to the left then to the right, where it became a long straightaway, an access corridor down the center of the ship. The vessel, whatever it was, was not wrecked. Behind her, the hatch closed and locked by itself. Air hissed and echoed, gears hummed as the inner door sealed itself and the outer one opened again to the deeps.

Stenciled in Ferrune at the intersection of every corridor and passageway was a reference: ⌐(x) – ↑(x), then: ⌐(x) – ↑(x). P9 – C11, she translated, P9 – C10 . . . Every fifth hatch added a placard: λ₀ ℞⌒ +)×S˹.

S for *submersible*, she thought, or *submarine*. The submarine *Rainbow*.

"Hallo?" There was no reply.

She followed passageway 9, faced on the starboard side with white steel entry hatches. Crew's quarters, she guessed.

Nearly to the end of the passage, she froze. Over the hatchway at C2 was mounted a crest, an emblem. Smaller than she remembered, but there was no mistaking.

Fastened to the steel was the image of a two-headed serpent: arrows in one claw, thunderbolts in the other, a fierce wicked thing, the color of emerald and coal, graven upon an oval of white.

She swallowed. How could an image . . . From . . . Has someone, she thought, somehow, read my mind . . . ?

Beneath confusion she noticed and questioned as always, observing, missing no detail, leaving reaction and emotion for a different time. Over the serpent had been slashed in Ferrune, one word in red paint:)S⊣ℓ

"*Note*," she translated. The word baffled her.

She climbed to the emblem, her paws trembling up the steel web of the passageway, examined the letters.

The word had been painted by paw. It wasn't an *e*, the last character, but an exclamation point. Over the fierce picture had been painted the word *Not!*

How had a submarine come to the bottom of Loch Stoat; how could it mount an emblem that only Shamrock of all the ferrets in the world had imagined; why the scarlet word to mock it; *where is the crew?*

Under the weight of those questions, she dropped to the deck, stood away and took an eye-picture of the emblem: gazed steadily, closed her eyes, opened them. The image caught in her memory, line and color, every detail.

"Hallo!"

But for echoes of her call, the ship remained silent.

Now's a time to practice patience, thought Shamrock. Oh, patience, my weakest virtue.

The detective, fur nearly dry, continued through the last hatch at the end of the passageway, found herself standing on what appeared to be an airline flight deck, lit with the same even glow that filled the rest of the vessel.

Roomier than a flight deck, in fact, bounded about with a dozen silent viewscreens, banks of instruments and switches and control handles, crew station seats complete with wide seat belts, none of them occupied.

The walls unpainted, translucent blue-silver steel. She caught her breath. The walls were ferretmetal, and blazoned upon them an insignia in gold: two stars, one large, one small, joined by a sweeping curved pathway. The pattern from the cornfields.

She moved closer, observing, absorbing, analyzing, as though Mum and Dad had led her here by the paw, removed her blindfold, stepped back.

What is this place, Shamrock, what is it for? How was it built? By whom? When? Where? How did it come to Loch Stoat? Why have you been invited here, who opened the doors? What is the emblem? *What does this vessel mean?*

"I'm here!" Her voice echoed against the metal, as much her beginning statement of fact as a voice to be heard by another.

The place was empty, silent. No dials glowed, not a needle flickered.

Her eyes widened. Placards, instrument markings, labels, all of them were engraved in Ferrune. Oval ports looked into black water. Fastened to the sill of one port, a small blue vase, a silken flower within to make it homelike, a humble Shooting Star. . . .

The painting!

"S doesn't mean submarine," she whispered, numb. "*S is for starship!*"

Shamrock sank to the edge of the command seat, ahead of a half-circle of semi-couches. Not knowing she made a sound, she spoke into silence.

"This is where they sat, my ancestors, in these seats, they touched these controls, they flew this machine across the stars! They were *here!*"

They had come, her ancient fathers and mothers and the kits who would be Shamrock's great-grandparents hundreds of times removed, they had come in this ship, light-years from Ferra to Earth.

Her eyes filling with tears, the detective collapsed forward upon the control pedestal, face buried in her paws. Pressed against the metal of the console, her tears on the ancient instruments, she watched the landing in her mind, yearning toward her great-grandparents in wild discovering joy that felt like endless sorrow.

Visions unprompted.

There had been no Loch Stoat, then. When the first ferrets landed, this place was a level valley meadow. Softly had the ship touched the grass here as it had touched in fields to the south, gently had it settled to its final landing, magnetic engines at last gone quiet.

Behind her eyes she saw the ancients when they were young, when they were kits, brave and frightened at once, filled with resolve to make a home of this new place, a civilization built upon the Courtesies.

She felt their determination. They wouldn't write old history, they'd live it new. Why condemn the future, recording wars that didn't deserve to be held in memory, why pass word through time, immortalizing names that stood for hatred and battle?

These who mocked that fierce serpent had vowed to honor only the highest their culture had been in spite of it, they vowed to surpass that highest, themselves. The colonists had survived every hazard the universe could lay before them, for the sake of their kits and a new beginning.

Now Shamrock Ferret, one of those unborn who had called her parents to the stars, lay sobbing in love for ancestors long dead, alive again in her heart.

23

"WOULD YOU CARE for tea, Miss Shamrock?"

Burrows Ferret stood before the flight deck console, water-drops glistening still in his fur. Behind him, another animal, unrecognized through the detective's tears.

"Burrows!" As much a sob as a cry of delight.

"Yes, ma'am." He looked about the room. "You found it!"

"They came . . . all of them, they came from Ferra! *Burrows, this is their ship!*"

"It is."

"You knew?"

"No. We followed you down. We know now."

"The legend's true. We came from the stars!"

"You have a great deal of evidence, Miss Shamrock." He turned to the other animal, nodded, turned back.

"Burrows . . ." Shamrock rose and hugged her partner, buried her face in the soft fur of his chest, tears on sable. He stood quietly, sheltering her.

At last Burrows made his introduction: "Miss Shamrock, I'm pleased to present Miss Nutmeg Ferret, of Nutmeg—"

Shamrock gasped, whirled to the animal she had admired for so long. The charcoal dust had washed from the captain's fur in the long dive from the boat. Now, still wet, it shone that soft spice-color, the eyes unchanged, noticing all.

Smiling at the young detective's startlement, Nutmeg completed the introduction with a wave to Shamrock's partner: ". . . and Bergamont."

Shamrock turned, felt her knees weaken. "Mr. Burrows? You're Bergamont Ferret?"

"The late Bergamont Ferret," said her partner. "The erstwhile Bergamont. I stumble sometimes, when cameras come round."

"You charmed us from the beginning, Shamrock," said Nutmeg, "since before the beginning. The Case of the Invisible Clock, remarkable—twin ferrets, we discover—well done! And the Case of the Midnight Patterns. We were puzzled, everyone was, and when you found the artists, and the mouse explained . . ." Nutmeg nodded to the emblem on the wall. "How did you know the patterns were from *Rainbow*, before you found the ship?"

"I didn't." Shamrock smiled at her heroine. "But give me a day here, ma'am, and I'll tell you all about it." Her mind raced. So much to say! "Miss Nutmeg, the aqua-bees! Did you notice? Their hive is aboard this ship. Do you suppose that means . . ."

". . . they're not bees at all?" asked Nutmeg.

Shamrock's observer within stood back, happy: here she is, the kit who once hauled encyclopedias home from the library, standing now, sharing ideas and matching wits with the celebrated Nutmeg & Bergamont.

The stuff of family, it thought. With the adventures we choose and the mysteries we solve we build our own credentials, write our own introduction to others around the world who value adventure and mystery themselves.

Shamrock Ferret, become a celebrity? Bright as she is, thought the observer within, she'll enjoy it.

24

ONCE EVERY century, the atomic clock strikes *Open and Search*.

Once every century the external access door slides open near *Rainbow*'s dorsal thruster.

Once every century I am launched.

Arcs and radials, I hum. Thousand-paw radius, ten-thousand-paw, one megapaw, ten megapaws, a hundred.

NSSD: No Suitable Storage Device.

Return to ship.

Monitor Hive Environment Nominal, Data-Bees in Rest.

Reset clock.

Shut down.

Once every century, I search.

I have searched 106 times.

After the thirty-ninth century, the atmosphere changed from free nitrogen and oxygen to ice and then to water, the ship at the bottom of a deepening lake of this substance.

Recording, Cycle 107:

Instruction—*Open and Search.*

External Access Door—*Clear.*

Door—*Open.*

Data-Bee—*Launch.*

I hum through water.

I begin search, thousand-paw radius.

NSSD.

I hum through air.

I begin search, ten-thousand-paw radius.

SDL: Storage Device Located. Range: 2,127 paws. Azimuth: 283 degrees.

I return to ship.

I activate Data-Bee Hive Wake-Up sequence.

I lock door open.

I reset my mission identity from Search Bee to Transfer Bee.

I begin Ferret Information Transfer, Energy Conservation Protocol, Low Volume Transmission.

I access ship's data center.

I download first kilopack, Section One Outline:

    1. To Our Grandkits

    2. Who We Are

    3. History of Ferra

    4. Why We Came to Earth

    5. Reenergizing Rainbow

    6. Starship Operation

    7. Navigation, and the Way Home

    8. Ship's Logs and Records

    9. Technical Data

I return to door.

I launch.

I hum direct to palace, thence through air shafts to archive storage below main library.

I confirm upload will not interfere with ferret computer operating system.

I upload first kilopack Section One Outline into unused disc space.

I return to ship.

I access ship's data center.

I download next kilopack Section One in sequence.

I continue transfer in one-kilopack units with other data-bees to upload twenty thousand gigapacks or until alternate instructions from ferrets.

I override following century cycles as required until upload complete.

I like my job.

☁

Wings buzzing cobalt silver in the sunlight, dusky pearl under the moon, aqua-bees emerge in tiny splashes from Loch Stoat, trailing misty spray from their wings, on course for the palace in Mustelania. They are small, fly swiftly and are rarely seen, even at close range.

25

DARKNESS MIGHT have fallen on the loch above; within *Rainbow*, the light was cool and even, the three ferrets at the navigator's station, star charts for a desktop.

"You know the feeling, Miss Nutmeg," said Shamrock, warm and at home now with the one who had been her heroine. "When I looked over the hatch in the passageway, and there was the serpent . . ." She shrugged with delight.

"Proof?" asked the other, that quiet voice.

"Proof! Otherwise, my psychometry, it could have been a dream, my vision just a theory. No one would have believed it was a choice we made. He was an example, Avedoi Merek. One ferret, one personal decision, on his own: *I withdraw my consent from evil* . . ."

"The rest of them listened," said Nutmeg, "knowing he was right. And they withdrew their consent, as well. Was that it?"

"To this day! All of us do it, still. Not one deed, but millions: every animal, every choice, every day. All of us, a continuous, undying golden deed."

The celebrity smiled at her young colleague. "A solution so beautiful is probably true," she said. "But tell me—you can prove that it began with Avedoi Merek?"

The way Nutmeg asked, thought Shamrock . . . something was wrong.

She laser-flashed over her case. All was in order: the sign of a war-serpent that she could not know existed but for her vision: Avedoi Merek standing alone, choosing his highest right. Her discovery of that very emblem over the passageway in this sunken starship. Evidence.

It was the snake that proved the vision to me, thought Shamrock, and in that instant she caught the flaw that Nutmeg hinted: the difference between subjective and objective, between deduced and tangible.

Shamrock laughed, mortified, lifted her paws to cover her eyes. "Oh, bless my whiskers," she said, her voice muffled in the quiet. "The snake proved the case *to me!*"

The sign, the arrows and thunderbolts were concrete, evidence to examine in the passageway above the hatch at C2. But Shamrock's story, though true, was no proof that any golden deed had ever occurred.

Other ferrets would believe her, for ferrets honor the truth that each perceives, but other ferrets hadn't been in the council hall with her, hadn't vaulted across time to the fires of an ancient war, hadn't watched civilization turn on the point of Avedoi Merek's example, the declaration of his highest right. All of this had been Shamrock Ferret's perception, it belonged to no other animal alive.

At last she folded her paws in her lap, her smile a little sad. She knew what had happened, and she would be alone in her knowing for so long as she lived.

"We can win them all, Miss Shamrock," said Burrows, "but we don't do it very often."

Nutmeg rose. "Have you considered," she said softly, "that you may have solved a case, a different one, which has never been opened?"

Shamrock shook her head.

Nutmeg caught Burrows' eye, and he nodded, go ahead.

"Let's call it the Case of the Missing Magnet. Have you ever wondered, Miss Shamrock, why ferrets love celebrities? You have. You know we love them because we're curious, and we're a civilization of models for each other. What other culture but ours calls on celebrity to show its highest morality?" _ WE ARE IN deep shit

"None," said Shamrock. "But the Courtesies are in our hearts, ma'am, they're the first morals we learn."

"The Courtesies are ideas," said Nutmeg. "Each of us, we live our own example of kindness and respect, of excellence in whatever we do, of how to think and speak and act in any situation. But celebrities are our examples. They start with nothing but a dream, most of them, they find the courage to follow what they know is right, no matter what. If I've been an example for you, Miss Shamrock; today you're an example for me."

"You're an example for everyone, Nutmeg! 'Now why would this be?' When anyone finds a mystery, they start with your words, they—"

Burrows cut her off, not harsh but firm. "She's asking you to be an example, too, Miss Shamrock. She's asking you to join her. Onstage, in front of the world."

The interruption was an act so astonishing that his partner was left midsentence, her mouth open, staring at him.

"If you would let go your humility," Burrows continued, "this would be no surprise. You are a brilliant detective, insightful, original, entertaining, unafraid. You cannot light such a firework of mind without expecting others to notice, and notice we have. We've been watching since you were a kit, and now it's time for others to watch, too."

"You've been watching . . . ?"

"We gave you tests, some cases we didn't solve," said Nutmeg. "But with us or without, you're on your way, Shamrock, and before long you'll be known around the world. It's not easy, all day every day, standing for the best in everyone. But there is a network. We can help."

"You're kind to believe in me, Miss Nutmeg, but I don't want to be a celebrity."

"Why not?" The words a little sad. Will she pass every test but this?

"The attention, the glare, the photos, newsferrets asking what you think, and why, always why . . ."

If soft words could shout, Nutmeg Ferret's did that moment. "Always-why is the way you grew up! Always-why is the love that drives you on! And beyond always-why is always-how. Kits around the world will pin your picture to their bedroom wall: 'How would Shamrock solve my case? How would Shamrock think if she were here? What would Shamrock do if she were me?'

"They won't know they're building their morality on your example, yours and other celebrities', but that's what they'll do. Your highest right will become theirs, Shamrock Ferret. If you slip, so will they!"

"Or you can retire," said Burrows, with a little smile. "There we can't help you much."

"What if I fail," she said, "what if I miss my highest right, what if I let them down?"

"Thought experiment, Miss Shamrock," said Nutmeg. "Can you imagine yourself setting out to become the highest, the most brilliant animal you know how to be, *and failing?*"

For the next hour, Shamrock wandered alone through the passageways of the starship, considering her highest right. She had been offered a chance to touch the lives of millions of kits. Accept, and she must give up her personal privacy for the rest of her life. Accept, and never again could she appear in public, no matter how courteous that public might be, without someone knowing who she was, connecting her with an ideal of mind and spirit, expecting her to shine that forth at all times in all places.

In her psychometry she held an object in her paws, sifting out with her spirit to find what it could tell of its past. Now the object held her, the starship Rainbow surrounding her with its ferretmetal memories, crew and colonists long dead, all of them seeking a world that would never again lift up the thoughtless to lead the unknowing into war.

Examples.

A vision passed through her heart: long ago, some ferrets had forgotten that others beside themselves love their mates and their kits, that others beside themselves cherish freedom to fashion all manner of invention and business and comedy and art.

How easy, forgetting, for Us and Them to arise, one fearing the other, one defending from the other.

Another vision washed over her: aftermath. Mates and kits now dead and dying, all at once the scorched survivors understood each other. As he spoke those few words to Ferra, common sense found in Avedoi Merek a spirit who with one breath, one personal decision, cast off evil.

When all that we love lies in ruins, how simple it is to vow from the deepest well of our soul:

Whatever harm I would do to another, I shall do first to myself.
So do all of us, promise. Every elder, every peer, every kit:
Before I harm you, I shall harm myself.
Before you harm me, you will harm yourself.
Therefore, as I refuse to harm myself, you shall live unharmed as well, you and your mates and your kits and your homes and your cities.
Therefore, as you refuse to harm yourself, I shall live unharmed as well, me and my mate and my kits and my homes and my cities.
Upon this promise stands unshatterable, adventurous peace.

So strong the hum of her vision that the detective swayed, reached for support to the steel of the hatch at P4 – C91.

Avedoi Merek had walked through fire, he and all the animals who had survived the war on Ferra, and the power of their drive, rejecting evil, had flung *Rainbow* across the stars.

The echoes of their promise swept across their great-grandkit, lifted her above fears for her future.

I shall make each choice and live each day to my highest sense of right.

Shamrock Ferret let go the steel. Kits need all the examples they can find. As Nutmeg stood for me, so let me stand, please, for one other kit.

She nodded, decision done. So shall it be. Good-bye, privacy.

Hours after her decision, through Stilton Ferret's MusTelCo media as well as through enthusiastic competitors around the world, a civilization learned that the legends of Ferra hadn't been fables at all.

Detective Lands Spaceship at Palace! cried the headlines, Burrows to work at once with the correction: Shamrock Ferret did not fly the starship nor did she land it, she merely discovered a craft that may have brought the first colonists, and the Courtesies, to Earth.

FerreTV ran its version of the correction: *Modest Sleuth Discovers Starship, Proves Ferret Way—Story at 11:00.*

"The first rule of celebrity," Burrows told her. "There will be distortion."

Shamrock hosted a two-disc videotour of *Rainbow*, the program running day and night for viewers hypnotized by its scenes on cable and network television and across the Ferretnet, with links for kits to sites on astronomy, physics, metallurgy, particle mechanics, psychology, aviation, space technology, archaeology, history, mythology, underwater exploration, psychic science and advertising.

She could not prove that one golden deed had changed the world forever, switched its polarity from negative to positive. In time, she didn't care. It is not what we prove to others, that matters to the heart, but what we know within.

Her book, *Imagining Fact: Avedoi Merek in the Council of Ferra*, appeared on the *Mustelid Weekly* bestseller list, just below Danielle Ferret's *Veronique's Kit*.

Both books moved down a place in the next issue as Avedoi Merek's *The Ferret Way* hit the top of the list—a first, said the tabloids, for an author over a hundred centuries old.

26

FAR DOWN A street of ferret houses, nearly to the end, stood the home of Oliver Ferret, still a kit but smart as any creature alive, his neighbors thought, when it came to puzzles.

He loved riddles and mysteries, his mind a sponge for patterns. He discovered, watching the empty static of an unused television channel, that by willing it so, he could make whirling cyclones of black and white appear on the screen, turn them clockwise, now counterclockwise, shift them into squares, into letters of the alphabet, into words that came from within.

The kit had intuitions for the way nature works, why clouds tumble as they do, and rivers and winds about hills and mountains. Now was he beginning to dream the way stars work, and atoms, and where the atoms begin and why.

⌣

"That's it, yes!" said the photographer for *Behind the Mask*, his face hidden in camera and telephoto lens, photoflash popping softly from the reflector on its stand. "Very nice. The star map a little closer, please, Miss Shamrock? Yes. Perfect. Very nice. Thank you. Forget the camera now, just go ahead and finish up with Jillibar. I'll get a couple of pickup shots while you talk, if that's all right?"

"Certainly," said Shamrock.

The writer had been waiting, patient to finish her interview. *Behind the Mask* wasn't a photo magazine, but this would be a big spread and photos were important. Some scenes though, she thought, photos can't show. She touched the button of her recorder.

"A lot of our readers are young," said Jillibar Ferret. "If you could give one idea to kits, Miss Shamrock . . . if you could say one word to yourself when you were a kit, what would you say?"

One word, thought Shamrock, one idea. "Trust," she said. "There's a light, when we close our eyes, the light of what we want to do more than anything else in all the world. Trust that light. Follow, wherever it leads."

The writer listened to silence after the sentence, touched the recorder off.

"That's it. Thank you so much, Miss Shamrock. We appreciate your time this afternoon. May I call when the story's done, check that I've got it right?"

"Whenever you wish," said the detective. She smiled at the writer. "There's a lot to say, isn't there?"

Jillibar Ferret nodded. "Somehow, I think you'll get your chance to say everything you want to say."

Her visitors gone, Shamrock slipped downstairs from her midtown office, a hidden passage to the alleyway entrance.

"Don't forget to turn it on before you knock on the door," she said, adjusting the flower-camera in Burrows' scarf. "I need to watch, but he'll notice everything, and if you're fussing with this . . ."

"Don't you worry," said her partner, rubbing chalk to lighten his mask, brushing his fur backward here and there. "I did it for you, didn't I?"

"M-hm." She nodded. "And I knew something was up."

She took the brush as he finished, set it on a shelf. "Do not call Oliver by name; you do not know his name, remember. And you're going to stop next door, this time. He's going to ask the neighbors . . ."

"Of course," said Burrows. "I forgot, with you. But you managed to turn out all right, Miss Shamrock. You passed your tests, though you may have suspected . . ." He nodded briskly to the detective, stepped out the door to his *Paws of Knowledge* van, every bit the salesferret.

Shamrock Ferret laughed. "Oh, Mr. Burrows," she called, shaking her head, "you might want to take this along."

He gritted his teeth in alarm, returned for his sample volume, a book by now a little tattered:

Paws of Knowledge, Volume 13: Megalith to Nudibranch.

— end —

Book 2

Budgeron and Danielle

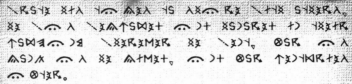

The Ferret and the Stars

IN THE BEGINNING, all the ferrets were gathered together, and one by one each was given its gift from the stars, through which might come each animal's happiness. Some were given strength and speed, others the talents for discovery, for invention and design.

When all the gifts had been given, one ferret remained. He stood alone and felt the starlight upon him, but could see no change in the spirit he had always been.

He pointed his nose upward, trusting, and asked how he might find his way, for he loved the light and knew that the path to his destiny had been opened even though it could not be seen with the eye.

"Your gift waits at the center of your heart," whispered the stars. "For to you has been given the power to show visions of all the other animals, of different pasts and presents, of could-be's and why-not's. To you has been given the magic to write the stories which will arch across time to touch the souls of kits unborn."

Listening, the last ferret was filled with joy, for it was so. As he turned within and found animals and adventures to make him laugh and cry and learn, and as he wrote his tales to share with others, he *was welcomed and honored in their company wherever he went, for as long as he lived, and for centuries after.*

Giving our visions and stories and characters to become friends to others lifts not only ourselves but the world and all its futures.

- Antonius Ferret, *Fables*

1

Budgeron Ferret drew the shades of his tiny attic writing room, unplugged the wall lamp, slipped a white silk scarf around his neck.

What's wrong? he thought in the gloom. Can my trouble be the ceremony itself?

Hollow, tense, he turned to his task, the tips of his ears bending now and then against the low angled ceiling of the room. He lifted the typewriter from the desk, set it on the floor. From the closet he took a wide green blotter, a rosewood case, an ancient oil lamp. He set the case gently at the rear of the desktop, the blotter in front, squaring the edges precisely, placed the lamp alongside.

He was a handsome ferret, the golden fur of his body darkening to ink at the tip of his tail. The mask around his eyes, equally dark, shaped a crisp W, a feature that other animals found compelling.

If it's my ceremony that's wrong, he thought, how do I fix it? Does it work because I believe it will work? What happens if I stop believing?

Next the writer struck a match and touched it to the lamp, a flame never lit but for this occasion. He watched the glow lift and settle, the color of an ancient key, peaceful soft reflections in polished silver.

Placing the chair just so in front of the desk, he seated himself. Everything the same, it had to be, as the day he wrote the first sentence.

Sliding open one of two small drawers, he lifted a tiny crystal pot of violet ink and set it in its place on the desk. He removed the cork and put it carefully by the jar, closed the drawer.

From the second drawer he selected a goose-feather quill, its point clean and bright. He laid the quill carefully to the right of the ink and cork.

He nodded, satisfied. Save for the growing terror within him, all was in order.

With the side of his paw he polished the rosewood case, slowly opened the lid. His heart fluttered as he touched his unfinished manuscript.

Where Ferrets Walk
by
Budgeron Ferret

Though he knew it word for word, he read his book yet another time.

Sadly, Count Urbain de Rothskit stood upon his paws by the edge of the castle turret and watched rosy-whiskered dawn push her nose under the tent of night.

The . . .

Here the manuscript ended.

Thus launched into the process of creation, the author sighed. It had a wonderful tension, he thought, yet something wasn't right with the novel that would set the world of ferret literature on its tail.

Did *sadly* mean "without happiness," which the writer intended, or "unfortunately," which he did not?

Was it necessary to write *stood upon his paws*? What else would his hero stand upon?

Did *by the edge of the castle turret* hint that Rothskit was about to jump? His Count was not suicidal.

Rosy-whiskered dawn sounded as fresh as the moment he wrote it, and he liked *the tent of night*. That was good.

He dipped quill-point to ink, lifted it toward the paper. It was time to continue the sentence.

He sighed again, waiting for the adventure that would follow *The . . .*

He wrote *dawn* . . . and stopped. He could not imagine a word to follow that one.

Silence curled in about him, tightening, the coils of a jungle constrictor.

2

IT'S THIN AIR, THE high country in Montana, and cold. It's hills and plains, sudden low cliffs cut by streams of liquid diamond, through lime-color clouds of summer alder and cottonwood.

Monty Ferret's Rainbow Sheep Resort and Ranchpaw Training Center was a dozen buildings at the center of open wilderness range, pasture and mountains and forest, parched desert and sudden deep lakes, stretching to the horizon in every direction.

"Hup! Hup! *Hya!*"

His first day at the Center, his new red bandana tied stiff and bright about his neck, ranchkit Budgeron Ferret had stood no taller than the middle bar of the corral, eyes wide at what he saw within.

"C'mon! *Go-go-go!*" Inside the corral, a burly ferret on a powerful delphin shouted and whistled, his mount stamped and snorted not ten paws from the pod of sheep.

Each of the woolly creatures a separate pure color, cherry and mint, lemon and plum, instead of stampeding, the Rainbows stood unfrightened, gazed in the direction of the ranchkits, curious to see the new arrivals. One lamb, blue as a twilight sky, yawned.

Monty Ferret, the sheep whisperer, rode to the edge of the corral, looked down upon his ten newest ranchkits.

"So you see," he said, the picture of calm, "shouting and carrying on, that's not goin' to get you anywhere with these animals. They're guests here same as you, except with them we have contracts for the best wool in the world."

He lifted his wide-brimmed ranchpaw hat, brushed back the fur of his brow. "These animals are cloned, they were born in a laboratory, but every Rainbow's an individual. They're beautiful, they're proud, they love the wilderness.

"The one thing they lack," he said, replacing his hat, "is outdoor skills. Their sense of direction isn't as good as yours and mine, they'll get to thinking and wander off, they'll forget to eat, sometimes. That's why you're here. You're going to be their guides, this season."

While he spoke to the young ferrets, the Rainbows turned and trotted near, as though they knew what was coming next.

"I suspect you brought some treats from the bunkhouse, kits. You might offer to share some, and watch how these animals behave. . . ."

Budgeron slipped his backpack to the ground, knelt and found the treats, alfalfa hay pressed in soybean oil, the shape and size of broccoli coins. The sheep stretched their noses toward the snacks, took them politely, nibbled them down and stretched for more.

Monty watched, continued his introduction. "Kits, life's not gonna be easy here this summer. Sunup comes early and you'll be runnin' hard till late, no more'n six naps a day."

The kits looked at each other, wordless.

"You've got a lot to learn about ridin', about livin' on the land, findin' your way through the forest and the plains, about always puttin' the Rainbows' comfort before your own. But you'll be ranchpaws by summer's end, and I reckon you'll find it's been worth your trouble."

Swiftly had the kits become friends, Budgeron and Strobe and Boa and Alla and the rest, their hammocks side by side in the bunkhouse, their places together in the dining hall, their delphins in adjoining stalls.

Together they curried their mounts and cleaned stables. They learned to saddle and bridle and ride, to orient themselves by sun and stars, a skill uninteresting to the happy-go-lucky Rainbows, who depended on the ranchpaws to know which way home and how long to get there.

Budgie Ferret had been different, that summer, from the other kits: he wore his crimson bandana and wide-brim ranchpaw hat as they did, he carried bedroll and canteen and many-blade utility knife, but as well he brought notebooks and pencils, packed carefully away in his saddlebag.

Spare moments he unwrapped these and wrote pictures of the land around him. He wrote scenes and dialogue, funny stories and scary ones, he wrote what he saw and thought and felt, homesick sometimes, exhilarated others, committing his heart to yellow notepaper.

For all this Western adventuring, he didn't count himself happy unless he had *done* something, unless he had taken some action upon the world around him, and that action was to write what he saw and what he thought.

At the end of the summer, bandana faded nearly to white by sun and rain, Budgeron Ferret had returned to the city self-reliant, independent, confident of his ability to survive in the wilderness and to be a worthy companion and leader to other animals.

On the bus home, he read his dusty, rain-spattered journal, bright colors and songs and scents of high-plains nights and noons, talks remembered word for word, tales of his friends along the trail and around the campfire.

In the pages, summer was alive again.

"I'll be a writer one day," he whispered.

Way down within, his muse listened. It stirred and happily sniffed the air.

3

IT HAD BEEN TWO thousand words a day, in the beginning, for more days than Budgie cared to count. Story after story to magazines, Budgeron Ferret received scores of rejection slips, rejection cards, rejection form letters, rejection letters with notes:

"Not quite . . ."

"Try us again . . ."

"Sorry about this one."

Taking these for encouragement, refusing to quit, he had made one sale, another, then sold a pair of adventure tales to the leading magazine for young ferrets.

"You have a particular charm, writing for kits," the editor had written. "You treat our readers as equals, you leave them higher than where you found them.

"Checks enclosed for *Lost on the Prairie* and *Hard Ride to Devil's Fork*. We solicit such additional stories as you feel would be at home in *Kits' Gazette*."

Long-term he would be no kits' writer, he thought, but he liked the compliment, pinned the letter to his office wall.

His first book struck without warning, wrote itself in one bright flash, a kit's journey through the seasons and through a lifetime. *One Paw, Two Paws, Three Paws, Four Paws* sold at once, his first publishing contract.

"*YES!*" he had cried to his empty office. "*Thank you, stars!*"

Within, his muse had smiled.

Surfing a wave of exhilaration, Budgeron Ferret gave his notice at the Black Ermine, found a waiter to replace him, served tables one final day to say good-bye to his friends, turned full-time to his stories.

He had become a writer.

He talked to himself, brave hope through the silence that is a writer's home. "The alphabet is public domain," he said. "Every letter I need is in front of me this minute, on my keyboard now, enough for a thousand books! All I have to do is find the right order for the letters, one after the other. . . ."

Yet, it isn't letters that make a writer, and he knew it. It's ideas that do that, characters come alive, the alphabet a net of light one throws to catch the spinning what-ifs, the pinwheel star systems of the mind, hauling them close for the pleasure of like spirits.

One Paw, Two Paws . . . was published to few reviews and modest sales. Some parents bought the slim volume to read to their kits, others bought it regardless of age, for the kit within.

"The ones who buy your book," his publisher told him, "they love it. But it's been slow catching on."

Neither a bestseller nor a stone disappeared in the pond of literature, his first book sold quietly and steadily without advertisement, one ferret occasionally telling another that it was a happy read.

Mornings found him in the park, then, not rich, not famous, an established young writer. About his neck the knitted scarf from his mother against the autumn breeze, on his lap a pad of yellow notepaper, in his paw a felt-tip pen, in his heart ferrets zany and brave, ferrets unlearned and ferrets wise, all of them characters to tell his stories, characters with stories of their own to tell.

Quality through quantity. He wrote the words and taped them, a thin motto at the top of his writing pad, and that's the way it seemed to be. How his work improved with practice! The more he wrote, the deeper and broader grew his stories, the easier they became to write.

There was something about the air, those mornings in the park, that moved him. It made no difference if he didn't feel inspired, if he didn't feel like writing, if he didn't know what words to put on the paper. He sat at his favorite bench, listened to the birds, then touched pen to pad and he wrote.

The more he wrote, the more there was to write, two thousand words a day, most often more. How much to say from what he had lived and thought, how much to tell about the family of Budgeron look-alikes, scouts and swashbucklers that vaulted and spun through his mind!

Three hours gone in an eye-blink at the park, he'd bring his pad of yellow paper home and type the words he'd written.

"*Words on paper!*" he told himself. "Words in the air don't matter. If I don't have words on paper I'm not a writer, I'm a talker! No words on paper, how can I improve a sentence? No words on paper, what's to work with, what's to send the publisher, Budgeron?

"So simple. No mystery. *WORDS ON PAPER!*"

He printed the sign in big letters, pinned it to the wall in front of his desk.

Typing finished, a sliver of fruit, a raisin or two, a vitamin cookie. Afternoons he edited his stories, rewriting until he could improve them no more. Then he typed it all again, fresh.

Into the drawer each tale would go at last, to cool for weeks while the next one began. Finally another read, another rewrite, and when he could no longer contain his excitement over the finished work, into its envelope and off it would go to the publisher.

No cover letter to the editor, in those envelopes. No *I hope you'll like the story.*

"Of course I hope you'll like the story," he said to his walls, "or I wouldn't have sent it!"

He kissed his manuscripts good-bye, before he dropped them in the mail, each on its own, no author nearby to help. "Don't be frightened," he whispered at the mailbox. "Speak for yourself!"

To be writing well and yet get rejections, Budgeron Ferret discovered, that is no fun. But a good story returned, he'd shake his head at the house that sent it back, stamp a new envelope and ship it out straightaway to the next, unchanged, until finally one of them had the sense to realize that it beheld the work of Budgeron Ferret, quality writer.

"The day will come," he vowed once, unhappy with the mail, "I am going to build a writing room in my house. I will build that room and I will paper the walls with these very rejection slips, and I will stand in the middle of the room, and I will laugh at you all!"

⌢⌣

Just home from the park one Tuesday, answering his telephone, he heard a snarl of lions, menacing, a glad sound from his kithood.

He listened patiently as the snarls faded into the jungle. "Hi, Willow," he said at last.

From the receiver her soft, earthy voice. "Hi, Budge. I need to know how my brother the famous writer is spending his day."

"You know how I'm spending my day," he said. "I'm writing. Let me guess: you've got something on your mind, you can't wait to tell me. Why am I all of a sudden a famous writer?"

"What I was wondering . . ." she said, "have I ever told you about the volunteer at school? She comes once a week and reads to my kits while I run to staff meetings and other things educational?"

"You've told me about her. That's Danielle, remember?"

"Have I? She's such a dear, Budgeron. Everyone loves Danielle. Guess what's her favorite kits' book and why you're a famous writer?"

"I don't know, Willow. Why am I a famous writer?"

"*One Paw, Two Paws . . . !* She loves your book! I didn't tell her that Budgeron Ferret is my very own brother, and I thought maybe it would be nice for you two to get together, you could at least say hello. Her mind's so much like yours. . . ."

"Willow!"

"You don't meet anybody, Budgie! You need friends!"

"I have friends! They're called *characters*, Willow, and I write them onto paper." He sighed, explaining. "This is that time in my life when I work hard, when I learn to be good at my job. Later, I have friends."

"She's bright, too, a warm and loving animal. She loves kits and they love her. You'd have a wonderful time!"

"I'm sure we would, sometime. Sometime when I'm not struggling to survive, which is what I'm doing right now."

"Oh, Budgie!"

"I love you, Willow. I'm writing now."

A wolf barked, angry, in the telephone. Her brother laughed, hung up the receiver, turned back to his manuscript. Friends? Someday. The relationship that mattered now was the one with the page in front of him.

4

He HAD NOTICED her for several weeks, a slender figure who came early mornings, Monday through Thursday, to the same spot by the lakeside, a bag of seeds in her paw for the sparrows, bread for the ducks. She would spread the food around her, sit quietly as the creatures came nearby for their breakfast. Then she would open a book and read. She always came alone, he noticed, she always brought food for the park animals, always a book to read.

Other ferrets would come and go, kits on an off-school day with their little sailboats, with bell-balls to chase on the grass, grown-up animals with cameras for the park scenes, or sketchpads and pencils.

She was, like himself, a constant.

She'd noticed him, too, he thought, she had to. Same scarf every day, same yellow pad. What she couldn't know was that he sat here Friday mornings, too, and weekends.

They sat not so very far apart, and respecting privacy, never did they say hello.

The days passed, his writing broken and distracted as he watched her stretch her slender paw and offer food to the geese and ducks. They weren't afraid, came close, content when she left that she had given them all she could.

She departed early after her visit one Thursday morning. Budgeron, having lost the thread of his writing, studied trees in the opposite direction.

When he turned back, she was gone, ducks and a single goose pecking the crumbs she had left.

Odd, he thought, that she should leave so suddenly. He looked again. The place was empty but for a book, lying on the grass where she had been. He rose and looked for her down the pathway through the park, but there was no sign of her.

"You left your book," he said quietly. How could she do that? Was she late for work, late for a meeting, that she had rushed away without it?

"Shall I rescue it," he said, "hold it till tomorrow?"

At last his highest sense of right told him to take her book under his protection, return it to her when next she came. He could think of no reason why she would deliberately have left it behind.

He walked to the place, knew before he touched the cover, lifted the book with the strangest sense of destiny.

It was *One Paw, Two Paws*, it was his own book she had left on the grass.

His heart raced. He looked up for her once again, feeling himself an intimate stranger, in spite of his best intentions toward her privacy, entering the life of the young animal with whom he shared the green morning hours.

On his way home, her book in his paw, he realized: tomorrow would be Friday. She would not return to the park until Monday next.

And then, that moment, he knew.

⌢

The halls were crowded with kits, and he asked one of them where Willow Ferret's classroom could be found. "That way, sir." The little one stood tall, pointed. "At the end of the hall, it's room 410."

"Thank you," said Budgeron.

"You're welcome! I'm . . ." The kit paused, remembering. "I'm glad to have been of help!" Then, thrilled with the chance to have practiced a courtesy lesson with a stranger, he dropped to his four paws and scampered away.

Ah, the Major Courtesies class, Budgeron remembered, and the advanced Minor Courtesies. *Whatever harm I would do another, I shall first do to myself.*

How many times he had used that principle, how much remorse it had saved! Manners for Ferrets, what a pleasure that class had been, and The Power of Polite. Only when he was grown had he realized how important, how instantly practical it was, the simplest kindness and caring to others—respect for elders, respect for peers, respect for kits.

He found the door and a placard, *Miss Willow Ferret*, looked through the glass. His sister was nowhere to be seen.

The class was beginning, kits settling in a half-circle around a trim grown-up animal. She turned, reaching for a book, glanced up and saw him, watching, the writer in his knitted scarf. A quick wave of her paw, a dazzling smile, then she turned back to the kits.

A flood of warmth swept through him, a wall of heat. It was Danielle Ferret with whom he had been sharing his green mornings, Danielle and he alone together day by day. Danielle who loved her park and her ducks and her books.

As he watched through the door glass, over her shoulder at the youngsters, the volunteer waited till they were settled and quiet, all noses and whiskers, all the little masks turned toward her. Then she began to read.

"Once upon a time," he heard faintly, through the glass, "by the edge of a great ocean, there was a party of kits, out for a romp. Adventurous they were, but not very wise . . ."

Budgeron watched for a long moment, then he smiled. He turned and walked down the corridor and out of the school. There was no hurry. He would meet her in the park come Monday, he would bring the book, and seeds and bread crumbs, and he would say hello to Danielle Ferret.

5

IN THE GLOW OF the polished old lamp, Budgeron Ferret looked back on those days and yearned for confidence once again.

Why can't I finish the first page? he thought. What follows rosy-whiskered dawn pushing her nose under the tent of night?

There came a gentle knock at the door, and it opened the width of a small paw. "Budgie," called Danielle softly. "Breakfast any-time . . ."

The door eased shut.

The writer sighed. Time passes swiftly on an empty mind, the morning wasted by. He rose from the desk, blew out the lamp, replaced the page in its gleaming box.

He cleaned the quill, set it back in its drawer, put the crystal ink pot, blotter and manuscript away, lifted the typewriter back to the desk.

His literary supernova had not yet lit off, and for the first time he feared that perhaps it never would.

6

DANIELLE FERRET met him in the little kitchen, a beautiful animal: fur brushed and shining, an oval of snow around her ebon mask, her eyes bright to see him.

He sat at the table, smoothed the mended gingham in front of him with his paw, felt the tiny stitches that healed the torn cloth.

How lucky can I get? he thought. She could have had any ferret she wished, for her mate. And she chose me.

"Happy Wednesday," she said, "happy Waffle Day." She placed his favorite breakfast in front of him, crisp orange-butter goodness, a pitcher of warm honey, a glass of milk. "How's the book this morning?"

"It's coming along," he told her.

"Two thousand words today?" She knew his writing pace for kits' stories.

He hadn't mentioned that his classic-literary-novel pace was slower.

"One," he said. All morning, and he had written "dawn." He took a bite of breakfast, in order not to speak.

"Anything you'd want to read to me, Budge? I'd love to hear . . ."

He nodded. "These are wonderful waffles, Danielle. Thank you."

"You're having a little trouble with it, aren't you?" She watched his eyes. "Just a little?"

She stood and walked around the table, leaned down and touched her nose to his, looked at him close up, unblinking, solemn. "You are a great writer, Budgeron Ferret, a great writer, and I won't hear anything different. You will change the world with your words. You will!"

She moved back, nodded *that's that*. Then she took her seat again across the table.

"Danielle . . ." How can she believe in me? he thought. Writing so hard, so long, just a few stories in kits' magazines and one small book to show for it. Drawers of rejection slips, us in this little apartment. Not my apartment, hers. My novel is doomed.

"We have a beautiful future, Budgeron."

"What makes you so *sure*?"

Before she could say, the kitchen clock struck six. She looked up, startled that the time had gone. "Nearly eleven," she said. "I'll be late."

She rose from the table, bent to kiss his nose, lifted her pawdicure bag from its place by the door.

"I just know, sweetheart!" she said. "Write from your highest!"

"It won't be long, Danielle," he told her, filled for a moment with her hope and vision. "Someday you won't have to work."

She flashed him a smile. "I like my work and you know it. Everyone has a story. All day, I make paws bright and listen to stories. All day, every day, chapters in a book, if I write what I hear. We can both be writers!" She waved brightly. "See you tonight, hon."

"Love you," he said.

He smiled, after she left, stirred by his mate's belief. *I can write this book!* I'm born a writer. I read stories when I was a kit, I listened to stories, I wrote stories. *The Polar Bear and the Bad Badger. What Happened to Charlie Chickadee? The Lonely Grasshopper.* Three stories before they trusted me with ink, and those were fine stories, I love them still! *How can I believe I am not a writer?*

Filled with conviction, trusting experience, he rose and climbed the stairs to his writing room, flung himself gladly into his chair. Write from my highest? Write what I know? Write what matters to me? Easy!

Not bothering so much as to square his typewriter to the desk, his paws blurred at once over the keys. He wrote a story that appeared unplanned before him, a flashing of wings, an adventure that filled him with pleasure. Indifferent to all but the scenes within his mind, he stood out of the way of his story and he wrote faster than he had written in a very long time.

7

"DANIELLE, THE littlest kit could have tumbled me with a pounce when Federico told me who she was!"

The pawdicurist stopped at the news to come, her claw-buffer frozen in the air. "She wasn't who you thought, Enriquette?"

"I could have sworn! You'd have done the same. They made a match like royalty, they were so perfect together!"

"'Such a beautiful little thing . . .' Could you believe I said that to poor Federico, reminding him it might be time to settle down:

'Such a beautiful little thing!' I'm seeing white veil, I'm hearing 'We Two Ferrets,' I'm tasting winter snow-water. . . ." Enriquette's voice trailed off.

"And what was wrong with that?" asked Danielle. She set her client's left front paw softly into a bowl of warm oil and fresh lavender petals, crystal marbles at the bottom to touch. She lifted the right front paw, patted it dry, began to buff the claws, not too softly, not too brisk, a moth sound in the quiet. Where is this story going?

"Why, his tail bottlebrushed, he looked at me as if I had just toddled out of the burrow. He took her paw and he said, 'Enriquette, my dear, I'd like you to meet my sister!'"

Danielle caught her breath, shocked.

Her mask the color of ginger, the pawdicurist's elegant client trembled with glee at her own gaffe. "Well, when we touched noses, I couldn't help it, I started laughing. I was going to marry poor Federico to his own sister!"

Her clients at Pretty Paws were her friends. Danielle loved them, she cared that they were happy. Each morning before work, the salon's youngest pawdicurist stopped at the flower stalls for fragrant petals, and as she came to know the flower ferrets, listening to their cheerful gossip, she found who was ordering flowers for whom.

She made her own exfoliating scrubs for the paws, candle-warmed paraffin and essential-oil treatments, mixed a rainbow of pastels into moisturizing creams of cocoa butter and fresh flowers, scented lotions and wraps, carefully she selected paw files and pumice stones. Bright old ferret jigs and reels played in her cubicle. At the end of the session she gave each client a last few minutes of paw reflexology and sent them on their way.

Danielle Ferret collected true-life stories. The more bizarre and startling, the more they clung to her mind, exotic gems treasured and carefully stored.

Though she hadn't dared to set the stories down in notes, for the minutes between clients she moved herself into their lives, relived their adventures with a smile and sometimes a tear for the choices they had made.

On her walk home of an evening not long after, dodging traffic, one animal in a sea of others, she considered writing for the hundredth time since those careless words to Budgeron: we can both be writers. All these stories within . . .

Now she knew it could be so, if she wanted. Of course she would never be a writer of Budgeron's stature. The only way he could stall his success would be for him to stop writing, and that would never happen. Her mate would change ferret culture, lift it higher than ever it had been.

Yet there's no reason why I couldn't write, too, she thought, some little tales, the kind I love to hear. What fun that would be!

Charmed with the idea, she failed to notice the taxicab drifting high speed around the corner, rushing uptown.

Budgeron has his future, she was thinking as she stepped into the street, and I have mine as well. It would be fun, both of us writing. I could learn . . .

Denison "Lion" Ferret did not question why the trim animal ahead had lost her mind. He did not think, but spun the wheel hard right, stabbed the brakes beyond the edge of rolling friction, a screech that trembled window glass three stories high, blue smoke exploding from all tires.

Ferrets left and right heard and saw, flew to rescue, instant reflexes too late to save her.

Instead of sliding broadside into Danielle, Lion's cab lurched sideways to a stop a tenth-second from her body, close enough that the driver could reach from his window and touch her paw.

Which he did. He looked up into eyes wide with fright, the pedestrian clutching her pawdicure bag for security.

A sigh of relief from the cabdriver. "I guess it's not your time, miss."

At once they were surrounded by others, Lion's cab and the crowd of help still wreathed in a cloud of burnt rubber. The traffic light changed, the would-be rescuers found all parties alive and well, the smoke drifted away.

Danielle gasped once, and then again. She covered his paw with her own. "I'm so sorry . . . what a foolish thing! I was thinking . . . I didn't look . . ." She turned to the crowd. "He saved my life!"

Her paw trembled on Lion's, he steadied her a second longer. "It's all right now, miss," he said. "It's over."

She nodded, starting to breathe again. "Thank you!"

He removed his paw from hers. "Mighty powerful dreams, walking like that into traffic. You take care now and make those dreams come true!"

The driver touched the brim of his cap to her and his machine moved away.

Trembling still as the crowd reminded her to be careful and went its way back to the sidewalks, Danielle wondered. Had the driver been an angel ferret, handing her a new life, a new life writing? Not the Great Ferret Novel, but something—stories of ordinary animals, the kind she loved to hear.

She looked both ways at the next corner, crossed when the light changed to walk.

I mustn't write what I've been told, she thought, but what harm in fitting parts here, parts there, no one could recognize? A collection of stories, just for fun.

A moment later, she slowed and stopped on the sidewalk, others hurrying past, left and right. Not a collection. A novel! A *romance* novel!

There's no reason in the world why I can't, she thought. For the fun of it, of course, just for fun. It may never be good enough to publish, but what a pleasure, the pages accumulating, the book taking shape, even if I'd be its only reader.

She ran up the steps to the apartment, slowed at the door.

For the fun of it.

She was too shy to share her plan with Budgeron. He was the writer, published time and again, she the novice, untalented, a kit at a grown-up's game.

She'd tell him later.

She turned the knob and entered.

"I'm home!"

A call from above, the sound of paws on the stairs. "Danielle! Welcome home!" A different Budgeron from the morning, her mate met her with a glad hug. "How was your day?"

She remembered her clients and their stories, and her decision. "Wonderful! How was yours?"

"Do you know what? Guess what."

"The book is finished," she said, kidding.

He nodded, as happy as she had ever seen him.

"I can't believe it, Budgie! It's finished? *Where Ferrets Walk* is finished? Congratulations, dearest wonderful best writer in the whole world!"

"*Where Ferrets Walk*?" he said. "Oh. No. That's not finished. I wrote a different book. What's finished is *Bevo the Hummingbird!*"

"*Bevo . . .*"

He nodded. "Remember, I told you? When I was a kit. My mom made stuffed animals for me. Bevo was the first, he slept on my pillow. And the story came—*whoof!*—it was already there. All I had to do was type."

"Why, of course! *Bevo the Hummingbird!* Do you love it?"

She could tell, the look in his eyes.

She touched his paw. "Read it to me?"

"Maybe you'd like to read it yourself. I need to know where the story slows for you, where you lose interest, where it's—"

"Read it to me," she said. "Please, Budgeron. I need to hear it. Your voice."

Her mate knew better than to argue. She had her reasons, always she had her reasons. Later she could read the story to herself.

He brought the manuscript to the kitchen table, a plump sheaf of pages neatly typed.

What happened, Budge? she wanted to ask. Why all of a sudden can you fly through this story, write it in a flash, when week after week your literary novel slows you to stone?

But she said not a word. She sat at the kitchen table while he settled in his chair, she closed her eyes and listened.

"*It was midnight when Bevo woke,*" he began. "*All about him, the sky was dark. The trees were dark. The moon was dark, and the stars.*"

For an hour he read, until:

"'*Happy at last with the creature he had chosen to be, Bevo the Hummingbird tucked his bill under his wing and fell fast asleep.*'"

He looked to his mate. "*The End*," he added.

Danielle opened her eyes, saw her husband through a curtain of tears.

"Budgeron," she said softly. "Oh, Budge. It's beautiful!"

"The raccoons," he asked. "Are they a little too . . . uncivilized?"

"Too nothing!" she cried. "I love the raccoons! It's the most beautiful warm touching story I've ever heard in my life!"

"Maybe when you read it—"

"*Budgie! Listen!* What have you wanted to do since you were a kit? Don't you know? Like *One Paw, Two Paws!* You've done it again!"

Tears glistened still in the writer's eyes from the touching moments of his own story. He trusted her judgment. He had always told his mate that she had a grand story sense, and now she was telling him that his little book had promise. He agreed. To have touched him so, he knew it did.

He quivered with what had happened that day, his writing a whirlwind that left him breathing fast. He had not invented the story. It had been there all along, unwritten: beginning, middle, end. Every scene, every incident necessary, every one of them had to be, inevitable.

The hummingbird had picked up his self-consciousness and his fears and dashed them aside, uncaring. Bevo had used the ferret's paws, used his thoughts and experience and vocabulary to tell a story that had to be told. Now it was finished, the author churned in its wake, left to glue himself back together as best he could.

Was it publishable? He was still too close to the tale to judge, but he didn't need to struggle for some verdict. It felt perfect, somehow, the story made him happier than any he had written.

Tomorrow he would ask how he had done it, and find no answer. For now, all that mattered was that Bevo the Hummingbird, with all that he dreamed and all that he stood for, had somehow been touched with magic and come to life.

Hurray! the writer thought. A few days smoothing, a little polish, off it goes to the publisher. What good practice! Now to do the same with my novel!

Within, a sigh, crestfallen. Whisper of an unseen voice: Am I a failure as a muse?

8

DANIELLE FERRET HAD promised that she would write for the fun of it.

She expected that with time and practice, the words would come quiet and orderly. She expected that whatever character she might invent would be flat and wooden for a long while. She expected to look at a blank page one and begin a long search for her first word.

What Danielle didn't expect was that her first page would explode with the likes of Veronique Sibhoan Ferret, a willful animal caught time and again in webs of her own spinning, in schemes so complicated that her author could barely imagine how they had started or what would happen next.

As Danielle watched the page wide-eyed, as she sometimes stopped and raised a paw to cover her open mouth, Veronique played with the hearts of others the way a kit plays with bell-balls—the more of them tumbling at once, the better the little flirt liked the game.

They're toys, she thought of the strong and gentle males around her. *Of what use are toys except for play?*

One moment innocent, the next mad for power, the night-masked Veronique laughed to shock her own author as much as to electrify readers of *Miss Mischief.*

By the seventy-fourth page, Veronique was openly plotting to deceive her roommate's long-lost Swedish half brother, Telegaard, fallen hopelessly in love with the vixen.

"You shall never know my name," Danielle's heroine cried to him. *"But if you must, call me . . . Valka!"*

How the vamp had discovered the name of Telegaard's secret

first love, the author would not know for many pages. But discover it she had, and Veronique took the name shamelessly, as a leopard, remorseless, devours a different hunter's kill.

All that the pawdicurist once heard within the walls of her cubicle, innocent misunderstandings and exaggerated stories told in the ferret way, to make fun of the teller herself, they tilted and shifted, came spinning out in harlequin suits and sinister intrigues as the author wrote, watching her pages dumbfounded.

From the time they are kits, ferrets are patiently instructed always to live to their highest sense of right. They are showered with love, treated with respect by their parents and by every other animal of their culture. No matter the path they choose for themselves, they run it with grace and honesty and pride.

In a land without envy or malice, without evil or crime or war, in a world of esteem for self and others, the least of ferrets knows that it is equal to the greatest, and they treat each other so.

Never had it been wondered: what if something went wrong, somehow, what if there could be such a thing as a *naughty ferret*? What would she say, how would she act?

Now and here, in the ink from her own pen, Danielle watched Veronique Sibhoan slink forth, she who lived for the moment, self-centered, thoughtless of consequences, uncaring of the highest right.

How shall I shatter that romance? She dangled her toes in the warm ripple-pond, watching the light shimmer in her own dark fur. How shall I split Carlos and Rikka? After I've finished with Telegaard, I want to play with her raven-whiskered captain for a while. . . .

With a horrified flash of her paw, Danielle swept her manuscript from the kitchen table, a blizzard of snowsheets to the floor.

How can it be, she thought, my husband at the top of the stairs working to bring the Great Ferret Novel into the world, and me below, helping this wicked animal to life!

She gathered the papers left and right, crumpled them, willed her saucy temptress never to draw another breath. Into the fireplace they went, Danielle striking the match. May Budgeron never know what I have done. . . .

Her paw shook, though; the match burned alone, suspended in air.

Veronique's barely more than a kit, the author thought, she's just pretending to be a naughty ferret. Tumbled away in a hurricane as a newborn, raised by squirrels, untrained in courtesy or friendship or the power of kindness to others, she means no harm. Her challenge is that she must learn grace and understanding from life itself, on her own.

The flame waited.

What kind of creature am I, who would destroy one whose only crime is that she hasn't found her way to love? And how do I know that those she seeks to bring down may not be noble enough to lift her up, instead?

The match burned lower, and finally Danielle let it fall, a lingering trail of smoke.

Budgeron creates literature, she thought. I write a dalliance for grown-ups, a book for the moment. Both are important. Both are fun.

The author lifted the pages, smoothed them against the floor, sat there and read her last lines again. A naughty ferret, indeed. Still, by the end of the story Veronique will have lived the consequences of all that she has done, and how she will have grown!

Danielle settled herself once again at the kitchen table, raised her pen, let the story continue.

"Veronique," asked the captain, stepping from the old entrance tunnel into the light, "have you seen my bowl of raisins?" Her host blinked in the sunshine. "They were here a minute ago."

"Raisins, Carlos?" She swallowed the last one, the bowl fallen silently to the grass beneath the picnic table. "No, I don't see them," she said. "They're not here now. . . ."

9

W‍HEN B‍UDGERON F‍ERRET came down the stairs next Waffle Day, Danielle knew he was in trouble.

She flashed her glorious smile, hugged him with one paw, the other holding a plate of golden crispness.

His nose twitched in the warm aroma.

The two ferrets sat at their little table. Danielle offered an amber pitcher. "Honey, sweet?"

A wan smile from her mate.

She watched his face. "A thousand words today?"

"There's something I need to tell you, Danielle."

She waited.

His eyes downcast, he took a breath. "The novel is not going well. It is worse than not going well. I wrote a hundred words today and they are all wrong."

He lifted his head, looked at her in anguish. "I tried, Danielle! I flew into that story same as I did with Bevo, but instead of the Count writing himself, instead of the story blasting through me like some wild-away freight train, it . . . I'm pushing on a stone wall. No. I'm pushing on a sponge, a wet sponge. No crash, no fire. Nothing."

He lifted his eyes to the ceiling, waffle untouched. "*Where Ferrets Walk* is a wonderful title, Danielle, a literary genius of a title. All it needs is some . . . and I am *home free*, I am no kits' writer, I'll be an *author!*" He took a breath. "I'll be a real author, at last."

He sighed. "Nothing. I don't have a whisper, what happens to Count Urbain de Rothskit. I like his name, but you know, I really don't like the animal himself. He comes from some different world, he looks down his whiskers at me: I'm not worthy to write his story. He shuts me off!"

He spoke as if he were warning the Count himself: "If I do not get that ferret moving before long, if I have to wait there with my quill and beg for words, I swear, Danielle, something strange is going to happen to him!"

She listened. How can my book be such adventure for me, she thought, and his such pain for dear Budgeron, his big novel? Before the answer could unfold its own reasons, the clock chimed thirteen.

"You've got to run," said her husband, his voice lifeless.

"I'll stay home today."

He stirred himself to the edge of confidence. "Nonsense. Thanks for listening. By the time you get home, I'll have a great chapter finished and the Count's going to be brushed and bushy-tailed!"

She didn't move. "I've never seen you so down, Budge. Wouldn't you rather I stay? l can bring you some orange juice, nice and cold, later on. I think I'd rather stay."

"No. Really. It means a lot that you'd offer, and I'd ask you to stay if this were really bad. Honest. I would. But I am a professional writer. I am not the pawn of my characters. Soon as you're out that door, I'm going to have a little meeting with Monsieur le Count. . . ."

She smiled, but did not move.

"I will be kind but firm with him, Danielle. Really. Off you go to work. If we don't have groceries, if there'll be no waffles next Wednesday, *that* will be disaster!"

His wife laughed, then rose and kissed him. "That's my Budgie," she said. "Never quit!"

She took her bag from the hook on the door. "See you tonight," she said. "And don't you be too hard on the Count."

10

THE TOP OF THE page was embossed, gold on white, *Books for Kits: A Division of Ferret House Press.*

"Dear Budgeron Ferret," the letter began.

"It is with considerable pleasure that we at Ferret House Press must tell you that we find your story *Bevo the Hummingbird* a delight. Rarely do we encounter such charm and grace in a book for young ferrets, or a theme so uplifting.

"Enclosed is a proposed contract for publication. Because of the demonstrated success of *One Paw, Two Paws . . .* , we would be particularly pleased to become the publisher of this story. We have taken the liberty of increasing the advance payment over our standard terms, and raising the royalty percentage.

"We hope that you will consider ours to be the winning bid for world rights to your story. If you would care to send it to other publishers, however, please feel free to do so, and allow us the opportunity to top whatever terms they might offer.

"With thanks for the kindness of your consideration, we remain, your obedient servants . . ."

Danielle had taken the letter from her husband's frozen paw after he had stumbled down from the office and appeared, wordless, in the kitchen.

She read it once again, aloud. She glanced through the contract attached, saw that the advance payment was an amount many times larger than their life savings.

"Budgie, I think . . . ," she said, dazed. "I think . . ."

She gave the letter back. The pressure of the paper against his numbed paw was enough to topple her husband's body slowly backward to the floor. Danielle, for her part, collapsed more or less straight down.

The clock chimed sixteen, and after that it was quiet in the kitchen.

<u>11</u>

FIVE KILOPAWS WEST of Side-Hop, Colorado, the house rambled over the high range: east of the mountains, south of the river. Soft hills, rising and falling, the colors of a sparkling shallow sea, shimmering like a broad summer moat around them.

Who would have thought, they asked each other, that solitude could become priceless?

With the publisher's advance and high hopes for the success of *Bevo the Hummingbird*, the two ferrets had given up their apartment and moved to the land of Budgie's kithood summer.

Here amid the splendor towering above, whispering below, the author planned to start a new life with Danielle, and to finish his epic novel at last. Surely in this haven from stress he could now find and master his reluctant muse.

From the porch on a fine day they could see their gate, away in the valley. In the months since they had moved, they had heard no sound of traffic or horn, they had seen no other animal save for their friend and ranchpaw Slim, out mornings riding fence.

With the two ferrets lived the hush of wind in the cottonwoods, the whisper of sunlight by day and moonlight in the dark. Peace rustled down on them like a fluffy deep comforter.

In that precious calm the two of them talked and walked. Her husband taught her to care for their delphins Dusty and Lucky, to bridle and mount and take them on long rides. Danielle came to love those times, and she and Budgeron could be found together nearly every morning in the saddle, deep in the quiet of the land.

For all their change and comfort, however, never did they forget what parents and culture had taught: the more gifts we're given, the more we can pass along to other creatures.

His book now a bestseller on the kits'-book list, Budgeron Ferret spent five nights a week in a drawing room he had furnished especially for work on his epic novel. Quill and lamp no longer in the closet, they stood full-time on his desk.

What a gift it would be, *Where Ferrets Walk*, if he could somehow finish the story.

Yet no muse appeared. In fact, he found in time that not only did he lack a muse for this most important work of his life, but he had somehow attracted a wicked anti-muse, whose every whisper told him how worthless he was, how bad his writing, how hopeless to wish that his work would grace the libraries or even the nightstands of the literati, of the studied sophisticates in the city he had just departed.

In his office gleamed a new computer, and here he kept the mundane: business correspondence, interviews, a copy of the Bevo story, letters to family and friends.

From this computer Budgie declined his publisher's request for a second Bevo book with a short note: "While I am delighted that my hummingbird has become a success for us all," he wrote, "I am at work on a major historical novel, which I shall submit for your interest when it is finished."

He wandered off, then, to the kitchen, laid out a platter of celery and peanut butter, ringed it in a circle of grapes. He ambled to the porch, where Danielle sat in front of what until lately had been her husband's typewriter.

"Hi, dear," she said absently as he slid into the chair alongside.

The keys rose and fell under her paws, an even, steady click of steels against ribbon and paper. He watched her eyes, knew what she was seeing. She was not looking at the paper in the machine or at the words, but through them, into a different world from this one. Scenes moved, changing, close-ups and long shots, actors turning on the set, she reporting the drama as it played in front of her.

He sat near for a long while. How different it is, he thought, writing for fun! He watched the tiny smiles that came and went on her face as the story surprised her, caught her off-balance.

At that moment, Danielle was watching bad Veronique accept, with a flutter of her lashes, an engagement necklace from a ferret whom she had not the least intention of marrying.

"Gunnar, you are kind! Much too kind for the likes of this poor mustelid!"

He slipped the diamonds about her lovely sable fur, sparkles upon sheen.

Veronique turned and gave him a radiant smile. "Do you like them, dearest?"

Without waiting for him to respond, and for a lark, she dashed the poor animal with ice water.

Danielle caught her breath, then laughed, typing steadily.

Budgeron rose without a sound, leaving the plate of snacks on the side table for his mate.

She turned her face toward him, yet her eyes held on the scene within the white paper. "I love you, Budgie," she said, from another universe.

12

SHE CAME TO HIM in the kitchen, a coral-color paper in her paw as he installed a shelf above the window. She extended it to him without a word, so that he put down his bracket and hammer.

"Why, that looks familiar," he said, but did not take the paper from her. "Let me guess . . ."

He watched her eyes, sad glow of a tear in each, gathered her to him in a gentle embrace.

As she clung close against his chest, as her tears fell, he quoted from memory.

"'Dear Writer: Thank you for your submission. Unfortunately, your manuscript does not meet our publishing needs at this time. Sincerely, The Editors,'" he said. "Is that what it says on the slip?"

She nodded. "Then at the bottom," she sniffed, "somebody wrote, 'Nice try. Too controversial.'" She was trembling.

He held her away to see her face. "You got a 'Nice try' on your first submission? Danielle, that's wonderful!" He enfolded her again. "Why, my stories, they sent five of them back, printed slips, before I got my first 'Nice try'!"

"They rejected *Miss Mischief.* . . ."

He felt the trembling. She had failed. It had started as a game, writing for fun. Yet she had done her best, she had laughed with Veronique and she had cried and she had held her breath for that animal, day after day, months till her book was finished, till it was fiction no longer. She loved her heroine and the patient friends who had shown her the way.

Now they're dead, she thought. Veronique, Telegaard, Lisette, wise Balfour. All of them. Rejected.

Budgeron stroked the fur of her neck. "Yes. They've rejected your book. They didn't want it, they sent it back."

He moved half a step, to look in her eyes. "One of the editors liked it, though. She was outvoted, but she liked it enough to tell you her truth and to write that note."

Danielle sighed, released herself from his embrace, brushed her tears, took control of her feelings. "Oh, well. I wrote it for fun, anyway. It felt so good, to finish that manuscript, and write, 'The End'!"

"The two most beautiful words in the language," he said. He did not return to his work. "What are you going to do?"

"I'm sure somebody needs a pawdicurist in town."

"There are worse jobs," he said. He reached for the shelf bracket. "Do you love your book, Danielle?"

"You know I do, Budgie. I wouldn't change a page! Veronique tries to be bad, but she doesn't know how. She's got a wonderful heart, and in the end, the very ferrets she's been mean to are the ones who save her." Tears fell once again. "Oh, Budgeron, I love them! I love my book!"

Calm and strong, her mate stood close, held her again. "If you love your book, what are you going to do with it?"

She stiffened. "I'm not going to throw it away," she cried, "*I will not!*"

"No."

"Why are you looking at me? What am I supposed to do with my book now?" She was close to tears again. "*It's been rejected!*"

"Who rejected it?"

"Does it matter? Bottlebrush Press. They sent it back!"

"Besides Bottlebrush, how many publishers are there in Manhattan?"

"Many," she sniffed. "But if Bottlebrush didn't like it . . ."

"No one else will? Have you ever heard of a book rejected at one house, rejected at ten or twenty, then gets published the twenty-first time and comes out a bestseller?"

He looked at her severely, professor to a kit. "Danielle, it's not whether a publisher likes your book that matters, it's whether *you* like it! When you believe in your story, you're not looking for a whole company to publish it, you're looking for one editor, one animal from your true family, the same taste as yours, same loves, same excitements, and that ferret happens to work at a publishing house, determined to fight if she must to see your book in print!"

Danielle brightened. "And this ferret, you're saying, may be at some other house, not Bottlebrush?"

He nodded.

"So you're saying I ought to try again?"

He did not respond.

"And all it's going to cost me is a return envelope, and the postage?"

He nodded.

"And someday someone's going to accept my book?"

"If they don't, you have another rejection slip for your collection."

A wan smile. "How can I lose?"

The little animal hugged her mate, bounced off to find the address of another publisher.

The kitchen shelves were installed by sunset.

13

Budgeron Ferret woke into darkness, breathing hard. The dream that had struck him once had struck again.

A host of animals was calling to him, bears and birds, snakes and wolves and giraffes, voices across a bright lake. No words but his own name, begging his notice.

"Budgeron . . ."

"Budgie . . ."

"B-ron!"

"Budgidear . . ."

"Boucheron-Bvuhlova . . ."

All the voices at once, each calling softly.

He was stepping toward the lake when he heard the sound of hooves on turf. Then a giant delphin swept down from the hills, the animal and ferret rider in ancient colors. They looked neither left nor right, the dark figure in the saddle urging his mount to greater speed.

The two struck the water a violent blur, sheets of spray flying.

They galloped through, wild thunders, and were gone, echoes of hooves fading into silence. When the water curtains fell behind them, the voices across the lake were silent.

Empty grass.

No one called his name.

Budgeron Ferret lay in the dark, trembling.

14

THAT WAS A HARD summer for Danielle Ferret and her manuscript.

The former pawdicurist received another rejection, from a different house, this time "Not quite!" written by paw over the printed text.

Three weeks later, the next, from Sleekwhisker Books:

"Dear Danielle Ferret:

"To say that we were startled upon reading your novel, *Miss Mischief*, would be an understatement. It has caused quite a stir in the office, and, I must admit, some controversy.

"Our sense of right, of course, suggests that we decline your submission as the actions of your heroine are not in the highest traditions of ferret literature and culture.

"Thank you for sending your story. Your writing has fine pacing and adventure. We wish you great success in your future writing and hope you will allow us to consider your next manuscript.

"JoBeth A. Ferret, Associate Editor"

Weeks after her sixth submission, this time to Ferret House Press, she frowned at the mail. Ferret House did not return her manuscript, but sent a rejection envelope anyway.

My husband writes a bestseller for your company, she blazed, you could at least send back my manuscript! Then, shocked at her outburst, she apologized to the stars and realized that she had made no agreement with the company to return her manuscript, and it was in no way bound to do so.

Not eager to see how Ferret House had phrased the rejection, she put the envelope aside.

It wasn't until evening that she opened the mail: bills, an interview request for Budgeron from *Kits Adventure*, the letter from Ferret House.

She sighed. She would paper the walls . . .

"Dear Danielle Ferret:

"Of course you know that your novel, *Miss Mischief*, is a story of behavior that every ferret would consider unacceptable.

"On the other paw, we find your story to be irresistible entertainment. While we certainly do not approve of Veronique Sibhoan's motives or choices, we cannot but admire her determination and infectious insouciance.

"In addition, the power of the manuscript's final chapter, to us, justifies all that has led to it. Veronique is indeed a kit from difficult beginnings, with much to learn about loving, and she learns it with the grandest bravura, at the last possible second.

"Usually we have a clear sense of the sales potential of the books we publish. With your story, we do not. Whether book-loving ferrets will embrace *Miss Mischief* or revile her, we cannot say.

"However, we believe that Veronique speaks for herself, and that holding her whiskers high, unashamed, she will dare her readers to be her judge.

"The offer attached is a modest one, because of the risk in publishing a novel without precedent. You will notice, however, that should the book sell a large number of copies, your profit participation will increase.

"With thanks for the kindness of your consideration that Ferret House Press might be your publisher, we remain, your obedient servants,

"Vauxhall Ferret, President"

Budgie looked up from his desk into a dark satin mask radiant with triumph. He took the letter from her paw, read it, let it drop to the floor. Without rising, he swept his mate into his arms, the two nearly crashing to the floor from the overloaded office chair. He felt sobs of relief against his shoulder, soaking him in happy tears.

"Danielle." His words muffled against her fur. "You did it. Congratulations. You worked hard, day after day, and you did it!"

"Oh, Budgie," she sobbed, "you know it wasn't work. I watched Veronique and I wrote what she did. That little vixen . . ."

After a time he set her on her paws, then stood and went to the kitchen, returned with the bottle of winter snow-water, saved just above freezing for celebrations.

Danielle was wreathed in delight. "I didn't change a word, Budgeron! I put the same manuscript in a different envelope and I sent it out another time!"

"Why didn't you try Ferret House first thing? They're my publisher!"

"That's why," she said. "Ferret House is *your* publisher. I didn't want . . ." She smiled. "Until I got desperate, I didn't want them to think I was asking for favors."

He touched her nose. "Silly kit! Do you think a publisher is going to spend a fortune publishing your book, some favor to you? How many favors before they're out of business? They're publishing your book because they love your story as much as you do!" He grinned at her. "And because they intend to earn a lot of money from *Miss Mischief.*"

The two animals talked long into the night about what Danielle's future might bring, and sunrise found them in front of the fireplace, nestled in each other's fur, asleep.

15

BUDGERON READ what he had finished that morning:

" . . . *only from that vantage will I be able to study the moon and planets as I need, test my theory of our origins. Yes, I believe it will be necessary to move this entire castle, stone by stone, to the top of the mountain.*"

"*My dear Count!*" *said the burgomeister.* "*What will say the Duke de Mustille? Will not your castle on yon hill fall squarely in view from his own?*"

"*We have spoken about this. He finds my home a pleasure to his eye, and does not object.*"

"*But—*"

"*Further, I shall pay handsomely every animal that lifts a paw to help me. It is a grand work, that upon which I am embarked. . . .*"

"*Wrong. Wrong! Wrong!*" The writer dashed his quill to the blotter, violet ink spraying the soft green.

My kits' stories are life, he thought, action and colors everywhere.

My novel, it's stilted, it's false, it's *dull*, turns me to wood. *And I'm the author!* Oh! my poor reader . . .

The truth swept over him, a mantle of stone and lead: *I've forgotten how to write.*

In the long silence that followed, his eyes closed, his nose sank low. It felt like dying, the light ebbing from his mind. This time, though, with the darkness came a voice within, a dragon from the night of his soul.

Who do you think you are, Budgie Ferret? What kind of a fraud, you dare call yourself a writer? Do you so love pain that you torture yourself this way?

He did not respond.

Who cares about you? Your book is no book, and you know it. The pages are sand, worthless. The novel was worthless from the start, it is worthless still, it will be worthless when you finally give up and tear it to shreds.

What a fool you are! To believe that any animal will ever read a word you write about Urbain de Rothskit, or care. A fool, Budgie. You make everything just so, you light your Lamp of Wisdom, and you ply your fancy quill. Go on, Great Writer, try it now! Try hard. What's the next sentence? And why bother? The blank page, it had some value as paper. You wrote on it. Now it's trash.

In slowest motion, the once-proud, once-confident Budgeron Ferret tilted forward in anguish, until his nose and whiskers rested on the soft blotter.

The ink dried on the fallen quill.

The dragon did not disappear.

Your thoughts are logs, jammed in a river, not connected, crazy angles. Your ideas are rocks. Not even. Your ideas are common pebbles, they mean nothing, they're worth less.

Worth less.

Great minds wrote the classics, ages past, and now along comes Budgeron Ferret thinking he's going to write a literary novel that will change the world? Is that likely?

The animal on the desk moved but only enough that its head rested no longer upon its nose, but upon the side of its face. Its eyes closed.

I'm asking. Is it likely that any novel you can imagine will ever change the world, which was getting along fine before ever you were born and is managing to get along fine without you this very minute?

Silence.

What are the odds that might happen? One in a million? One in how many millions? Are you different from any other creature who ever lived . . . are you so different, let alone better, that any word you write for the halls of literature deserves to be read?

Silence.

Surely there is a better way to spend your time than Where Ferrets Walk. *What a foolish title! What a foolish animal you are!*

Then, in a giant echoing whisper, the dragon recited the names of the great ferret writers through the ages. It was no celebration, but a dirge to hopelessness.

. . . Barthenai . . . Emander . . . Avedoi Merek . . . Chiao Jung-wei . . . Miguelita Ferez . . .

With each name, the dragon trusted that Budgie's esteem for his own light would sink a little farther into darkness.

The trust was not misplaced. The next time the writer touched the quill, and it was quite some time later, was to clean the point of dried ink, and put it away. I'm finished, he thought.

Ceremony closed and done, for reasons he would not know for a long time hence, something happened that had never happened before. That morning the broken writer heard the voice again, this time soft but filled with life, whispering through the wall of mighty names, dissolving them, shattering their darkness:

They spoke for their time, Budgeron Ferret. Who shall speak for yours?

The voice echoed within him, all ferocity gone, it shocked and soothed in the same moment.

The stories you tell, it said, *the characters you bring to life, Budgeron Ferret, shall never die.*

Then it was gone, in its place not chaos but silence.

Followed, not long after, by the fragrance of orange-butter waffles.

16

AT BREAKFAST ON the porch, he swallowed his despair, told his wife once again that he had thrown out his day's work. Not a word had he added to *Where Ferrets Walk*.

"But I have a feeling, Danielle," he said. "It's going to be big. Urbain de Rothskit's going to stand with the classics. The classics . . ." Is that so? he asked himself. He reached for the honey pitcher.

"I know it," she said, a quarter of a waffle on her plate, and that barely touched. "You know why? Because there's soul in your writing. Not soul. No. What am I trying to say? There's something in everything you do . . . it's in *One Paw, Two Paws* . . . , it's in *Bevo*. I care about Bevo because he's got my heart in his wings. He's Bevo, but he's me, too! I don't know how you do that. I can't write that way. Veronique's not me. She's not any ferret I've ever known. She's fiction, but Bevo . . . Bevo's *real!*"

"That whole book is waiting for me upstairs," he told her. "But it's in the dark, hidden away. I wish it could come the way the kits' stories come to me *dook-dook!* A flash of light, there they are!" He cut a giant piece of waffle with the side of his fork, ate it without losing his thought.

"Oi guff Urbon'f go'n to tak a lon tom." He reached for the milk, swallowed, noticed his wife's furrowed brow.

"I guess Urbain's going to take a long time," he repeated. "I'm not sure who he is, even, yet."

She nodded. "Classics must come slow. Anybody else would have given up on that book by now."

"Professional writer's an amateur who didn't quit," he reminded her. Then, for brighter conversation: "How's Novel Number Two?"

She smiled, sniffed the air. "It's coming along. Three thousand, sometimes five thousand words a day."

He laughed. "You're kidding. I mean really. How's it doing?"

"Really, Budge. Yesterday I wrote two chapters, fifty-two hundred words."

A sigh of understanding from her mate. "That's a long day writing."

She wrung one paw gently against another. "I wanted to slow down today, but Chantelle wants to run. I can feel it."

The sky turned high over the ferrets' little house, the wind sifting here and there, tamed by the porch so that it barely ruffled their fur, trembled their whiskers.

He decided to tell her. "I can't write kits' books anymore."

She looked up at him, surprised, frightened. "Oh? Why can't you write whatever you feel like writing?"

"They'll get in the way when it's time to publish *Where Ferrets Walk*."

She looked at him, puzzled. "Get in the way?"

"When my novel comes out, I want the world to take me seriously."

"Do you take Antonius seriously?"

"Danielle, he's an ancient, classical . . ."

"*The Ferret Fables*. Aren't those kits' stories?"

"I mean the modern reading public. Grown-ups. They'll think I write for kits. They won't read *Where Ferrets Walk* because Budgeron Ferret writes for kits."

Danielle smiled at her mate. "That's your fear speaking, isn't it? You know that's not true. It's not true for you, it's not true for anybody: 'I won't read his novel because he's written books for kits.' Readers love good books. What about Thartha? We'll read books by a *hedgehog* when she writes great stories!"

17

A NIGHT OF DESPAIR, sleep like torn leaves, blowing, the scrape of claws on stone. *No matter how much I . . . this isn't working. It's never going to work.*

By dawn, not even the sun could lift his spirits. He would not survive unless he could be honest with his mate, he knew it.

So did she, setting breakfast upon the table.

"Something's wrong, Budge."

Silence for an answer, and a sigh.

"I'm not sure why I wanted to be a writer," he said at last. "Do I so love pain?" He nibbled a slice of mango, put it down. "Every day's the same. Do you want to know the truth? The novel is not coming. I'll never finish it. I don't love it, I don't even like it. It's empty. Disaster. A dragon showed up, he flamed me, Danielle, and he gnashed me to pulp. I'm a failure. I was lucky with *One Paw, Two Paws*, I was lucky with *Bevo the Hummingbird*. I'll never publish another book. We'll have to sell the ranch."

She crunched undismayed on almond-butter toast. "So who is this dragon, anyway?"

He blinked. "Hm? What do you mean, 'who is this?'"

"What's your dragon's name?"

The writer thought for a moment. Why, yes, it does have a name. "Cinnamon."

"What's Cinnamon look like?"

"Oh, come on, Danielle . . ."

"No, really, Budgie. If he's going to destroy you, at least you get to look at him, don't you?"

The writer closed his eyes, remembered. "He's bigger than the house, Danielle. He's blue, with wavy yellow stripes, he was painted from a merry-go-round. Teeth big green emeralds, sharp. Breathes flames, purple fire. Wings, but he doesn't fly."

"Your dragon won't fly?" she said, watching him over her toast. "Do you find that interesting?"

"You're sounding like a philosopher ferret, Danielle. No, he won't fly. And he doesn't want me to fly. Ever."

She looked at him wisely, nodded. "Does he have a title?"

"Title?"

"What's his job?"

"He's the Big . . . he's the Chief Really Bad Dragon."

"Can he hurt you?"

"He wants to. He wants to destroy me, he wants to stop me from writing, stop me from doing anything beautiful, ever again."

"Can he do it?"

Her mate was still. "Yes."

She set her toast gently on the table, leaned toward him. "How, Budgie?"

"He'll destroy me when I believe what he says."

"Are you frightened?"

"Yes."

"Let's see." Danielle leaned back. "Cinnamon's a flame-breathing Chief Really Bad Dragon three stories tall, scary colors, purple fire, but he can't destroy you unless you do the job yourself. To do that, you've got to believe . . . what do you have to believe?"

That instant, the dragon burst alive, scorched through her husband's terror: "*I'm a fraud, nobody cares what I think, my ideas are fake, my title's foolish, I'm foolish, I'll never write a book, I'll never change the world, I'll never do anything beautiful, I'm a failure, I'm worthless!*"

Budgie's eyes like spiral dinner plates, the echoes slashed cymbal razors through the ferrets' kitchen, deafening. The broken writer collapsed inside, fell back in his chair, eyes closed, tears of frustration beginning.

Danielle stunned into silence, the fur of her tail standing straight.

Then, slowly, as though she were one of those advanced souls who walk among ferrets, she took a deep breath, turned within, called her highest truth. When it answered, she held it fast.

She reached across the table, put her paw upon her mate's, spoke what she had been given to say.

"That's not you talking, Budgie, it's Cinnamon. Those aren't your fears, those are Cinnamon's fears! *Your dragon needs your help!*"

Budgeron opened his eyes, exhausted, unbelieving. "He wants to destroy me, Danielle. He wants to kill me!"

She listened to herself, scarcely believing it was her own voice. "Every image within us, every idea, comes to test our love," she heard herself say. "Even dragons. Cinnamon wants to be your friend, he wants to serve you, *he doesn't know how!*"

"He could start by not killing me. . . ."

Danielle blinked, reached to hold the blaze of inner light before it faded. "Give him a different job," she rushed on. "Not your destroyer. *Your bodyguard!* That dragon's your *muse!* Let him bring you ideas, let him light a ring of fire about you as you write, let him shield your characters from doubt, till they're finished at last and fly where you nor Cinnamon can ever go!"

Then the light was gone, a starburst vanished back to her center.

She was quiet for a long while, her husband staring at her.

She shrugged. "It's a thought. . . ."

18

Upstairs in his writing room, Budgeron Ferret closed his eyes, imagined a friend. Not my fear, he thought, I call forth my love, my most playful creativity . . .

"Cinnamon . . . "

No further than a whisper, there was a rustling in his mind, and a new Cinnamon, a thoughtful, devoted dragon, looked down upon the writer.

"What I wanted to tell you," said the great soft voice, "came from yourself. You already know. Urbain de Rothskit has something to say, but it's not for *Where Ferrets Walk*."

The writer listened. "Are you saying that I can't write historical novels?"

Ah, mortals, thought the dragon. They love to learn, they love to forget. "No," he said gently. "I'm saying you don't want to. You cannot write books that you do not love."

Budgeron pounded his paw on the table in frustration. "So what *can* I write, Cinnamon? You've hammered me flat, telling me what a failure I am!"

"I'm sorry," said the dragon. "I was afraid, it was the only way I knew to warn you, when I called you a failure. I meant, a failure you are with *Where Ferrets Walk*. Other books, you're a wonderful writer!"

"Thank you," said the writer. "I do have feelings."

"I'm sorry."

A long silence. "So what's my secret? No novel, no Rothskit? Now what? How do I write?"

"You've known it all along," said the creature. "The stories you wrote as a kit, *One Paw, Two Paws . . . , Bevo the Hummingbird.* What do they have in common?"

Anyone else, watching, would have seen a solitary ferret at the desk, unmoving, tranced in thought, computer screen humming blank before him.

Yet the author trembled with excitement, his heart raced in the midst of the test from this sudden new friend, his dragon muse.

"What do they have in common," Cinnamon prodded, "that your grand novel does not share?"

Instead of speaking, the writer's paws moved on the keyboard, he typed his answer:

I had fun, writing!

The muse waited, for the test was not complete.

I did not think about the writing, I stood aside, I got out of its way and let it happen.

A longer silence.

I was not critical of the writing while I wrote. It didn't matter what the reader thought, what the editor thought, it didn't matter what I thought. I let my story be what it wanted to be.

Budgeron heard a great sigh. "I don't edit," said the dragon, "but let's say you wanted to reduce those three to rules you might tape to your computer for now, or maybe for the rest of your life."

The writer clung to doubt, for safety. "Assuming I have a life."

The dragon smiled. "Assuming . . ."

Budgeron Ferret read what he had written. The fewest possible words. He cleared the screen.

Have fun, he wrote. Then:

Don't think. And:

Don't care.

"Ah!" breathed the dragon. "Simple. Fail-proof. True for any creative adventure."

The writer leaned forward, tense as a ski jumper launched down an icy chute. "Tape and scissors . . ."

"Not yet," said Cinnamon. "Test them. Test them on *Where Ferrets Walk*."

Budgeron nodded impatiently, alone in his room. Of course.

"*Have fun?* No!" he said aloud. "That book was work. The opposite of fun, it terrorized me!

"*Don't think?* Ha! Mind squeezed flat, thinking. Instead of flying through the story I was *calculating*—should Rothskit do this, or this, or that? Should he do nothing? Maybe something else ought to happen now. . . ."

He nodded, agreeing with himself, beginning to understand.

"*Don't care?* Wrong. How I cared! Look out, world, here comes Budgeron Ferret! Hello, Medal of Avedoi Merek! What scarf shall I wear for the ceremony in Mustelania, when the Queen proclaims I've joined the greatest writers?"

It was true. How he had cared about that novel! How worried he had been, caring! Worried to a halt, a tin woodferret rusted under showers of stress.

"H'm." Cinnamon cleared his throat, interrupting. "See that? Each rule you followed, when you wrote your best. Each you broke, forcing *Where Ferrets Walk*.

"There's a time to work on a book and you know it," said the muse. "There's a time to think about the story, a time to care about your readers, your publisher, about rhythm and timing and grammar and spelling and punctuation, about design and advertising and publicity. But none of those times, Budgeron, is *when you're writing!*"

The dragon whispered, for underline, "None of those times is when you're writing."

Cinnamon craned his sea-blue neck, twisting to peer over the ferret's shoulder, to read the computer screen and quote correctly. "'*Have fun. Don't think. Don't care.*'"

"Thank you, Cinnamon."

"It's what I was trying to tell you. I had to get you away from Urbain de Rothskit. That book would have crushed—"

"Don't wreck it, don't wreck it, Cinnamon," cried the author in his mind. "Let me write!"

"Of course." With that, the giant lifted its head. In one movement, nearly a dance, he breathed a flaming circle about the writer, a wall leaping far above the animal's head. Yet from the flames came only a gentle warmth, as from a heart in love.

"You are proof from doubt, Budgeron Ferret," said his muse. "Have fun, and write."

All at once, listening, the writer was swept in a kaleidoscope of images, a colorswirl of possibility. Any character he could imagine was already enchanted. He felt a vast network of connections reaching out from him, drawing in.

Cinnamon towering, keeping the peace beyond that steep round fire, Budgeron Ferret was filled with hope and decision. Gone was the tension of quill and violet ink, the agony of which word to follow the last.

HAVE FUN! DON'T THINK! DON'T CARE!

Later he might come back to Count Urbain de Rothskit. Now, watching his paws move faster over the keyboard, he listened to his rules, and obeyed.

19

His manuscript was finished in a week, the same week that Danielle signed her contract for *Miss Mischief* with Ferret House Press.

After she brought a little snack for them to the porch that afternoon—watermelon sliced thin, currants on top—before she settled to her writing, he turned to her.

"Thank you, Danielle."

"You're welcome, Budgeron."

"What do you think?" he asked.

She smiled. "What do I think about what?"

"The new Bevo manuscript."

"A new Bevo? Where, Budge?"

He offered her a sheaf of pages, harvest of his pleasure, writing.

"Budgeron!" she cried, and read the title page. "'*Bevo and the Bee Bandits*'!"

An hour later, Danielle was in tears. "How I love Bevo," she sniffed from her pawkerchief, "How I love *you*, Budgeron!"

He warmed in her praise, but listened to caution. "Are the bee bandits, at the start, are they too . . . well, too mean, keeping the flowers to themselves?"

"Well, they're not *ferrets*, Budgie! Those particular bees had room to grow, and Bevo did what no one else could . . . he showed them that flowers bloom for all the animals! I wouldn't change a word."

"It's first draft," he said.

"Perfect. I wouldn't change a word. I couldn't improve the story one bit. But you're the author." She smiled at him, a massive weight lifted. "You can change any word you want."

He took the manuscript from her, and the two animals sat together on the porch, the one drawing her typewriter near, continuing her second romance novel, the other . . .

The other licked the tip of his pen, began reading *Bee Bandits* from the top, listening to the sound of the story in his mind. Was the rhythm of the words as it must be?

Under his breath, he tested the meter, barely whispering.

"*'Bevo hummed his way through the meadow, one flower to the next,'*" he read, then the same syllables again, for the flow of them:

"Da-da *dah* da-dah da-da-da-dah, *da* da-dah da-da-dah . . ."

He liked the rise and fall of it. He changed nothing in the sentence, went down the page.

The second pass through his manuscript, he looked for the same word too often used. He smiled. Use a word once, the mind clings desperate, needs to use it again, right away. A writer sets boundaries: No.

Third pass, he cut every *just*, deleted each *very*, enjoying the way the sentences crisped and sharpened as they disappeared. It's all right to write those words first draft, he thought, it's not all right to print them later. With his pencil he worked a magic: the shorter the sentence, the more meaning it carries.

A mess of a sentence? he thought. Simple fix: don't print it. Cut it out. All the reader sees is what goes to press, final draft. It's not skill as a writer that matters, it's skill as a re-writer, over and again, each pass smoother, easier to read, till the final is a summer breeze over the harp of a reader's mind, soft telepathy. Open our eyes to these patterns of ink on paper, and in silence we hear voices, watch ferrets dance, fly with them on adventures we'd never imagine otherwise.

Fourth pass, he applied a different rule: the only synonym for *said* is *said*, and that one used sparingly. Don't use the word at all if you can get away with it. Show the character doing something, then follow with dialogue . . . you don't need *said*.

Once he had apologized to Danielle that his were little stories for young ferrets, reminded her that his real destiny was *Where Ferrets Walk*. Yet in the quiet poet-garden of his heart, he loved his hummingbird. The tales that had come twice, now, divine flashes from some mystical nowhere, they thrilled him, brought him to laughter and to tears. He didn't know how to write any better than this.

So turned the summer afternoon, the two fluffy animals together, barely a paw's distance one from the other, each alert, unspeaking, trotting deep into vastly different worlds.

20

"DEAR DANIELLE,

"I send this letter along with your first royalty statement to tell you that Veronique seems to be finding quite a few readers. There's word of mouth building for the book, and I'm happy to tell you that a week from Sunday, *Miss Mischief* will appear as number 13 on the *Mustelid Weekly* bestseller list.

"Congratulations from all of us at Ferret House!

"As we agreed, of course, we are expanding our advertising budget for the book.

"We respect your privacy, Danielle, but you've become a curiosity, and we've had quite a number of requests for interviews. Would you consider the matter again and consider talking with the press about *Miss Mischief*? Might you be available for television interviews, perhaps for a book tour as Veronique goes up the list? Let us know at your early convenience—it could matter to sales.

"I must say, Danielle, that we can't wait to see your second novel. Of course we wouldn't want you to feel any pressure, but if we had a manuscript in our paws soon, a story as arresting as *Miss Mischief*, it would be possible to place it in our fall catalog and in bookstores by the holidays.

"We remain,

"Your friends and obedient servants,

"Beatrix Chateauroux Ferret, Vice President, Publicity Director"

The check that accompanied the letter was a quiet underline to her publisher's enthusiasm.

Like any first-time author, Danielle had been delighted simply to see her book in print. She hadn't considered what might happen if it were to become a bestseller.

Now she sat back in her writing chair, tapped the envelope softly at the side of her nose. If publishers measure success by numbers of copies sold, she thought, how do authors measure it—by the chaos it brings into their lives?

She was happy with their choice to move to Colorado, happy to stay with Budgeron on their ranch. What would he do if she went off on some many-city tour for her bestseller? Quality of life, she thought, is more important than book sales.

Danielle set the check aside. Then she stood, took the letter to the kitchen, tore it into small pieces and scattered them in the waste-basket. Bestseller or not, she wanted to stay at home.

21

NO SOONER HAD she fluffed the batter and ladled the first batch into the waffle iron than she heard a sound on the stairs. Budgeron Ferret appeared in the kitchen doorway, a sheet of paper in his paws.

"Done!" he cried. "I've finished my novel!"

She looked at him dumbfounded. "Finished, Budge? Did you say finished?"

"You heard it. I am done with *Where Ferrets Walk*!"

She took the page from him, scanned that old first paragraph and read the remainder:

> The dawn he watched was the beginning of his own new being.
>
> No more the burdens of aristocracy for this Rothskit, he thought. The theater has called, and I shall answer!
>
> With that he packed a single valise, left a note declaiming that he would rather live a full life as a thespian than a troubled one as a count, and set off across the horizon for the city, in search of his star.
>
> The End

Danielle looked up from the page. "Budgie?"

Her husband studied her, eyes alight, a great weight gone from his shoulders.

"This," she asked, "is *Where Ferrets Walk?*"

"I didn't want to leave it unfinished."

"Budgie?"

"It's a short literary novel. I realized, upstairs, that I don't write classics. It's a bestseller title, but I don't know how to write the book. It wasn't fun for me. Too heavy. Couldn't run."

"Don't throw this away," she said, handing the sheet to him. "I have a feeling . . ."

He touched the page in her paw. "No. It was everything I could do to keep from shredding it, upstairs."

"Budge . . ."

"Don't worry, Danielle. Sometimes the way to save a story is to throw it away. If it matters, it'll come back again, different clothes."

Not long after, as he installed a telephone extension under the kitchen cabinet, the phone rang at the instant Budgeron connected two wires, the sudden noise jerking him away as though he had touched raw voltage.

He answered on the third ring, while his wits returned.

"Why, Vauxhall! How good to hear your voice!" It was quiet as Budgeron listened to his publisher, to the one who had believed in him and in Bevo, who had fast become his friend.

"Not for us. Colorado summer: if you don't like the weather, wait five minutes, it'll change. . . ."

Danielle came to sit on a tall stool by the sunny kitchen island, listening to her mate's side of the conversation. Why the call? she wondered. *Something nice is going to happen, I know it.*

"Yes, sir. You could move your office from Manhattan to Side-Hop. There's a whole block empty by the feed store, you could rent it cheap."

A long silence. "You do? Vauxhall, thank you!"

She looked at him, raised her eyebrows, held her paws in front of her, more information, please. *What's he saying?*

"I'm so happy to hear that! I can't tell you how good it feels, that you would . . ."

This is no social call, she thought.

"That's a pretty big audience."

He turned to Danielle, made a wide face to say he couldn't believe what he was hearing. "Wow!" he whispered to her.

No matter that he couldn't believe it. She could. *There's no competition in writing,* she thought. *The only place Ferret House Press can get a Budgeron Ferret book, from now till the end of time, is from Budgeron Ferret. Anything else is imitation.*

"*Every* writer wants a publisher who's committed to the books. . . ."

Vauxhall, she thought, *wants another Bevo story. He would not have called unless the Bevo books were selling very well indeed.*

"Of course I will. I'll give it careful thought."

Danielle furrowed her brow, whiskers forward, thoughtful.

"I will. And hers to you, Vauxhall. Thanks for calling. Bye."

She waited. Then: "What did he say?"

Her husband looked at her in disbelief. "Vauxhall sends his warm regards."

"Yes. . . . *Tell me!*"

"He likes *Bevo and the Bee Bandits.*"

Danielle jumped from the stool and hugged her mate. "Of course he does! Hurray, Budgie!"

"He wants me to write Bevo books. It's not just the kits who like the stories, he says it's parents, too. Grown-ups. They're buying Bevo for gifts, now, and once that happens, he said there's no stopping."

"Did you tell him you don't want to get typecast, a kits' writer?"

"No."

"Why not?"

"You taught me better. Ferret House wants a contract for more books. Three more."

"A *three-book* contract?" At once she curbed her delight, watched him closely. "What do you think about that?"

"For so long I thought the novel was my destiny. Did I come here to write *Where Ferrets Walk*, then *not* to write it?"

"You were put on this planet to do your highest best," she said. "If it were your destiny to write Urbain de Rothskit, you'd write him and nothing in the world would be big enough or strong enough to keep you from it."

"*Where Ferrets Walk* was not my book, Danielle. I don't write literary novels!"

She heard beneath his words. No distress, no self-pity, Budgeron was no martyr speaking. A fundamental change had happened within him, before her eyes.

She smiled at him. "'*Listen to your life,*'" she quoted from *Bee Bandits*, "'*it's telling you all you need to know about the creature you can become.*'"

He listened, stretched luxuriously against the kitchen island, feeling more relaxed than he had been in a long time. "I think my life's telling me to stay away from quill pens and exotic ink for a bit. Forever, I think. The creature I want to be, right now, is the one who writes the adventures of Bevo the Hummingbird."

22

AT NOON, TWO DAYS later, Danielle Ferret heard a sound from the living room, a cry, a scream from her mate shattering the gentle noise of her typewriter.

"*Budgie!*" In a flash she was up, her chair flying midair away from the writing table, she a sable blur into the house.

She found him frozen at the television set, his fur standing straight, his tail bottlebrushed, one paw both reaching and repelling the screen. "Danielle . . ."

Her eyes followed his paw; she gasped:

Where Ferrets Walk

The title dissolved to a book-lined study, a slow zoom to a close-up of a distinguished host in soft hat and satin ascot, turning a giant globe with one paw.

"Good afternoon. I'm Brytham Ferret. Welcome to *Where Ferrets Walk.*"

The two animals watched, openmouthed.

"Our program this week takes us to the coldest spot on earth, where one risks one's life even to visit . . ."

The study faded, the narrator continuing, his voice carrying over a scene of ice and snow blown horizontal by a great wind. ". . . where Lola Evine Ferret has set up her camp. She is under siege, night and day, by the wind and the cold. It is a siege that she is determined to survive."

From the snow, the face of a sturdy ferret appeared, layered in heavy scarf and parka hood, frost clinging to her mask, to eyelashes and whiskers.

The narrator spoke directly into the scene. "It looks a little chilly, Lola!"

The adventurer laughed over the storm. "Why, no, Brytham, this is one of our warmer days. . . ."

Danielle touched a button and the screen faded to black.

She turned to her husband, her face a veil of shock.

"*Where Ferrets Walk?* Budgeron, how could they . . ."

He fell into his soft old chair. "A great title, but not for me." He laughed, free as a song. "I write for kits!"

There was silence for a little while, both animals watching the dark screen, reflecting on coincidence.

"Nothing just happens, does it, Danielle?" he said at last. "How long did it take for me to get the message? Urbain de Rothskit never took off, not at all. My dragon roaring *Don't write that book, it's going nowhere!* He says my characters will live forever: I think Rothskit, he means Bevo. No sooner do I let the big novel go, my publisher calls, he doesn't want a big novel, he wants a Bevo series. I turn on the television, *Where Ferrets Walk* is nobody's book, it's a TV show!"

She smiled at him. "What's the difference between dedicated and stubborn?"

"Why, Danielle," he replied, "dedicated, we're in tune with our life. Stubborn, we're not!"

23

NEXT SPRING, THEY were in print, pyramids of them in bookstore windows: *Bevo Makes a Promise. Bevo in the Haunted House. Bevo Takes a Nap.*

All that Budgeron Ferret had hoped for *Where Ferrets Walk* came true for Bevo the Hummingbird, each new title more popular than the one before. *Bevo Takes a Nap* was hailed on the lofty pages of *Mustelid Weekly*: "The most absorbing volume on the nature of imagination this reviewer has read—words for kits, meanings for ferrets everywhere."

Danielle delivered her second novel to Ferret House that summer. As shocking as *Miss Mischief*, the exotic Chantelle-Dijon Ferret ravaged a swath through three continents, wider than naughty Veronique's. Chantelle's startling white mask and her secret quests for the good of ferrets everywhere earned *Forbidden Questions* an opening spot at number 4 on the *MW* bestseller list, just below the author's first book.

They were on the way from Side-Hop to Moss Canyon for delphin treats, humming around the curve south of the city, they saw it at the same instant.

"*Budgeron!*"

At once their little truck pulled off the road and rolled to a stop, dwarfed under a billboard the size of a jumbo jet:

MUSTELIDS READ DANIELLE FERRET
KITS READ BEVO
AT BOOKSTORES EVERYWHERE

The two sat transfixed, the sign towering over them. Then, out of the silence, her voice:

"What have we done?"

Until that moment the ranch at Side-Hop might as well have been a glass dome over the writers, sealing them away from the shock waves, the one gentle and the other scandalous, that their books were causing among readers.

Manuscripts had been reams of paper from Side-Hop Office Supply, stories that they read to each other, puzzling, smoothing, polishing, correcting over and again till they disappeared in the mails.

Stories changed into contracts and royalty checks. In time, each of them accepted that their books were bestsellers. They were happy for this, but writers do not turn through the day in amazement that their books are appreciated. All the excitement distant to them, news reports from far-off places.

The billboard towering above, however, was no report. It stood 80 paws high, 150 wide, the letters three times taller than Budgeron himself, carbon ink against sun white. Ferret House had increased its advertising budget as promised.

"If this is happening in Colorado . . ." he said.

". . . what have we done?" she murmured.

In time the truck moved on, the driver and his mate silent.

When they loaded oats and grains and fresh apples from the yard at Manny Ferret's Delphin Treats, the clerk at the feed table looked at their invoice, looked again.

"You'd be no relation to *the* Budgeron Ferret, now, would you be?"

"Do you have mangoes?" Danielle asked at once. "My little Dusty loves dried mangoes."

"We certainly do, ma'am. In fact, they're right in front of you, on the counter."

They retreated west to Side-Hop, reaching the quiet of the ranch by nightfall.

The two ferrets, they loved telling stories. The gifts they offered were the worlds of their imagination: the saucy lands of Danielle's heroines, the enchanted territory of Bevo's innocent adventures. When we give sparingly, ferrets are taught, sparingly are we rewarded. When we give worlds, we are rewarded vastly.

They had prepared for what they could plan and control: hours at the computer and the typewriter, writing to deadlines, discussions long-distance with editors and book designers and subrights sales-ferrets at their international desks.

Yet neither had given more than a passing thought to what they could not control: the storms of curiosity their books would sweep down upon them, the forests of choice, the fields of surprise ahead.

From that moment under the towering letters, their lives would never be the same.

24

"WHOA, LUCKY," said Budgeron, shifting his weight in the saddle. "Whoa down."

The chestnut delphin slowed to a stop, Danielle halting alongside on Dusty.

Sunup found the two at the far edge of their property, out of sight from their ranch house in the savannas to the north. Wicker saddles creaked softly beneath the riders, cool air fragrant with prairie grass and cottonwood about them. The Little Side-Hop River bent in a wide curve nearby, a few paws deep over patches of watercress and smooth round stones.

"Vauxhall's leaving it up to us, a book tour. Good for sales, he said, but I'm not sure I want to go, Danielle. The city was all I knew till I got away to Monty's that summer, and then city again after that. Now I'm happy here. I don't want to go back to cities."

She laid her reins lightly on Dusty's mane. "I love it here, too."

"We don't need to go on tour. We don't need to sell books. They're already selling."

She nodded.

"We have everything we want in Side-Hop."

The barest breeze began, early sun warming the hillside. Here and again, the silent flap and flash of butterflies.

"What do you think?" he asked. "What should we do?"

"I don't know *should*."

He smiled, leaned forward in the saddle, massaged Lucky's neck. "What do you want to do?"

"I'd like to go."

"Why?"

"To see how it feels," she said. "I think, out there, we may be celebrities. I don't know what that feels like. I'd love to meet our readers."

"Cities?"

"It won't be for long. I don't mind cities. That used to be home." She reached across the space between them, touched his faded old ranchpaw bandana. "A tour sounds like fun, doesn't it? A vacation, a little break from writing? We'll learn a lot. And if we don't, that's the end of it."

"Remember the billboard? We'll be mobbed."

She smiled at the image. "Ferrets don't mob, Budgie. If readers come to say hello, I'd be happy to meet them. Wouldn't you?"

He smiled, shyly. "I am a little curious . . ." Then: "Danielle . . ."

She looked at him.

"This is going to be your tour. You know that, don't you?"

"It's going to be our tour," she said. "Both of ours."

He shifted his weight forward; Lucky started a walk, heading for home. "It will be you and me, yes, but there's a difference between a kit's bestseller and an adult's bestseller. Vauxhall told us straight: it's *Miss Mischief*, it's Veronique that's got everyone startled. I'm going to stay in the background and watch. You know that's the way I like it, a little attention goes a long way with me. I'll have my moments with the kits, but you're going to be the one out front."

Danielle nodded, but inside she who had read to kits knew the truth: her books wouldn't be in ferret libraries a century from now, Budgeron's would.

25

THE TWO WRITERS left Side-Hop for Manhattan one sun-blue morning on a sleek polished business jet, courtesy of media magnate Stilton Ferret, distant relative and close friend of Vauxhall.

The captain met them as they boarded, a powerful animal dressed in pilot's cap, sunglasses, a scarf of deepsky blue and four golden stripes. As the writers reached the top of the airstair steps, the officer removed his glasses:

"Howdy, ranchpaws."

Budgeron was tumbled in a wave of delight, a voice from his past. He knew that smile.

"*Strobe!*" he cried. "I can't believe . . . *Strobe!*"

The friends embraced, time collapsing around them: the flash of Monty's vast ranch, their whistles and cries over the thunder of Rainbows on a run, the clang of old-West dinner bells.

The captain stood back and looked at the writer. "Comin' up in the world, are you, Budge?"

"Well, I'll be." Budgeron turned to his wife. "Danielle, here he is! This is Strobe, from my ranchkit days!"

The flier took her paw, touched it gently to his nose. "My pleasure to meet you, ma'am."

His friend was taller, leaner than Budgie remembered; he wore the air of command as easily as his captain's scarf.

"You can step this way, if you'd like," he said.

The jet sparkled, full-length couches of finest Rainbow wool, soft chairs, dining tables of polished wood, the corporate logo inlaid golden letters: *MusTelCo.*

"The president's lounge has the best view," said the captain. "Long way from a saddle on a sheep drive, though I suspect you may have guessed that." He winked at his friend, went forward to the flight deck, leaving his passengers in the care of a flight steward and two attendants.

After takeoff the captain invited the writers to the cockpit. Danielle, drowsy already from the whisper of sky by her window, elected to nap on the president's couch.

Budgeron went forward to the seat tactfully vacated by the co-pilot and donned the officer's headset. Flight and engine instruments spread before him, through the broad windshield a view of the world as he had never seen it, Strobe sitting relaxed at the controls to his left.

They cruised in bright sunlight at an altitude of thirty-seven kilo-paws, Earth unrolling below as the two stitched in the seasons since they were ranchkits.

Once Strobe held up his paw to Budgeron, pressed the microphone button on his control wheel. "Minneapolis Center," he said, "Mustel Two Zero, level at three seven zero." Then he turned once more to the friend he had known since before he had learned to ride.

"Things moved on. Seemed like no sooner home from Monty Ferret's Rainbow Sheep Resort and Ranchpaw Training Center," he said, "than it was time to drop out of college and meet some airplanes."

"You quit school?"

The flier nodded. "One semester in academia, Budge, that was enough for me. I told my folks they could save the money. I wanted Action . . ."

Budgie joined him, a line the ranchkits had shouted so often: ". . . Adventure! Romance on the High Plains!"

They laughed together.

"I found it all, flying, Budge. Student pilot, mail flier, crop seeder, flight instructor, charter pilot, freight dog, airlines . . . a lot of flying."

Strobe lapsed into quiet, remembering, then continued, "I didn't know my roommate from school was going to become quite the media mogul. Stilton found me again, asked me if I'd look over his airplanes, make some suggestions. I did. After a while, he asked me to be his chief pilot." The captain smiled. "Sure beats sloggin' through mountains at night, Budge, covered in ice, dodgin' treetops, wishin' you were somewhere else, preferably warm and On The Ground."

"I'm proud of you, Strobe," said Budgeron. Cathode-ray tubes showed airways in green lines, compass heading in white, airports passing below in blue. His friend had mastered all of this.

"Proud of you, too. May angel ferrets help me if I ever need to survive, putting words on paper!"

The writer learned, cruising just under the speed of sound, that their ranchkit pal Boa had joined the Ferret Rescue Service, stationed on the storm coast of Washington State.

"What he could do with tools!" said Budgeron. "Remember that old tractor, back of the delphin barn?"

"Rusted shut," said the pilot. "Even Monty said, 'Not much hope, kit, that machine's gone.' Remember?"

"Boa had to show us."

"Good old Boa," the captain said. "I'd like to see him again, before too much longer."

"Alla?"

"Last I heard, Alla was digging up ancient cities."

"She did it! She's an archaeologist!"

The captain nodded. "She called once, a while ago, through New York on her way to Persia. We had dinner, she couldn't talk enough . . . 'We've found the lost city of Pheretima!' That's some vast big palace under the sand, I guess. Cut out of the rocks. Our little ranchkit figured out where it was buried. 'Facts behind the legends! Where did we come from?' You know Alla. She gets her mind set. . . ."

Over Cleveland, the pilot gave Budgeron a flight lesson, gentle turns, small climbs and descents. "You learn flying in five minutes," he said, "you spend the rest of your life practicing."

The writer practiced, easing the jet left and right, surprised at how swiftly it answered his touch. "I'd show you some extras," the pilot said, "but there's this bell goes off down in the Air Traffic Control Center. We go three hundred paws off our altitude, they get all excited, call and ask us what's wrong. It's more fun, on a nice day, flying the biplane down low than it is the jet up high. Maybe we could do that sometime."

"I'd like that. Don't forget." Budgeron took his paws from the controls, gave the airplane back to the captain. "Are you married, Strobe?"

His friend smiled. "Odd you should ask. Not long ago, I would've told you it wouldn't happen. Last month I met Stormy. She was flying south over the Siskiyous, through some ferocious weather, flying a cargo plane, warned me about it on the radio. I was flying north, warned her about the storm I'd just come through south. Turned out we both landed at Redding, had dinner together, we've called each other since. She's a good kit, a good pilot." He paused. "I'm crazy about her, Budge."

Starting their descent into Manhattan, the copilot returned. Budgeron gave up his seat and stepped back into the luxury behind the flight deck.

Landed, engines shut down at the terminal, the captain swung out of his seat, smiled to them. "I guess I can tell you now. I'm scared of heights and scared of crowds. When that door opens, you two are on your own!"

Danielle hugged him warmly. "Thank you, Strobe. It couldn't have been better, you showing up for Budgie today."

"It was him showed up for me, ma'am."

The flight steward touched Strobe's shoulder. "Exit door's clear to open, sir."

"If you two survive what's about to happen," said the pilot, "I'll see you for the flight to Boston. Good luck, old friend!"

Strobe gripped Budgeron's paw again, touched his cap to

Danielle, then pressed a button by the entrance and the door slid upward.

A sea of fur surrounded the arrival gate, fur in colors of snow through polished coal, a crowd of dark-mask faces, light masks, faces maskless, paws waving. *Welcome Danielle Ferret!* painted on signs. *Welcome Budgeron!* Kits in hummingbird hats, *Bevo Loves Me* embroidered.

Danielle swallowed, looked at her mate. "I didn't expect . . . ," she called over the noise of the crowd.

He patted her, reassuring. "This is fun."

She touched above her ears, self-conscious. "Is my hat on straight?"

Black velvet, soft and shiny, a bill of polished brass angled so low it nearly hid her eyes. He touched her fur lightly. "You're beautiful."

She led the way, smiles and waves for the first crowd of fans she had ever met.

Now Budgeron followed Danielle and watched, proud of his mate. They love her saucy heroines, he thought, so they love the author who brought them to life.

As they took a breath to plunge into the crowd, a young animal appeared, held up her paw.

"I'm Beatrix Chateauroux," she said over the noise, "Ferret House Press. We've got a table set up . . . cameras . . ."

They touched noses, left and right, and the publicist led the way through the crowd. No one pawed the authors, no one pushed or shoved. A path opened ahead of them from the crowd's respect and courtesy.

Beatrix touched a switch on the microphone. "Welcome, everybody!" she said. *"Welcome Danielle and Budgeron Ferret!"*

The cheers and waves redoubled, signs in many colors, tilting left and right:

We Love You Danielle Though We're Not So Sure About Veronique!

Call Me . . . Valka!

Here Comes Veronique!

Two kits atop their parents' shoulders, holding a banner: *Hurray for Bevo!!*

"On behalf . . . ," said Beatrix. Cheers. "On behalf . . ."

The cheers continued, and finally the publicist passed the microphone to Danielle.

"Thank you, Manhattan," she said. "It's wonderful to be here!"

Budgeron Ferret didn't know whether he was watching a marvelous transformation or discovering what had been there all along. Danielle, the volunteer reader to city kits, the pawdicurist friend to each of her clients, the writer who invented naughty ferrets turned nearly as noble as the readers for whom she wrote, was an angel in the cameras.

"Why, she's a star!" He nearly turned to see who had spoken when he realized they were his own words. His mate was as born to celebrity as queens are born to rule.

"If Veronique were here," Danielle said quietly, letting the microphone amplify her calm, "she'd be planning a way to steal the spotlights. But it's just Budgeron and me, and we're so glad that you came to say hello."

The cameras loved her. Her brushed fur reflected television floodlights in rippling silver sheens, it sparkled bronze and gold in the swish of flashbulbs. Her image in the monitors, from the jaunty angle of her cap to the tip of her ebony tail, was chiseled elegance.

Danielle wasn't acting, she was enjoying every animal in the crowd, and everyone knew it.

Budgeron looked into the faces of her fans, imagined they were mirrors of the one onstage in front of them. They wanted her to be charming, to be spicy and unexpected, they wanted her to reflect their own inner selves and they were not disappointed. The love between writer and readers, as she spoke, was a warm aura that filled the room with light.

He felt a tug at his knee, looked down to see a kit standing by her father, her mask still faint as dust. She clutched a stuffed hummingbird half her size, and Budgeron knelt to her level, below the sea of fur.

"Thank you for Bevo," she said softly, thoughtful of the crowd listening to Danielle, watching Budgeron with solemn dark eyes.

"You're welcome!" The writer patted her Bevo doll. "I'm happy he's your friend."

"They weren't bad bees." The dark round eyes held his own. "They're my friends, too."

The room blurred for Budgeron Ferret. He hugged the kit and rose, touched her father thanks, brushed his eyes with a paw. This is what writing's about, he thought. You hold an image within, you love the sight of it, and you hand it to a reader. Images, ideas, characters, dialogue, all these things come like torches, to warm and to light and to pass from one of us to another.

"She loves *Bee Bandits,*" her father said. "We just got *Bevo Takes a Nap.* Her grandmother read it, she called this morning, told me stop whatever I was doing, go down now, today, and buy this book for Kimra! Then we saw in the paper that you were going to be here."

"Thank you," said Budgie, "thanks for coming."

"Would you mind?" The father opened a bag, produced the book and a pen.

Budgeron steadied the book on his knee, wrote, *Kimra! The bees are your friends always,* and signed his name. Then he sketched a kit and a hummingbird and a bee, flying together toward a cloud.

He closed the book and returned it with the pen to the father.

There was a burst of applause as Danielle finished her talk. Beatrix took the microphone, told the crowd that Danielle and Budgeron would be happy to sign books for a while, then they had to be off for television interviews downtown.

So went the first hour of their book tour.

26

Piet and Olga Ferret owned Black Mask Books, in the heart of the city. Now they watched as patiently as their customers, curious to find what kind of animals these writers might be.

Their business was books, their love was books, as well. The touch of a fine cover, the delight of a thoughtful phrase or a funny one in ink and paper, the lift of a beautiful story, the sparkle in a reader's eye: "It's just what I was looking for!"—these made their lives and their work a glad place.

"Welcome to Black Mask!" said Olga. Would they notice, she thought, the hours we spent painting banners, would the writers see the posters and advertising, their books stacked floor to ceiling, three tries getting them all to balance?

"Thank you," said Budgeron. "We . . ."

"Beautiful!" said Danielle, embracing her, touching noses. "How much time you've taken for us! And the little bees circling . . ."

Piet looked at his mate and relaxed. Business would be good, but more important today, customers would meet the souls behind the best-sellers, would know that books are not mystery, they come from the hearts of ferrets as easy to meet and talk with as these two. They were one family, writers and booksellers, it warmed them both to meet.

Readers stood in line, talking with each other, making friends as they waited, most of the way around the block. Over the door a taut banner:

Mustelids read DANIELLE FERRET
Kits read Bevo

Surprising owners and readers alike, Danielle trotted down the line, touching noses here and there with her readers, told them thanks for coming, then bounded inside to the table at which she would sign their books.

"That's different," said Olga, watching.

"Nice touch," her mate replied.

Unlike the publishers who had rejected the manuscript of Danielle's first book, Olga and Piet knew it for a bestseller at once, ordered a hundred copies from the Ferret House rep. Within days, they had followed with an order for three hundred more.

"*Veronique's so naughty!*" her readers told Danielle over and again while she wrote their names and signed her own. "If my mother knew I was reading *Miss Mischief* . . ."

"If my mother knew I was *writing* it," said Danielle, and they'd laugh together, two conspirators, author and reader.

The more she met them in person, the more Danielle loved and respected the ones who read her book. Most of all, she learned, they're playful. They know their highest sense of right and they live by it, every one of them decent loving animals. Yet every one of them eager to pretend that within there roams an impudent, a defiant, a brazen ferret, shocking friends and family with every free-spirit leap and bounce.

Meeting readers was a telepathic burst of understanding, each of them to the other, and they laughed without words in the minute they shared together. Contact energy crackled through the meetings; it would take hours, later, for the writer to settle down.

"I write for fun," she told her readers. Yet it was more than fun that they found in her books, she thought, and as she signed she reached for the answer. It was an *unleashing* that happened, when certain animals opened her pages and entered her world.

Her husband had told her long ago that she didn't need to please everyone with her stories—if a book pleases only half of one percent of the reading public, though no one else bought a single copy, it will be a massive bestseller.

"It's not that you're different from me, Danielle, that I like your books," one reader told her while she signed *Forbidden Questions,* "it's that you're the same!"

Budgeron's place might as well have been another world. Hers was a square desk, a solid square sign with her name and photograph. His was round, a cloud of feather hummingbirds suspended from threads, turning in the air.

No lines of ferrets standing patiently for his signature but clumps of kits, sometimes brushed and orderly, sometimes animal-wrestling, mouths wide, little fangs bared, tails bottlebrushed and flailing before their minute with the writer.

Many brought crayoned pictures of Bevo, presents to the author. Suddenly poised and polite as their turn came to have books signed, the littlest of them turned shy, too bashful to touch noses with Bevo's creator.

He signed and sketched in their books, hoping his Bevo-drawing and words for them might be valued later on.

What would this have been, he thought, if instead of Bevo this book were *Where Ferrets Walk*? There'd be no kits here, no unruly thumping about, but everyone grown-up, solemn and literary. Deadly dull.

The television show's choosing its title was the best thing that could have happened to his troublesome novel. He smiled to himself as he signed. Whatever will become of Count Urbain de Rothskit?

The next kit was barely tall enough to see over the edge of his table, the only sign of her a snowy chin on the wooden edge, a dusty mask and tiny whiskers, two black eyes, a little voice:

"Will you write *Bevo Meets the Count* for me?"

The writer caught his breath, thunderstruck. "Excuse me? *What did you say?*"

The eyes did not blink. "Write *Bevo Meets the Count*, please."

The writer stared speechless at the kit, turned openmouthed to her mother, unbelieving.

The parent shrugged. "It's just an idea."

"Where did she . . . how did she . . . ?" said Budgeron, a shock of confusion. "Did she say *Bevo Meets the Count*?"

"She's having trouble with numbers."

"Numbers?" He leaned forward, hoping to understand.

"She wanted me to ask you to write *Bevo Learns to Count* and I told her she could ask you herself."

Budgeron Ferret began to laugh. He stood, lifted the kit to the table, where she looked up puzzled and solemn to her mother. What had she done? Kits waiting, and their parents, smiled at the sight.

"Forgive me," said Budgeron to the kit's mother. "I thought she said . . . What she said, it's brilliant, it's a stroke of unbelievable . . ."

He threw up his paws, helpless before coincidence.

He took his seat again, asked her name, then wrote: *Seraja! Thank you for saving my life! From Urbain de Rothskit and . . . Budgeron Ferret.*

Still smiling, he handed the book down to her and she took it, huge in her little paws.

"Thank you, Budgeron Ferret," she said.

"You're welcome." *You have no idea what you've done, Seraja*, he thought. *That's* what his destiny wants for Urbain de Rothskit! *He meets Bevo the Hummingbird!*

And yet, as he watched them depart, the kit and her mother turned and winked to him in exactly the same instant, then raised their paws together, a synchronized wave good-bye before they set off again and disappeared from sight.

A shock of strange went through the writer, one shock, then another.

What was that? what happened? Was it coincidence, I didn't hear what she said, or did I hear that little voice perfectly well? Did those two come to have a book signed or were . . . or were they angel ferrets disguised, or philosopher ferrets, come to hand me a story I would never have found without them?

He watched the place where they had disappeared, the open doorway to the street, sidewalk crowds passing by. Ferrets don't wink like that, he thought, not a mother and her kit together, knowing the depths of another's heart.

Of course, *Bevo Meets the Count!* he thought. Brilliant brilliant brilliant! The *contrast* between the two, one the very spirit of light, the other heavy and lost. When they meet! What will the Count discover? Will he find something more profound in the little hummingbird than in all of Europe's aristocracy?

Whoever you are, the writer thought, turning back to his table, mortals or discarnates or wise and thoughtful creatures . . . thank you!

When the next kit held her book up to be signed, the writer watched her closely. "What do you know," he asked the little face, "about angel ferrets?"

27

THEIR HOTEL SUITE was not far from Ferret House Press. Convenient and expensive, thought Budgeron. Sixty floors above Madison Avenue, the corner window looked out across the city, north to the park, west to the river and beyond. Beyond was Colorado.

He missed his home. He missed the morning air, he missed the hills and the river, he missed Slim and Lucky and Dusty. He remembered when he had loved the city for its excitement and drive; now those qualities made him yearn for the slow side of life, the peace of Side-Hop, the solitude of the ranch.

From their suite's center table burst a massive spray of flowers, a curving rainbow turned still life over a bottle of sparkling snow-water and a card from the publisher: For Danielle Ferret—Miss Success. The card was a miniature bestseller list, Miss Mischief circled in scarlet.

On a side table stood a wicker basket of small chocolates, lifted nearly airborne by cherry-color balloons. Painted on the basket: *For Bevo—The World's Favorite Hummingbird!*

Budgeron turned from the window, walked into the next room, sighed and collapsed into the deep satin hammock.

"What do you think?" he said. "How's it going?"

She appeared in the doorway, looking tired. "It's hard. It's fun. I miss home."

"We'll be home before we know it. Only seventeen more cities."

Fatigue faded to determination. "I'm glad we came. I like my readers."

"Me, too. Mine are different from yours."

She brightened. "What happened? I looked over and you were . . . startled. Something happened."

Budgie told her about the strange incident, the coincidence, twice he misunderstood what the kit had said.

Danielle shrugged. "Philosopher ferrets."

"Maybe. And what would they say? 'Forget the coincidence, *write the story!*'" Budgie looked to the ceiling, an ornate white-on-blue fresco of classic Greek ferrets. "What would Urbain de Rothskit do if he met Bevo? He'd simplify! And if he simplified, what would he find in all the world that mattered most to him?"

The two of them talked till late on the grand satin hammock.

Before they slept, Danielle turned to her mate. "Are we successful writers, Budgie, you and me?"

He thought about it. "Do we love our books?"

28

H<small>E WOKE WHILE</small> the city slept, unable to silence the little voice: "Will you write *Bevo Meets the Count* for me?"

No computer, no typewriter, he slipped silently from Danielle's side, found his pen and note cards. He padded softly to the living room of the suite, touched the lamp switch, curled in the corner of the sofa.

It was all there, the story, barely a whisper from Cinnamon. Simple, breathtaking, inevitable. He watched it happen, he wrote what he saw:

Away in the sky, a speeding sunlight dot above the snowy clouds of Hungary, flew a tiny lime-ruby streak. Bevo the Hummingbird was off to find Count Urbain de Rothskit, the actor ferret who had awed and charmed a continent.

The tiny bird could not imagine why, but as he rolled and dived through the mist toward Rothskit's castle, he knew that the Count was frightened. . . .

29

H<small>OURS LATER, AFTER</small> the interview for *Celebrity Ferrets* and before an afternoon of satellite television appearances, Danielle and Budgeron met with Vauxhall and the staff of Ferret House Press in the executive conference room.

It was a catered lunch: palettes of bright fruits, swirls of walnut butter, flakes of chocolate, Colorado mountain snow-water while the animals talked.

Until they saw them together in one room, the writers hadn't known how many ferrets worked to bring their books to the marketplace. The art director was there, Tricie, a little shy around the powerhouse her designs had helped to create. Danielle's editor, Marla, of course, met for the first time in the fur. Erich from Production, Angella from Copyediting, Paul from Subrights, Bonbon from Advertising, Mirabelle, Beatrix's assistant, from Publicity . . . animals funny and thoughtful, eager and retiring, ferrets who, like the owners of the Black Mask, lived under the magic of the printed word.

A giant paw covered her own. "Markham Ferret, *Inks on Paper.* I want to thank you for a lot of business lately! Wouldn't miss the chance to meet you, Miss Danielle, if I had to stop the press!" He grinned. "Of course I didn't have to do that . . ."

Vauxhall had invited librarians as well, friends of years, stories to tell.

"*One Paw, Two Paws*, Budgeron, our collection went to five copies, then ten, checked out all the time! Katherine looked at me one day, your book returned one minute, it went out the next, she told me, 'Darryl, it's going to happen to this kit! We'll do well to keep an eye on Budgeron Ferret!'"

Librarians cherish collections, booksellers count sales, Budgie thought. What matters for both is ideas to readers.

For everyone in the room, writers were not merely interesting ferrets, they were essential to life. Without writers, none of them would be here . . . the kindness to the visitors was beyond courtesy, it was as kindness to parents, every bit genuine.

In a while all took their places at the table and Beatrix joined the meeting, handing a sheaf of papers to the company president, finding a chair across the table from the writers.

"Are you two holding up all right?" she asked. "Paws tired from the autographing?"

"Stronger and stronger," said Budgeron, flexing his paw. It was true because he said it was. Had they admitted fatigue, the two would have been exhausted.

The publicist smiled. "You like the meetings, face-to-face?"

He nodded. "My readers are guests in my mind while I write. I like them there, but they're awfully quiet."

"They tell me I'm not alone," said Danielle. "I may have an odd sense of humor, but so do they."

Beatrix nodded. "I stood in line yesterday, talked with a lot of your readers. They're not going to go out to become the Veronique of Fifty-seventh Street, but they're awfully fond of her, they like her pepper. They're fond of you, too, Danielle."

Budgie sensed something in the air. He listened to Beatrix, but he watched Vauxhall studying the papers she had set before him.

The president looked up, glanced at the tall old clock in the corner, pendulum swinging as it had for decades. Talk around the table went still.

"You have a busy schedule, you two. Satellite interviews, then *City at Night*, then you're off to Boston?"

"We've confirmed, Vauxhall," said Beatrix. "Half an hour on *Round the World* from Boston, before the *Sunrise* show."

The president nodded, smoothed his whiskers. "Budgeron, Danielle," he said. "Ferret House has been in business a long time. Some of us have worked here quite a while. And we've found something that happens over and again. You probably know this, but it's why we're together right now. An idea gathers to itself everyone it needs in order to be born."

The ferrets of the staff nodded to themselves. It was true.

"The idea of Bevo found Budgeron to write him. Veronique found Danielle. Then after a while Bevo and Veronique found all of us at Ferret House. Now they're flying to readers around the world. An exciting business, publishing; it never gets old."

Vauxhall leaned toward the two. Silver fur gleamed in his mask, his face the picture of the thoughtful, distinguished book-ferret. "From everyone at Ferret House, we're happy you're here. I expect that you two will be getting all the attention you can stand, and maybe a little more. Frankly, we can't print your books fast enough. *Bevo*'s as successful a book as kits' publishing has seen, *Miss Mischief* is in her fourth printing . . ."

Beatrix held up a paw close to her body, claws spread wide.

". . . in her fifth printing," said the president. "I know you've got a lot on your minds just now, but I want you to know that we'll do whatever we can to keep you happy with Ferret House for a long time."

There was a ripple of applause from the animals who had worked so hard to turn the writers' ideas from manuscript into copies in every bookstore. They didn't envy them, they didn't want to be Danielle or Budgeron, but glad they were to know that their own work and skills had launched the authors' books into the world, made it a more exciting place for readers.

Budgeron turned to watch his mate. Fur brushed, eyes bright under the bill of a crimson cap, her mask sharp and clear, she sat poised and lovely.

"Thank you, Vauxhall," she said, "thank you all. You believed in Budgeron from the beginning, you brought me aboard when no one else wanted Veronique. We won't forget."

Beatrix had taken a call on her cell phone, now she nodded to the president.

"Your limousine awaits," he said, and rose. So did everyone else in the room. "Thank you, Danielle, thank you, Budgeron, for taking time with us all this morning. I trust you'll enjoy what's about to happen to you. You have a quiet place, there in Colorado?"

They nodded.

"Maybe you'll want a bit more land around you if you can." It was a congratulation and a warning. "Before too long that's going to mean a lot, a quiet place to write." Vauxhall extended his paw to Budgie, then to Danielle. "Have a good tour."

In the limousine, Beatrix handed Danielle the latest copy of the tour schedule, along with a large white envelope, then turned to the driver.

"To the studio, please, Gabby."

"There's just one small change in the afternoon," Beatrix said to the writers. "We're swapping the satellite interview for the Houston station with the one for Wichita. Not to worry. We'll have a card up, under the camera, with the city and the interviewer's name. Oh, and I almost forgot. We had a call from Cheyenne-Montana Productions. Are the film rights for *Miss Mischief* available?"

Danielle looked to Budgeron, startled.

He told her what she already knew: "That's Jasmine Ferret." He grinned at his mate. "It's about time she called."

30

Now THE WHITE envelope from Ferret House lay open on the deep silk hammock in the penthouse suite of the Boston Princess Hotel.

"I've never heard of so much money in my life!" said Danielle for the third time since they'd read the offer from Ferret House. "Budgeron, do they want to pay me this . . . this fortune, just to run off and have a good time writing?"

Her mate lay back into the luxury of the great hammock. "No, dear, they want to pay you this fortune for three finished manuscripts. Of course they'd like you to have a good time writing, but it's those stories that Ferret House wants in its paws. The sooner the better, a bonus for sooner."

She stepped into the hammock, rested her head near his, went suddenly silent. At last she sighed. "Shall I do it? We don't need the money. . . ."

"It isn't about money, Danielle. It's about your writing, it's about your characters, your spirit, about what you mean to readers. You give who you are, the money follows. What you do with the money, there's a different test."

"The publicity, the crowds," she said, bringing his fears out for another look. "Do you want to be a celebrity, Budgeron?"

"Do we decide? We're famous if other animals say we are. We can't control what they think. Somebody's never heard of us: 'So who's Danielle? Who's Budgeron Ferret?' Celebrity's not up to us, it's up to them."

"We could stop writing. . . ."

He stared at her.

"Well, we could," she said.

"I'd like to see you try."

She laughed. "Could you?"

"Of course I could. Soon as I finish *Bevo Meets the Count*. After that, I'm out of ideas."

He nodded, happy for his mate and for the adventures ahead. We chose this life, he thought, we asked for it, and now it's showed up on our doorstep.

31

HER CHARACTERS visited Danielle Ferret day and night, chatty spirits unable to end the séance with their author.

Awake in the dark, Budgeron listened to the sound of her pen on the notepad, a small sliding hiss in the dark, ink on paper, words she would puzzle over in daylight, glad for her notebook, deciphering tilted night-words into scenes that would have disappeared by dawn.

He breathed in silence, not to disturb her.

Not that she needs notes, he thought. Danielle Ferret never starved for ideas. More than any other animal he had met, his mate knew the ferret condition, the turns and mysteries of ferret relationships. And as she knew, she wrote.

The sound stopped, the sleek head sank into her pillow. Then she lifted her head barely clear of the pillow and turned to her mate. "I love you," she murmured in the dark, the next second back to sleep.

He was stunned in warmth. Incredible that she would say that, not a tenth awake!

What have I done, he thought, that I deserve this beautiful creature to love me?

Budgeron Ferret sighed happily, reached a paw to soothe the animal beside him. She relaxed at his touch, turned toward him in sleep. In a moment her breathing was deep and even once more.

He closed his eyes. Writing. What a blessing to have been given the talent; what a test, learning to use it.

Then he slept.

It was an ancient city, in his dream, buildings of granite, streets of cobblestone around the town square. And yet the rooftops . . . he knew those rooftops.

Budgeron Ferret, an audience of one, listened to the town crier, a black sable ferret in red cap and golden scarf, reading aloud from a wide parchment scroll:

"'You have found what every writer has found before, what every writer who follows must find as well.'"

The crier looked at him over the scroll, his eyes meeting Budgeron's. "And this, too, will you find . . ."

He spoke as if he were reading, but his eyes held Budgeron's: "The more ideas you have, the more shall you be given!"

Behind the crier, Budgie saw the roofs of those houses again, the top of one so deeply familiar. . . .

"You enchant an inner family of characters who will come if you invite, each bringing stories for you to set in words."

There was a long silence, waiting.

"*Do you invite?*"

"Me?" he replied in his dream. "Do I invite? Invite who? Ideas? Characters?"

The same question, firmly asked: "Do you invite? Yea or nay?"

He was not accustomed to his dreams demanding answers. "Yea, I invite!"

The crier looked at him, nodded, those black eyes watching his own. "So let it be."

Then the ferret rolled the scroll firmly, tied it with a dusky ribbon. Whatever ceremony there had been was over.

"So let it be," he said once again to Budgeron, the voice warm and informal. Then he was gone.

The writer turned in the dark, sleepy, puzzled. A message dream. What was the message? What did it mean?

32

T HE WIND EASED along the meadow beside the Little Side-Hop River, grass and cattails swaying in the last hour of day, hill shadows stretching eastward toward the dark.

"It's beautiful here, Budgeron."

He nodded.

"Look down the meadow," she said. "If we galloped fast enough, do you think we could fly? Up from the grass, into the sunset, out over the housetops of all the cities . . ."

The words struck him like thunder. Over the housetops. The housetops . . .

The image from sleep came rushing back, the town crier, the housetop of his dream. Of course! It was his own roof he had seen, the top of his kithood home!

He closed his eyes tightly, reaching for the image from sleep. Why? Because, he thought, because . . .

"Budge?" Danielle called, gentle, not to interfere. "Where are you?"

"*Dandelion!*" he cried. "*Buttercup!*"

At once they crowded round, set loose by remembering. In the attic! They're still there! All his friends, all the animal dolls his mother had sewn and stuffed for him.

Danielle touched the reins, Dusty trotted close.

"Growing up, Danielle," he said, aflood in memory, "it wasn't just Bevo! There were dozens Mom made for me! Dandelion and Buttercup were baby giraffes, sisters, yellow-flower pajamas. Did I tell you?"

He looked at her, his mind full of bright times back then. "I'd pick an animal from the shelf, we'd sleep and dream together, adventures every night!"

His mate smiled, seeing the pajamas.

"Once I picked the sisters," he told her. "Dandelion said, 'Let's imagine we're going to Africa.' Not Buttercup: 'I'm scared of Africa. It's full of wild animals. I don't want to go.'"

He grinned, telling the story. "'*You're a giraffe!*' said Dandelion. 'You *are* a wild animal! You *came* from Africa!'

"Buttercup stared at her sister, Danielle. 'In my jammies?'"

Danielle laughed at the picture, for the joy that Budgeron had found in the sunlight of his memory.

"And there was my bat, my amazing bat, Bvuhlgahri. He took me to Mustelania, to the palace." Budgeron slipped into the brooding, low voice of the kithood creature: "'Your Majesties, may I introduce Boucheron-Bvuhlova . . .'"

His eyes were bright in the sunset, remembering. "The stories, Danielle, the stories!"

"Your mother. How many animals did she . . . ?"

"Twenty! More! Aviator Bear, White Buffalo, my dragon . . ."

"Dragon? What color dragon?"

"Blue, wavy yellow stripes . . ."

"Oh . . ."

"Seahorse, Hedgehog, Dinosaur, Orca Whale, Blue Whale, Raccoon, Zebra . . ."

"Where did you . . . ?"

"Every night. We'd travel the world, Danielle, everywhere. Petey, three feathers left, my peacock from Hawaii . . ."

"Budgie Ferret's friends," she said quietly. "Where are they now?"

"They're in the attic, right now. All of them. They're in the attic, back home. . . ."

No sooner in from the stable, he raced to the telephone, lifted the receiver, dialed.

"Hi, Mom!"

☻

Into Side-Hop airport, Express Mail, arrived boxes 1 of 4 through 4 of 4. In each box, old friends: yarn smiles and bright shoe-button eyes through faded colors and careful patches stitched. Petey the bird in box 1, Dandelion and Buttercup traveling together in box 3, Zebie and Camie with them.

For anxious moments Budgeron thought his bat had been lost. Then at the bottom of box 4: "*Bvuhlgahri!*"

The black had faded to gray, but there he was, same soft wings and fluffy face, same high radar-squeak when the ferret squeezed his velvet body.

The writer was a kit once more. "Bvuhlgahri, can we fly again? Do you remember?"

In his dream, the writer had invited his friends to return, and return they had, into his waking life.

Before sunset their shelf was fixed in place, same as it had been long ago, within reach of a paw from the hammock. The old stories could be dreamed anew.

⌒

Budgie Ferret's Friends, the books were called.

The first manuscript of the series went directly to Vauxhall Ferret.

The day it arrived, the president and chief executive officer of Ferret House Press canceled his appointments, closed the door to his office high above Madison Avenue.

There being no cover letter, Vauxhall began as would any other reader, at the title page.

The pages flowed through his paws, exotic blossoms in warm honey.

Budgie's passage to Africa, holding tight the manes of twin giraffes, the night on the veldt when all the creatures told their stories, the scene at the Great Waterfall where they parted, at the entrance to The Undiscovered Place. His discovery of the secret that wild animals keep for ferrets everywhere. The test of the Gift, and Budgeron's return, giraffes once again become fluffy dolls upon his bedroom shelf. His Final Question, and proof of every ferret's Wild Powers.

Vauxhall read the book through, then turned to page one and read it again, slowly.

When he had read the last page once more, he put the manuscript down and looked out his window.

It means so much, he thought, to live a life that makes a difference. How can an animal do that? How can a writer touch a keyboard far away, without a sound, reach me here in the city and remind me who I am? Books, he thought. Books.

33

O<small>NCE IN A WHILE</small>, in the silence under Western star-fields, Budgeron Ferret was brushed by the life that might have been, had ever he finished his giant novel.

Now and again random images flickered from sleep: the author of *Where Ferrets Walk* the keynote speaker at writers' conventions, Budgeron Ferret in formal ascot, the Avedoi Medal for Literature gleaming at his throat.

A different future, he sighed, missing that different past.

Then in the dark, for the first time, he realized, that's no life that might have been! I couldn't write that book, I couldn't force that life to happen! I still can't; I don't want to.

I don't like literary novels!

He eased from the hammock, not to disturb Danielle, and padded to his writing room. Today, he thought, I am open to whirlwinds, adventures with any character, any inner friend who needs my paws to tell a story. I am open to write what I enjoy.

On his desk from the day before, two letters, reader mail. Curious, he lifted the first.

It was printed with the Mustelanian coat of arms, beneath it in small sharp letters: *The Palace.*

"Dear Budgeron Ferret,

"In the short while since we were chosen from the Librarians and elected King and Queen of Mustelania, we have had many tests, many decisions to make about our past and future and our highest right.

"Not long ago we realized that the principles we've needed in our decisions are the ones you wrote so simply in *One Paw, Two Paws, Three Paws, Four Paws.* Your book is a focus of the highest ferret wisdom—what we loved as kits we practice today to lead the kingdom.

"Thank you for our education."

It was signed in sweeping letters: *Prestwick & Francesca Ferret.*

The second letter was neatly printed by a pencil evidently held in a very small paw.

"Dear Budgeron,

"I love Bevo the Hummingbird.

"Sometimes when I need to know the right thing to do, I ask Bevo in my mind.

"But before he tells me I already know and he likes that a lot."

It was signed in careful, slow cursive: *Bosco Ferret.*

The writer held both letters. He had not written the Great Ferret Novel. He was not invited to writers' conferences or to literary teas. His opinion was not sought by the press.

He lived, however, with a loving, brilliant mate on a hilltop ranch deep in a gentle countryside. He shared his mind and skills with his muse, a large and thoughtful dragon.

Budgeron Ferret had chosen to be a writer. With his choice came poverty, loneliness, rejection, frustration, despair, perseverance, delight, attention, riches, love, understanding, fulfillment, a life of ideas that mattered to him, shared now and then with kings and kits.

Without thought, without care, words on paper for the fun of it, he closed his eyes and wrote what he saw:

The land where we touched was green as spring meadows, the mountain a color of summer maple, the fields below sheets of clover, the lake broad and deep as autumn. Atop the mountain, a palace of golden snow.

Upon the fields lay a village, thatch-roofed, misty smoke curling from chimneys as ferrets stirred awake.

I turned to Bvuhlgahri Bat, flown so far to bring me here.

"Mustelania," came the low, dark voice. *"And in the farthest, deepest depths of Loch Stoat, Boucheron-Bvuhlova, for a thousand years, a great serpent has waited."*

"Waited . . . ?"

Rushing on, paws blurring over his keyboard, the writer wondered: Is a serpent like a dragon? What color dragon?

"A thousand years, the serpent has waited," he said. *"For you."*

And so it happened, as rosy-whiskered dawn pushed her nose under the tent of night, that Budgeron Ferret's writing room dissolved, Mustelania coming alive about him.

He watched and wrote. What would happen next?

— end —

Book 3

Bethany

The Ferret and the Field-Mouse

A YOUNG FIELD-MOUSE, *being pursued by a cat, ran blindly and collided face-to-face with a ferret.*

"I am lost!" cried the mouse. "Escaping one doom, I have fallen into the paws of another!"

"It is true that you have fallen into my paws," replied the ferret. "Yet I am not doom but a creature like yourself, led by the destiny I choose, and by my highest right."

So saying, she carried the mouse to safety from the cat and set it free.

The mouse clasped its paws in gratitude. "How can I thank you for my life?"

"By one means only," said the ferret. "By preserving the life of another."

Then the ferret went her way, and never did the mouse see her again.

It is happier to save life than to allow it to perish, nobler to rescue from distress than to abandon others to their fate.

- Antonius Ferret, *Fables*

1

...wly above a cool summer dark, Katrinka
...ter and little brother, and set them
...the night. Walls of stone released
...' home, and the kits, freshly

...ne row of books on their bed-
...s waiting for the right instant.
...d Vincent together, and in that
...er paw and pulled forth the volume
...e book by feel, by the worn, bent cor-

...kits, before even glancing at the title she
ope... ...in mock surprise.

"M... ...what have we here?" said she. "Is this by any
chance ca... *...scue Ferrets at Sea?*"

So often ...ad she held the book and read the story that it was
long memorized, but the two cried, "Yes! Yes!" as though she had
magically plucked the volume from empty space.

"Then settle down, my kits," she said, "and I shall tell you the
story of the little ferrets who went to sea. . . ."

Bethany Nikka, the elder, snuggled into her favorite spot in the
hammock, chin on the edge of the warm fluff, nose and whiskers
pointed in rapt attention to her mother. Eyes already closed, she fell
deep into imagination, waiting.

Vincent lay alongside, one paw holding his stuffed hedgehog, rustling himself into the most comfortable position that the remaining hammock would allow. Someday, he knew, it would be his hammock alone. Tonight he was happy to be with his sister, he wanted her to have the best spot for herself.

"'Once upon a time,'" their mother began, "'by the edge of a great ocean, there was a party of kits, out for a romp. Adventurous they were, but not very wise, for they determined to sail from the land to the Forbidden Island offshore. . . .'"

Here she opened the book to show the picture of the adventurous-but-not-very-wise youngsters, clustering about a driftwood raft and bedsheet sail. Bethany nodded, eyes closed, for she saw the picture in her mind.

Oh, those foolish kits! she thought, for she knew that even as they left the shore a monstrous bubble-storm was frothing toward Forbidden Island, unseen and unknown to the voyagers.

She saw it while her mother read: the all-day sail to the island, the carefree ferrets swept there more by current than skill, she saw them tumbling ashore, exploring with no care for night approaching, ignorant of a sky signaling the storm ahead. She saw the flash, she heard the crack of thunder. The kits were trapped.

"What shall we do?" she whispered, barely moving her lips.

"'*What shall we do?*'" Katrinka read, holding up the picture, two pages wide, the six hapless ferrets stranded on a speck of land, surrounded by a wall of bubbles.

"What could be done?" both kits said, with their mother.

Bethany saw it all as it happened: the storm advancing ruthlessly; the great ships racing to port to escape the fury of an ocean gone wild; the poor kits clinging like furry flags to tree trunks before they were blown head over heels to the ground; the discovery by parents that their little ones were missing, with barely a bag of ferret food to sustain them; the storm raging on. At last the wind subsiding but the island and the sea about it smothered deep in bubbles, no way for land creatures to sail.

"'*What could be done?*'" their mother read.

"CALL THE RESCUE FERRETS!" cried the kits together.

"Exactly right," Katrinka said. *"Call the rescue ferrets!"* She turned the page.

Bethany watched the story unfold so clearly that she nearly stopped breathing. The clangor of the alarm bell on the dock of the Ferret Rescue Station, Captain Terry Ferret and his Alert Crew dashing to their posts, the low-thunder roar of twin engines lighting off, lines casting away a-splash in the wake of the sleek vessel setting forth on a mission of mercy.

Out from the channel came the rescue animals, the mass of bubbles parting ahead, flying aside as the bubblebreaker *Emily T. Ferret* sliced on a course to Forbidden Island.

So *brave!* Bethany thought as she pictured Captain Terry, though she knew he was too busy to acknowledge admiration.

He steered by dead reckoning, daring a straight-line compass course through the shipping lanes for the island, both engines at full throttle, his boat at flank speed, as fast as it could go. He watched his radar for returns from ships in his path, but the bubbles blurred the electric picture. More than radar he trusted the keen ears of his crew listening for echoes ahead to avoid a collision that would send them all to the bottom.

Meanwhile, the kits on the island, engulfed in bubbles, were holding paws so as not to be lost one from the other. They finished their rations, sharing their ferret food to the final crumb. They huddled close, shivering with cold, doubting they would live to see tomorrow's sunset. How foolish they had been to take such a trip for a lark, and how sorry they were now for having done so!

"Ship ahead, Captain!"

Bethany saw what Captain Terry Ferret saw, the sudden-looming radar blur of a human's freighter, come to a dead stop in the sea, blocking the way ahead.

"Right full rudder!" he cried to his helmsferret and the rescue boat careened wildly at top speed, spray and bubbles flying.

For a moment the black cliff of the freighter's hull loomed amid the snowy mass of foam, solid steel unmoving in the water but streaking midnight blurs alongside the high-speed ferret boat. Then it disappeared behind.

"Left rudder to course."

At last the rescue boat snaked its way, dead slow, through the reefs and shoals of Forbidden Island, Abington Ferret at the bow throwing a lead line and calling the depth.

"Mark, twenty paws!" he called. Then a toss and whistle of line in the air, and a splash as the boat moved ahead.

"Mark, fifteen paws!" Bubbles still blanketed the sea and the island, three times higher than the radar mast.

"Mark, twelve paws!"

"Anchor down," said the captain. "Siren, please."

Sharp blasts rent the air, four times over. Echoes from the invisible land nearby, and quiet.

"Again."

After the echoes, faintly, the sound of cheers.

The captain took the loudspeaker microphone. "Party on the island, this is rescue boat *Emily T. Ferret*. We are standing a hundred paws offshore, our siren every half minute. Approach to the edge of the water and our crew will pick you up. Do not swim for the boat. Our crew will pick you up."

The cheers came louder from shore, and "Hi! Hi!" from the survivors.

A few more siren blasts and Bosun's Mate Jingles Ferret appeared with the first of the wayward kits, bedraggled, covered in bubbles.

"Up you go, young fella," he said, lifting the kit to Joanna Ferret, the forward lookout, on deck. Then he turned back toward shore to retrieve the next of the adventurers.

The trip home to the rescue station took longer than the trip out. Though the bubbles had diminished, it was by no means a fit sea for more than half-cruise speed, even for a Ferret Rescue bubblebreaker.

As her mother turned the final page, the one with the picture of little Angela Ferret kissing Captain Terry, Bethany brushed back a tear, filled once more with admiration for the brave ferrets of the Rescue Service.

Her mother closed the book, and the room was silent. Then she rose and tucked their blankets close. "Good night, little ones."

Bethany took a breath, paused, spoke at last. "Someday, Mother, can I be a rescue ferret?"

Katrinka turned and beheld her daughter. Oh, my firstborn, she thought. So like your father.

"You can be anything you want to be, my Betha-Nikka," she said, "if only you love enough." She kissed her two kits, turned out the light.

Far from the small stone house, in the highlands near the roof of the world, philosopher ferrets had learned the same and called it wisdom: we find our happiness only when we follow what we most love in all the world.

It was not the last time Bethany Ferret would hear her favorite story, but it was the first, listening to her mother, that she knew she would one day stand upon the deck of her own rescue boat.

2

Not many humans know. On the edges of every sea, the Ferret Rescue Service stands with the Coast Guard and Coastal Patrol of every country that claims an ocean shore. It is the job of humans to rescue humans at risk in storm and shipboard disaster; it is the job of the ferrets to rescue seagoing animals in distress.

Adjoining each Coastal Patrol station lies a small base, home to those devoted and courageous ferrets who risk their lives to save others at sea. Ferret Rescue Service bases mirror the humans'—miniature living and dining quarters, maintenance bays and dry docks, and a small command center.

The FRS motto, *In Silentio Servamus*, tells its story. Quietly We Save: the goal and code of every animal who volunteers for the Service. They share a pride, these ferrets, that regardless of storm or oil or fire, rarely has a survivor of a stricken ship been lost once an FRS vessel has pulled alongside.

Their J-class rescue boats are small and light but strong, with powerful twin engines and fast on the water. Operated by a captain and crew of four sea ferrets, FRS rescue vessels have proven to be nearly unsinkable. In the course of their service, a few have been dragged down with shipwrecks or dashed to pieces in mountainous surf, but handled with skill and courage they are perfect for their mission.

Not so long after her mother had read her to sleep, having graduated from the arduous course of sea-ferret officer training, Ensign Bethany N. Ferret, FRS, reported for duty at the Maytime Rescue Base.

Maytime had been her choice by virtue of her standing at the top of her class. The base stood on a protected inlet along an otherwise rockbound coast, lashed in winter by ocean storms, surrounded in summer by a labyrinth of deadly currents. She had asked for action in service; at Maytime she was bound to get it.

She saluted. "Ensign Bethany Ferret reporting for duty, sir."

Commander Curtis Ferret looked up from the engine compartment of a J-boat, saw the trim figure dockside, returned her salute. First in her class, he thought, she's planning to be in command of her own boat before long. She's learned a lot, but there's so much more ahead. Poor kit. Lucky kit.

"What's the redline oil temperature for the engine of this boat, Ensign?"

Bethany was startled. She was expecting a welcome to the base, not a quiz.

"One hundred eighteen degrees Celsius, sir."

"What if the captain chooses to run the engine over-temperature?"

"Why, she can plan on the main bearings to seize, sir, she can plan on complete engine failure!"

The commander frowned, to cover his unseen smile. His new officer would command or die trying. "What if there are lives at stake, Ensign? What if she has to run her engines overtemp?"

"If she has to burn one, she'd best save the other, sir."

The senior officer surveyed the scorched metal. "That's what this captain did. Now we've got to rebuild the engine. And engines do not grow on bushes, Ensign."

"The captain saved how many lives, sir?"

He looked up sharply. "Twenty-five mice, three ship's cats, a pygmy marmoset. Twenty-nine lives."

"Yes, sir." His new officer stood at attention.

"Welcome to the base, Ensign," the commander said. "You picked some fine weather to report aboard. Enjoy it while you can." He turned back to the engine compartment. With the barometer falling, this boat would soon be called to service.

So began the adventure Bethany Ferret had sought. She was assigned as third officer aboard J-166, the rescue boat *Dauntless*, under the command of Captain Angio E. Ferret. From her first hour on board, she found the sea a more demanding classroom than any school she had known.

Always in some pre-dawn hour came rescue practice, over and again, in the sudden screeching whoop of the dockside alert siren. Amid the blasts, ferrets tumbled from hammocks into storm hats and life vests, scrambled for their stations. Sleep vaporized in the thunder of heavy engines bursting to life, darkness shattered in the arc of instant floodlights.

"Away the bowlines!" came the cry from the bridge. "Away the stern lines! Away the spring lines, away all lines! All ahead, flank!"

Twin searchlights stabbing ahead, twin hurricanes from the engines, white water flying from midships, sweeping into rooster tails astern.

From her station as Starboard High lookout, her face hidden in helmet and visor, Bethany raced through her station check, reporting herself ready for sea.

This is it! she thought. *Here's the life I wanted!* On the interphone, she listened to her captain call the Rescue Center.

"Maytime Control, J-166 is launched mid-channel seaward, standing by for vector and distance."

As often as not, that would be the end of the alert. "Roger, 166, your mid-channel time was fifty-eight seconds. This terminates the exercise. Return to base and stand by."

Other times, though, *Dauntless* would streak ahead, past the channel jetties into a sea of moonless black. She followed vectors from shore and her own lookouts to find some tiny motorboat or sailing vessel floating lights-out in the dark. Aboard, a crew of off-duty sea ferrets hiding belowdecks, curling themselves as small as possible, hoping to be overlooked by their rescuers.

"Seven survivors aboard, sir," Bethany had once reported, lookout turned rescuer, exhausted from dragging the dead weight of the distress-vessel animals to the deck of the *Dauntless*.

Angio Ferret had narrowed his eyes. Something was wrong. "We have all the survivors? Are you sure? Are all the survivors on board?"

The rescue would not be complete nor clock stopped until every creature in the practice was accounted for. She felt the captain's suspicion.

"Stand by, sir," she said. She dashed to the deck, past the survivors, relaxed and chatting now, forward of the bridge.

"*Searchlight!*" she called as she ran, and flew paw over paw down the stark-lit towline to the vessel just rescued. Scrambling aboard, she looked again from bow to stern. Just when she was certain there was no life on board, a shape in the sail locker caught her eye.

"All right," she said. "Come on, out you go!" Sure enough, a very young ferret had smuggled itself tightly under the canvas, scarcely daring to breathe. Bethany threw the sails aside, but even then the kit did not move, its eyes tightly shut.

"Gotcha." She lifted the youngster by the scruff of its neck, held it firmly in her teeth.

"I'm going to be a rescue ferret," it said in a tiny voice.

Bethany smiled in spite of herself. "Someday . . . ," she muttered.

The kit hung immobilized while she reappeared on deck, dashing up the towline over the waves into the glare of light. At last, aboard *Dauntless*, she set the kit with the other survivors, raced up the ladder to the bridge.

"Eight rescued aboard, sir," she panted.

"Are you sure, Ensign?"

"Yes, sir!"

The captain lifted his microphone. "J-166 has eight survivors aboard. The distress vessel is in tow."

"Roger, 166," came the reply. "Understand eight survivors. Exercise is terminated. Thirty-one minutes, twenty-five seconds. Return to base."

"Roger the time," said the captain, noting it in his log. "Returning to base."

He nodded to Bethany, releasing her to her lookout station.

"Oh, 166," came the voice from the Center, "can you tell us who found survivor number eight?"

The captain turned to his junior officer, puzzled by the question. "That was Ensign Bethany Ferret, located the last survivor."

"The very small survivor?" asked the voice on the radio.

Bethany nodded.

"That is affirmative," said the captain.

"Well done, *Dauntless*," said the Center. "Well done."

Angio Ferret nodded, a hint of a smile. There may have been a wager, he thought. He would not have been surprised to learn that survivor number eight had a close relative at the command center.

Bethany had run more than a dozen night missions before her first daytime alert.

Beyond her surprise at the alert siren going off in sunlight, the test was easier, she thought. She sighted the target vessel eleven minutes from the jetties, and though the seas were not smooth, *Dauntless* streaked top speed to its rescue station, lowered its skiff of rescuers, Bethany among them. The J-boat didn't require lookouts after the target was found.

Hard work, she thought. But her inner kit didn't care how hard it was. She had built this life from dreams in her hammock, and now the dreams were true.

Aloft once more in her lookout station, the distress boat in tow, Bethany saw the jetties from seaward for the first time in daylight, and what she saw stiffened her.

She pressed her interphone button, direct to the bridge. "*Vessel on the rocks!*" she called. "On the starboard jetty, sir!"

Waiting for the reply, her blood ran cold. That was no ordinary vessel, it was a rescue boat, a *J-boat*, stranded on the boulders!

She braced for the tilt of *Dauntless* to starboard, and the rush of her engines to aid. Neither happened.

Had the captain not heard? "Starboard High lookout to bridge, *we have a vessel on the rocks, sir!*"

"Roger, Starboard High," the captain answered. "The vessel's in sight."

Still J-166 proceeded at tow speed, her course unchanged.

Presently Bethany felt a movement behind her. She turned and saluted. "Welcome to Starboard High, sir!"

The skipper of *Dauntless* could be as tough and unyielding as the rocks themselves, a powerful animal who had worked his way from sea ferret third class to captain by native brilliance and devotion to the Service. As ever with the strongest of creatures, he rarely displayed his power, choosing courtesy instead, and understanding.

"At ease, Ensign." Angio Ferret touched her shoulder. "It's been there for a year now, Bethany," he said. "I thought I might tell you without your shipmates listening."

The lookout took her eyes from the gray wreckage, turned to him. "What happened, sir?" she asked. "Why?"

The officer sighed, lifted his cap and ran a paw through his fur. "She was returning from a night rescue, the seas were rough. More than rough . . . the channel radar buoy was dragged off station."

"But sir, she must have had the jetty on radar. . . ."

"By the time the captain realized what had happened, it was too late."

The younger ferret swallowed. "The crew, sir?"

"No one was lost. Survivors and crew jumped to the jetty and we picked them up straightaway. We left the wreck to remind us: Assume nothing. No mission's finished until our lines are fast to the dock."

Bethany watched the wreck, barely a hundred paws distant as *Dauntless* slid by. The bow showed above water at high tide, the name fading but legible: *Resolute*.

"But sir, the boat . . ."

"J-101 was the first of her class, the oldest vessel on station. We salvaged what we could. She's a good warning as we come and go. We won't lose another that way."

"But sir, the boat . . . ," she whispered.

The captain was down the ladder and returned to the bridge, yet Bethany's eyes stayed on the shattered metal stranded on the rocks. There was a yawning gash at the starboard waterline, a slice nearly half the length of the boat. The seas had jammed the hulk fast into the jetty. Most of *Resolute* went underwater on the high tides; she was pressed hard to the rocks on the lows. A lovely shape, sleek and trim despite the beatings, her twin lookout towers unscratched, defiant of the sea.

What a waste, the ferret thought. The oldest boat on the station, but so what? She's a *J-boat!* She can save lives!

Through her first tour, Bethany Ferret applied herself diligently to her duties as a sea-ferret officer. Night practice and day, emergency rescues, vessels in distress adrift at sea. The real events, though, were most of them less trying than the practice: vessels helpless, out of fuel at sea, vessels lost in fog, broken rudders and fouled propellers, animals to be rushed ashore.

Now and then a major gale blew in, but most shipping stood warned in advance, steering to the safety of deep water, far from lee shores and jagged rocks of the storm-coast.

In time, Ensign Bethany Ferret was promoted to lieutenant junior grade, thence to full lieutenant. Her superior officers rated her skills and her attitude outstanding, her courage unwavering. Every one checked the square: "An exemplary ferret, one in a hundred, an officer I would wish to serve aboard my ship." Soon she was first officer aboard *Dauntless.*

Never did Bethany Ferret forget the sight of J-101 on the rocks. Every time she put to sea and every time she returned to base, the young lieutenant shook her head over the loss, stranded there.

It was not time, then, that moved J-101 from the teeth of the land, it was Bethany's patient, relentless pursuit of an ideal. The earnest young ferret never raised her voice over the issue, she never argued against other viewpoints.

No one taught her, but she knew: more important than talent or gifts or education is the determination to make one's wish come true. The young officer, quite simply, had resolved to rescue J-101, and she was willing to endure any hardship to see that happen.

"The value of *Resolute* to the Ferret Rescue Service is inestimable," she wrote, from her tiny quarters aboard *Dauntless*. "Should this vessel be restored and save a single life, she would have paid for her own restoration. Should she save a hundred lives, there is no counting the return on the modest investment I propose."

In his office overlooking the docks, Commander Curtis Ferret turned the pages of her proposal, gray whiskers unmoving, his face impassive.

"I request that at little cost to the Ferret Rescue Service, on my own off-duty time and on the off-duty time of such sea ferrets who may wish to join me, that I receive permission to restore J-101, FRB *Resolute*, to alert-ready condition."

The base commander frowned. Her captain has told her the wreck has a purpose, he thought; is this becoming an obsession? How can she save lives while she's rebuilding boats? She's a promising officer and her job is at sea. Almost imperceptibly, he shook his head.

"At worst," Bethany wrote in her next letter, "the project will sharpen the knowledge and skills of its volunteers and make them better officers and sea ferrets. At best, the Maytime station will have an additional seaworthy, active-duty vessel to fulfill its mission requirements. This endeavor is in the best interests of the FRS, to save and protect seagoing vessels and animal lives aboard them."

The commander shook his head again, turned to gaze down from his office window at the boats that were his responsibility. He put her request aside.

Letter followed letter, as though *Resolute* were no derelict reminder but some enchanted sword-in-the-stone for an officer determined to pull her free for quests to come. Bethany Ferret made it clear that her wish was attainable, was valuable for the Rescue

Service, that every aspect of her plan would be positive. Patiently she explained how she would overcome each test the project would offer.

On August 14, as her captain watched, Bethany took command of *Dauntless* on the rescue of two paddlers, hamsters drifted to sea by offshore currents, squeaking with joy at the sight of the ferret vessel pulling alongside. The seas were moderate; skill was required to take the paddlers and their craft aboard without harm or damage. *The lieutenant accomplished the rescue without incident,* Angio wrote in the ship's log, no other comment being necessary.

Upon her return to dock, a messenger found her aboard, saluted, presented her with a sealed envelope. Lieutenant Bethany Ferret was requested and required to appear at 1500 hours in the office of the base commander.

At 1459 hours she arrived, combed and brushed, trembling a little, a thick envelope of project plans under her arm.

She entered the commander's office precisely on time, saluted. "Lieutenant Bethany Ferret reporting as ordered, sir."

The commander nodded. "Sit down, Lieutenant." He turned in his chair, watched the docks, the row of sleek, snow-colored J-boats nosed into their berths, *Strongpaw* and *Courageous* on alert, closest to the sea, crews aboard, ready for immediate launch.

The office of the base commander, like the animal himself, was lean and polished. There were books in shelves on three walls, a fading photo of an old E-boat, Lieutenant Curtis Ferret standing proudly with his crew at the ladder to the bridge. On a cabinet, encased in glass, stood a scale model of a J-boat, finished to the smallest detail. Next to it a color picture of three kits tumbling on the grass at lakeside.

For a long while, the senior ferret did not speak. He turned back to his desk, glanced again at Bethany's service file, reviewed a line from her personal history: *Officer's father, Artemis Ferret, plunged from bridge into white-water rapids attempting solo rescue of two kittens adrift on river ice. Both animals in distress were pushed to paws of shore personnel, surviving without injury. Rescuer lost in freezing water.*

The commander stood, lifted a book that was open on his desk. "I have something to read to you, Lieutenant, from the FRS operations manual. Are you ready to hear this?"

Bethany sat erect on the edge of the wooden chair, her eyes watching his. "Yes, sir, I am."

"Then listen carefully, please." He turned a page. "'*Service policy forbids the personal involvement of officers in the construction, maintenance or operation of FRS vessels except in performance of duties to which they have been assigned by the Service.*'"

The senior ferret sighed and closed the book. "Do you have any comment?"

"Yes, sir." *Except in performance of duties assigned* could only mean one thing.

The commander nodded. "Go ahead."

"*Thank you, sir!*"

"So this is no surprise."

"No, sir. You had no choice, sir. Sooner or later you had to let me do it."

The commander shook his head, a smile of surrender. He lifted a sealed envelope from his desk, handed it forth.

"Your orders, Lieutenant, are to salvage, overhaul and return to service our vessel J-101, the Ferret Rescue boat *Resolute*. When the work is complete, you are to command that vessel for her sea trials and active-duty service. May I quote, to the best of my recollection?"

The young ferret grasped the envelope, tears in her eyes. "Of course, sir."

The commander turned again to the window, watched a returning J-boat drift slowly into its berth, ferrets on deck heaving its bow and stern lines ashore. "*As this endeavor is in the best interests of the FRS and its mission to save and protect seagoing vessels and animal lives aboard them, you are requested and required to complete your mission as soon as ingenuity and perseverance can provide.*"

"Aye, aye, sir! Thank you, sir!"

She rose and stood wordless before him, wreathed in happiness. The commander gave her a salute of dismissal, to which she responded. Then she embraced the elder ferret in delight.

"Excuse me, sir," she said, recovering her dignity. "Thank you, sir. You'll be proud, sir. . . ."

"I'm already proud, Lieutenant. I'm expecting *Resolute* to stand alert this winter."

The young ferret caught her breath. It was an impossible schedule, to rebuild the boat and train a crew for rescue duty in two months' time.

"Aye, aye, sir!" She saluted and stepped toward the door.

"Oh, and one other thing."

Bethany turned. "Yes, sir?"

"If you need me to growl at somebody to make this happen, I trust you'll let me know."

She flashed a radiant smile. "I will, sir!"

⌣

Not the next week, as the commander had expected, but that very afternoon, magic began. Maytime's floating crane was somehow borrowed, and the hulk of *Resolute* was raised on slings from the rocks, by a crew of Bethany-charmed ferrets. By sunset the boat was in dry dock, red-tagged for express overhaul.

Not the next day but that evening the wreck swarmed with workers recruited by the lieutenant, unable to resist the intensity in those dark eyes when she came to them for help.

Welder ferrets' torches cut and patched, sparks and puddles of molten steel spilling firefalls through the night. A crew of burly sea ferrets heaving a hydraulic ram straightened and set crushed bulkheads; electricians tore looms of wiring from the sea-shattered bridge and replaced them with new. Armor-glass windows, overhauled instruments and electronics appeared at dockside as if by special delivery and were soon taken aboard. It was a steel orchestra swept over the edge of chaos: rivet guns, pneumatic hammers, high-speed grinding wheels, carpenter's saws, the boat crowded with every manner of specialist.

By dawn *Resolute*'s engines and generators had been winched free of the boat and trundled off to Powerplant Overhaul, her transmissions and driveshafts and propellers lifted out for inspection and balancing.

Shifts came and went as Bethany Ferret worked through, not noticing that she had tired at all. It was as though she had stored her sleep for this event; resolute as the boat she would command, she was everywhere at once, suggesting, ordering, flattering, pleading.

"You're saving lives," she told the engine ferrets below-decks. She hugged their chief, nearly twice her size. "Don't you want to be ready when the engines come back this afternoon, Boa? It's easier to check the radiators now than later. . . ."

"This afternoon, Lieutenant?" The big ferret smiled at her. "We only pulled 'em last week! They'll not be ready for ninety days!"

Bethany stood on tiptoe to whisper in his ear. "I traded our engines for two just out of overhaul."

The chief's eyes widened. His paw still on her shoulder, he called to his foreferret, "A move on, there, Billy! You want to get a good look at those cooling and exhaust systems right now, the fuel supply system, engine mounts and shaft bearings! Our lieutenant here tells me we got *lives* waiting on us!"

Noise engulfed the once-abandoned vessel, tools and fires and heavy-equipment engines, orders and commands flying, radios blaring the songs of WhitePaw, Dook and Zsa-Zsa and the Show Ferrets while all paws worked.

Gradually the haze around the dry dock changed from welding smoke to the flying dust of dry barnacles and old paint, then at last to a mist of new enamel, white as sea-spray, *Resolute* in black at her bows, *J-101* at her transom, *RESCUE* in flame-colored letters amidships.

At last, weeks from the afternoon she was taken from the rocks, the J-boat slipped back into the sea again, Lieutenant Bethany Ferret on the bridge. Her tail dragged with fatigue; she was thinner than she had been in the commander's office. Yet she trembled with excitement as her boat drifted loose-lined from dock. The ship's pennant fluttered in bright diagonal stripes, cherry-lemon colors flying from the crosstrees above, matching colors to the fresh crew-scarf tied neatly at Bethany's neck.

She pressed her interphone button. "Start Engine One, please, Boa."

"Starting One, ma'am," came the big ferret's voice in her headset.

The whir of the starter-motor, low at first, sliding swiftly up the scale to a sudden choking shudder, the whine blown away in heavy diesel thunder, rough and uneven for a moment, then quieter, smoother, the throttle drawn back.

She smiled. Life for my boat, she thought.

"Start Engine Two."

"Starting Two, ma'am."

The whir barely heard over the idle of the first engine, all at once J-101's second engine was firing, a faint cloud of black smoke from the exhaust. Bethany Ferret moved the telegraph handle forward.

"All engines ahead one-quarter."

"Ahead one-quarter, aye."

The boat trembled faintly, propellers turning.

She switched from interphone to the deck loudspeaker. "Away all lines," the officer said, her voice calm and even.

Mooring lines splashed into the water, hauled smartly aboard by paws from a volunteer crew.

A cheer went up from the pier, pride and relief, those exhausted animals glad with their new overhaul record, hoping not to see Lieutenant Bethany Ferret until they'd had a long rest.

Resolute's first trip was no more than a dozen boat-lengths, from dry dock to her berth alongside the other J-boats. There was much to be done before she'd be ready for sea: finishing crew and survivors' quarters belowdecks, crew selection and training exercises, sea trials for the boat and crew. A list of a hundred actions still needed before J-101 could back away from the berth into which she eased.

"All engines back a quarter," she said, spinning the helm hard to starboard.

"Back a quarter, aye."

Resolute inched sideways toward the rubber-shielded berth. "All engines stop."

"Engines stopped."

Now the boat drifted in silence. "Lines ashore," she said.

Ferrets sprang from deck to the land, fastened bow and stern and spring lines.

From the bridge to her hammock was only a few steps, yet Bethany barely made the distance. Her hat askew over her eyes, the gay new stripes of her crew-scarf still about her neck, she collapsed onto the blanket and fell instantly, profoundly asleep.

The fever of work continued in the days ahead, but at least, she thought, it's a fever I control. Instead of cajoling, pleading for the needs of her boat, Bethany was flooded in choices. She required four crew members. At once she had formal requests from a dozen sea ferrets and informal offers from a dozen more. An offer even from Boa, the big chief engine ferret from dry dock, who once had sworn he wanted a hammock on land and never go back to sea.

Her volunteers had watched her breathe her spirit into J-101, had seen her drag the vessel back to life by her own fierce will. They knew that she would demand as much of them: three paws for the boat and one paw for yourself, still they applied to serve under the young officer, so much did they admire her spirit.

In her cabin, Bethany had studied their résumés over and again, interviewed, watched the eyes and hearts of those who would be her crew.

The last application was from Ensign Vincent Ferret, arrived yesterday from Sea Ferret Officers' School, following his sister to Maytime.

She set it down and sighed. Oh, Vink, she thought. If I take you aboard, someday I'll be ordering you into danger, maybe into death. I'll never do that.

His application rejected, herself nearly asleep, she heard his voice in her mind: "I chose this life same as you did, sis. If I'm not under your command I'll be under somebody else's, same risks. I'll trust you more, work harder for you than for anyone. I'll do whatever you ask. Let me come!"

She shook her head and slept. In her dreams she watched herself slip *Resolute*'s candy-stripe crew-scarf about her brother's neck, and still asleep, she murmured, frightened for what she had done.

3
—

Not days were the pages of Bethany's diaries, nor months. She measured her life by events: by storms at sea, by vessels in distress. Not December 20, but the sinking of the *Mary Louise Ferret* and the rescue of no less than 328 crew, passengers and stowaway mice. Next, the shepherding of the *Queen Angela* into port when her rudder failed. Next, the saving of every ship's animal from the humans' deep-sea trawler *Lydia Shepard* before she capsized and went to the bottom.

When the alert siren sounded under gale flags, crews human and ferret fired their engines and launched between the Maytime jetties into the tempest, racing each other to be first to the vessel in distress. Ferret rescue boats were smaller but lighter, with greater power for their weight. In smooth seas they outran the humans' Coast Guard cutters, but in high seas and gale winds, great skill was required for the J-boats to win the race.

On station, the boats worked together, helping crippled vessels to port, standing by to save lives when ships went down. This job, for Bethany, made her life worth living.

Then, storm season nearly over, a strange order from the base commander. Bethany opened the envelope, read the single page and frowned. The crew of *Resolute* was requested and required to host one Chloe Ferret, a journalist on assignment to tell the stories of ferrets at risk. The commander trusted that Lieutenant Bethany N. Ferret would show all due courtesy to the visitor, as she would be responsible for the journalist's safety and comfort during her stay.

Bethany's heart fell. In the privacy of her quarters aboard ship, she dropped the orders on her tiny desk, leaned against her hammock. It's hard enough, she thought. Hard enough with survivors in panic, abandoning ship before they need to, hard enough with the seas, with waves higher than my boat. Now I need to do it with a *writer* on board?

She would have appealed to the commander, but such was her gratitude to him for command of *Resolute* that she responded that it would be her pleasure to host the journalist.

Boa asked it first, the crew assembled on deck to hear the orders: "Is this *the* Chloe Ferret, Cap'n? The same Chloe Ferret from Zsa-Zsa and the Show Ferrets?"

"Of course not," said Bethany. "That one's a singer, isn't she?"

"She's *famous*, ma'am!" said Dhimine Ferret, *Resolute's* Starboard High lookout and youngest of the crew. "Zsa-Zsa and the Show Ferrets are, well, celebrities! Chloe writes, too, for the big magazines."

"It's true, Captain," said Vincent Ferret. Her brother ever took care to address Bethany by her proper titles: *lieutenant* onshore, *captain* on board. Were the crew not so small, they would never have guessed the two were related. "She wrote a story about space ferrets in orbit, not long ago. She seems to like danger. Or maybe the appearance of danger, ma'am. I shouldn't say that rescue is exactly dangerous."

"She can sing for me," said Harley Ferret. "She can sing for me whenever she wants." Harley was *Resolute's* Port High lookout and the most reckless animal of the crew. Sleek and dashing along the very edge of sea-ferret regulations, occasionally flying over the bounds, Bethany had chosen him for his sheer daring, his choices to risk his life time and again to rescue animals at sea. More than once she had shielded him from consequences that would have grounded any other ferret—it was thanks to her that he still wore his crew-scarf.

"Fine with me," said Boa. "So long as she stays in her place, doesn't get in the way."

Bethany nodded. "When she wants to talk with us, we talk. I want you to tell it as it is, I want you to answer her questions. Just a few wild stories, Harley, not too many. If she wants to go along on training, she can. She'll stay with me on the bridge. When we get a rescue call, though, she goes ashore. After we're home we'll tell her the story, what happened, how we felt about it, whatever she wants to know."

Bethany Ferret did not often underestimate others. The truth, however, was that her young lookout was right—Chloe Ferret was a star. Wrapped in the world of her boat and her mission, Bethany did not imagine what that was to mean on the high seas.

4

THE KNOCK ON Bethany's cabin door was neither soft nor demanding.

"I'm looking for my room. . . ." The ferret who stood before her was dark and beautiful, her fur carefully brushed, whiskers combed. Her eyes were bright and inquisitive under a navy-style designer hat that would have set the lieutenant back a month's salary. "They told me this would be my ship."

"You must be Chloe," Bethany replied, offering her paw to the lovely creature, charmed in spite of herself. "I'm the captain. Welcome aboard."

"You're very young to be a captain, aren't you?"

The rescue ferret sighed. "Young but determined, they tell me."

The singer looked at her carefully, reading Bethany's eyes in the silence. Then she smiled, a warm hello. "We're going to be friends, aren't we?"

Bethany nodded, smiled back. "As long as you do everything I ask."

"I promise, Captain. Could you show me my room?"

"Of course. It's not far away, onshore. You'll have the VIP suite in the visiting officers' quarters. To be preferred, Miss Chloe, over sleeping on the boat."

"Call me Clo, please," the show ferret replied. "When I'm on a story, though, I don't sleep in suites. I need the experience, the real thing. I'd rather not be an observer."

"This time, you might want the suite. Crew's quarters are

assigned, of course. Survivors' quarters are not what we call luxurious. In fact, they're a little bare."

"They'll be fine. I'll just drop my bag and then could I meet your crew?"

Bethany shrugged, led the other down the companionway forward nearly to the chain locker, opened a door on the right, touched a light switch. "There's not much view, I'm afraid."

"Thank you. I didn't come for the view. I came to live your life."

The officer smiled at the audacity. "Happy to share it. Most of it, anyway: the routine, the training. Of course you won't join us when we're called on rescue, you understand."

"The regulations forbid it," said Chloe, "you can't be responsible for an observer in the way, you need as much room for survivors as possible."

"Exactly. The storm season's nearly over. But you'll find our training realistic."

There were no questions, the two understood each other perfectly. Storm season or not, Chloe Ferret had come to report a rescue firsthand, every exciting second of it, and she fully expected to do that. Bethany, for her part, was quite prepared to lock the writer onshore to keep her from endangering lives at sea.

Yet the young officer knew that the rock star's story would be in the best interests of the Service, that it would be read by thousands of kits ready to decide their lives and perhaps by a few ready to risk them for others.

The two emerged from the forward companionway at the moment that Boa came up the aft ladder from the engine room. In the instant that the engine ferret raised his paw to salute the officer, his eyes caught the visitor's, and he extended the salute, politely, to include her. He didn't notice that for a second, as their eyes met, she had stopped breathing.

Chloe turned her head to watch the big animal as he passed. "And he would be . . . ?"

"That's Boa," said Bethany. "Without Boa, you and I wouldn't be standing on this deck."

The reporter turned to look again, but the ferret was gone.

Normally, she would have held her tongue, but she had liked the officer at once, and she spoke her heart: "Bethany," she asked, "do you love him?"

The lieutenant laughed in surprise. The kind of question that makes good stories, she thought. "I love all my crew, Chloe. Of course I love Boa."

"The oddest thing, Captain," said the rock star, puzzled, shaking her head. "So do I."

☜

Through the afternoon, Bethany found that it was easy to be nice to her guest. A strange animal, she thought, testing her intuition. On one paw vivacious, engaging, open, charismatic. On the other she's shy, even a little frightened.

That evening, at the door to the station mess hall:

"After you," said Bethany. "Our crew table is on the port side . . . that's on the left."

But instead of entering, her beautiful visitor waited, shivered. "Give me a minute."

The lieutenant turned and stared. "Are you all right?"

"Fine," she said. "I need a second to breathe, to get ready." Then a quick smile of apology. "No matter how much you love other animals, you build walls when too many get too close. I need to tell myself to let down the walls."

Then Chloe squared her shoulders, took a breath and entered the Maytime Rescue Station mess hall, as poised as for the cover of *Rolling Stoat*.

At once conversation stopped, echoes dying away. Nearly a hundred faces turned to the door, every eye stared, unbelieving, absolute silence.

Chloe Ferret? *The* Chloe Ferret? *In the Maytime mess hall?*

The situation balanced on its edge. In a second there could have been a stampede of fans.

"Carry on," said Bethany, her voice firm and clear in the silent confusion. "Miss Chloe appreciates your welcome." She led the way, striding to the table by a towering steel placard, polished as a knight's shield, ebony letters under a field of stripes in red and yellow: *J-101 Resolute.*

With that, after a startled quiet, conversation returned to the room, though Bethany suspected the buzz of voices was about who had just walked through the door. A little fame must be sweet, she thought, but too much, I'll bet too much is a cake, stuffed down your throat.

Ensign Vincent Ferret, who had been chatting with his shipmates, sat up smartly when his sister arrived. "Crew table, 'tench-*hut!*"

The four animals stiffened in place, braced upright, eyes straight ahead, unmoving, around a table fairly loaded with food.

"At ease, *Resolute*," said Bethany, and her crew relaxed, turned to listen. She took her place at the head of the table, touched the empty chair to her right for their guest.

"You know Chloe Ferret," she said. "She doesn't know you."

From the other side of the table, her brother rose and nodded. "First Officer Vincent Ferret, ma'am. Glad to have you with us."

The chief engine ferret, twice the bulk of the first officer, struggled, half-rising. "We've met. Call me Boa, ma'am."

"I'm Harley," said the raffish sea ferret. He looked directly into her eyes, an instant longer than was quite proper.

"Dhimine," said the smallest ferret breathlessly, glancing away.

"The finest crew in the Rescue Service," said Bethany, firm and proud.

"Then I've come to the right place," said Chloe. "I want to know what it means to be the finest. I want to know what it's like to be you."

There was an awkward silence. Boa broke it without a word. He lifted a platter of zucchini-lemon fettuccine in one paw, a bowl of Sicilian summer salad in the other, offered them to their guest with a hint of a smile.

"We eat well," he said.

Their visitor laughed.

"What's it like to be us?" said Dhimine shyly. "Practice, practice, practice."

Harley nodded, helped himself to golden spaghetti pie and Mediterranean wheat-berry rolls. "You'll see. On a nice day, nothing we do is hard. The hard part's doing it at night, searchlights only go a hundred paws in the rain, less in the snow, the wind blowin' force nine, the tops of the waves in your teeth . . ."

"Some snow peas, Harley?" Bethany smiled, offered the cool distraction to her lookout.

He touched his chest, inclined his head politely in gallant response, accepted the tender greenery.

Chloe's eyes widened. "It's that bad?"

"No," said Boa, snapping a carrot stick in one huge paw. He grinned at the handsome lookout. "It's only that bad when there's a lady to impress."

"Tell her, Harley," said Bethany. "It's mostly routine, isn't it?"

The lookout nodded, chastened. "Yes, ma'am." He turned to Chloe, caught by those beautiful eyes. "Mostly we're an escort for a boat that's low on fuel, or one that's a little lost, or somebody's not feeling well, they need to get to shore in a hurry. Not a very exciting life. Routine, like the skipper says, mostly." His glance fell to his plate.

"Mostly routine," said the rock star, "but not always?" Her smile would have melted any animal.

Harley looked up happily, shrugged. "Not always."

"The rest is practice, Miss Chloe," said Dhimine. "Engine start and castoff, against the clock. First boat to clear the jetty. First boat to the rescue site. Lost Mouse, how many minutes to find him."

"It's always against time, Clo," Bethany explained, pouring high-mountain ice water for their guest. "Don't worry if you left your stopwatch at home, there are plenty on board."

The visitor lifted her head and looked about the room, seeing mostly eyes watching her. The tall shields distinguished the tables of the rescue crews, each animal wearing the bright silk scarves of her or his own boat's colors.

Under a field of yellow and blue lightning bolts: *J-131 Defiant.*

Red and green triangles: *J-139 Heavensent.*

Green and yellow polka dots: *J-143 Courageous.*

White and black diamonds: *J-160 Strongpaw*.

Blue and white checkerboard: *J-166 Dauntless*.

Gold and black stripes: *J-172 Stormhaven*.

How must it feel, Chloe wondered, to see those names appear from the gloom, in freezing wild black water, when one is near dying terrified? Could my story open there, out in the dark?

"Every crew's the best," she whispered.

Boa nodded. "To the poor soaked creatures they haul out of the sea, Miss Chloe, you bet they're the best!"

5

CHLOE APOLOGIZED for the hour she spent signing autographs after dinner, her baked stuffed pear untouched, her fragrant panforte barely nibbled despite its wondrous colors and spices. Then she and *Resolute*'s crew walked together from the mess hall to their boat, the moon and dock lights glimmering on the water alongside. It was low tide, the air thick with the smell of salt and the sea.

Dhimine asked shyly if Chloe planned to write a song about *Resolute*.

"Not a song," she said. "A story. I've always wondered about you. A lot of ferrets wonder who you are, what it's like. I want to tell the story."

"I wonder about you," said Dhimine. "I wonder about Zsa-Zsa and Mistinguette. Are you really like what they say in *Celebrity Ferrets*?"

Chloe laughed. "The press doesn't always print the whole story. Everybody thinks she's this wild ferret, but Zee-Zee's no party animal, not a bit. She reads. Ferret history. Archaeology. She loves old things. 'History is us-then calling to us-now,' she says."

Harley choked. "You're kidding! Zsa-Zsa the Show Ferret? She *reads*?"

"Encyclopedia with paws," said Chloe into the shocked silence. "And Mistinguette . . . Misty's got a heart as big as all outdoors. Our romantic. She's writing lyrics, singing, dancing, but all the time she's waiting for Mr. Wonderful to say hello and help her lift the world."

The gentlest of breezes whispered of summer coming.

"And what would they tell us," asked Bethany, "about you, Clo?"

The lovely brow furrowed for a moment. "'Clo's always moving,' they'd say. 'She's restless. She's looking for something she's never found.'"

The six animals boarded *Resolute,* each but one touching its cap with a paw, a salute to the FRS flag flying from the crosstrees over the bridge. Beyond lay the night, the stars glittering cool and careless above.

Good-nights, and the captain led the writer to her place in the survivors' quarters. "And what Clo's looking for is . . . ?"

Her guest paused at the door. "I don't know, Bethany." She touched the officer good-night, watched her as one friend watches another. "Do you know beauty that's beyond anything we can imagine? It's there, I know. One time, I want to see that beauty."

6

OVER THE NEXT weeks Bethany found that Chloe Ferret was no write-and-run journalist. Days she spent with the crew, helping as they buffed and polished *Resolute,* watching and listening from out of the way as they checked the boat's systems over and again.

She stood behind the captain on the bridge for the daily pre-patrol inspections, listened to her on the interphone.

"Starboard High station check, please."

"Main searchlight, on . . . ," came Dhimine's voice over the speakers, and the light from her tower blazed, glaring even in daylight. ". . . and off. Secondary is on . . . and off. Smoke flares, parachute flares, dye-markers and line-launchers are loaded and safe, circuit lights are green. Life raft is stored and safe. Pelorus—three-six-zero degrees . . ."

Chloe watched the compass-bearing indicator marked *Starboard High* swing through its dial in quarter-circle jumps as the lookout tracked her instrument around the horizon.

"What's a pelorus?" she asked.

Bethany touched the indicator. "It points to landmarks."

". . . two-seven-zero, and three-six-zero. Autocamera power is on, covers are off. Starboard High is ready for launch."

The captain clicked her stopwatch, noted the time without comment. "Port High station check," she called.

"Main searchlight is on . . . ," came Harley's voice.

Bethany insisted that each of her crew be trained to fill the duties of the other, that any of them be able to command the boat, if necessary. She required that each crew member school the others on his or her own station, which meant mainly that she and Boa held classes in engine operation and seaferretship.

Resolute held her own practice sessions when she was not standing alert duty, Dhimine and Harley on the bridge, easing the boat from the dock and running it high cruise on autopilot and radar to practice rescues, Boa firing line-launchers until he could lay a rescue rope on a bell-ball floating barely visible in the water.

Chloe listened and watched, even steered the boat from time to time. She pointed searchlights in the dark, then turned them off, once, and fired a parachute flare high above, to see how it felt.

"Like setting loose a great slow comet over the water," she wrote. "With a touch of my paw I turned night into noon for two minutes fourteen seconds."

Before long, secretly, she began to believe that she could run the boat herself, if she had to. Still she studied. Alongside her hammock in the survivors' quarters were research books: *History of the Ferret Rescue Service, Strategy and Tactics of Small-Animal Rescue at Sea, The Sea Ferret's Manual, Marine Engine Operator's Handbook, Small Boats in Heavy Seas, Lessons in Twin-Screw Boat-Handling, Ferret Heroes: Amazing Stories from the FRS.*

"You're happy here, Boa," she had said on one visit to the engine room. "You know this place, you love it. How many animals live lifetimes without finding what they love?"

The big ferret had looked up at her along the oiled side of the injector block he was installing. "I couldn't say, Miss Chloe," he had replied, "but it's my job to find it for me."

How we learn from our choices, thought the journalist, and how determined we are to practice our lessons!

"My mother told me," Vincent said as they returned late from night-rescue practice, "and I never forgot." He paused for a long while, the two of them watching the luminous spray fly from amidships. "'Vink, if you want to meet the one ferret who can fix any trouble, no matter how bad it is, the one who can bring you happiness when nobody else can do it—why, just look in the mirror and say hello.'"

"You can learn a lot about an animal," Chloe wrote that night, "when you find what gives it comfort." Bethany's comfort, she thought, came from welding separate animals into a disciplined, powerful force of love, then pitting that force against the elements. That was the core of her skill as a sea-ferret officer. The captain needed to know that love could conquer all, and she was willing to bet her life, if need be, to prove it.

Though Chloe filled a second notebook, and a third, in time she came to feel more one of *Resolute*'s family than a visiting outsider. If she had to be an observer, she thought, she'd be an intimate one.

Chloe eased so smoothly into the crew that the captain barely noticed the change. Boa taught the journalist the art of knots, and she practiced incessantly, till she could tie a Monkey's Fist in seconds, throw clove hitches like magic tricks, whip a bowline on a line's end with the snap of her wrist.

Boa confided that he had spent a summer in Montana, when he was a kit, at Monty Ferret's Rainbow Sheep Resort and Ranchpaw Training Center. Not a secret, yet a fact that he had shared with no one but the captain before. He told sea stories to the rock star, and when his Truth Fairy said the moral after each in a tiny mouse-voice (". . . and that's why we *never* leave open barrels of honey balanced on our engine hatches"), she laughed so that she leaned against him, helpless in tears.

One day, returning from practice at cruise speed, Bethany and Chloe stood alone on the bridge.

"Thank you, Captain."

"You're welcome, Clo." Bethany pressed her interphone button. "All ahead three-quarters, Chief, if you will."

"Ahead three-quarters, aye," replied Boa, the engines a wall of thunder behind his voice.

The rumble belowdecks rose and the boat lunged forward, its keel lifting. Glowing water flashed away to port and starboard, snow blasted across a sea the color of blurring ebony.

"Thanks for letting me in," said the writer. "I'm not used to that."

The captain grinned. "Everybody lets you in, Clo," she said. "They love you! You're magic!"

She touched the interphone selector. *"Lookouts for the jetty."*

"Port High," said Harley.

"Starboard High," said Dhimine.

Two pelorus repeaters swung to point a few degrees right of course. Followed by the third, from Ensign Vincent Ferret's position at the bow.

"Forward lookout's on the jetty," he called.

Bethany held *Resolute* on course, planning a right-angle entry to the channel. She could have navigated by radar, but electronics can fail, she knew, and when that happens only practice and skill can guide a boat.

"If celebrity's magic," said Chloe, "it's a screen, and I'm forever outside. Whatever I do that's not what they expect me to do, whatever I say that's not what they want me to say, they're disappointed; I'm not who they hoped. I wish sometimes somebody would see me and not some . . . some mirror flash they want me to be."

"I don't think you're a mirror flash," said Bethany. "I don't think Boa does. Or even Dhimine, anymore. She's over being shy, she tells you her secrets."

"That's why my thanks, Captain."

The officer touched the bill of her working cap, her rescue-cap, marked and creased now with sun and salt and practice. "We're here to serve."

As the days passed, Bethany forgot that Chloe Ferret was not a product of the sea-ferret training system, that her discipline was personal and not Service-taught. The captain forgot, in short, that Chloe was not her crew, she was a rock star.

7

ON APRIL 17, the vessel *Deepsea Explorer* turned from the Gulf of Alaska, following the gray whale migration course west of Canada, measuring the currents along the way, comparing temperatures with the ocean surrounding, counting plankton. It was the last leg of a voyage filled with discovery.

Aboard were one calico cat, a Shetland sheepdog, an Indonesian parrot, seventy-six ship's rats and thirty-five mice who had crept aboard seeking adventure where they could find it. Also aboard were forty-four humans, crew and scientists, each with a thousand questions for the oceans and the distant skies. Like electronic nets, computer disks once blank were now stuffed with answers. Secure in sealed containers lay fresh discoveries about animal life from the trees of Malaysia to the depths of the Mindanao Trench, whispers from the planet's farthest atmospheres. Caught in those disks was the last cry from the sea to the creatures who depend upon it for their lives.

The low-pressure system that moved in from the west as they passed Vancouver Island and the Strait of Juan de Fuca was at first no more than a curl on the horizon, an apostrophe to a successful voyage. No one ashore or at sea expected that strange sky to be any more than a photo opportunity for satellites.

In four days, though, *Deepsea Explorer* wallowed not so far to windward of the rocks north of Maytime, pounded by force-eight winds and giant swells beyond the ship's capacity to resist. From time to time, the bow of the ship was lifted and balanced aloft in empty air, till *Explorer*'s seams began to part forward and her pumps could no longer keep the ocean out. Not long past midnight, she called for escort, for a rescue ship to stand alongside for safety.

Minutes later, her stern lifting clear in a sudden monster wave, came a thuddering screech of spinning failing steel that deafened the storm itself. Bent while turning nearly full speed, the starboard propeller shaft tore itself apart, shearing great holes in the ship as it did, water flooding forward.

The call for escort changed. "Mayday, Mayday, Mayday! This is

Deepsea Explorer, Deepsea Explorer. We have lost our starboard propeller shaft, we have lost our rudder, the forward hold and engine room are flooding. Our position is three-point-two miles on the two-six-two-degree bearing from the Moray Reef radio beacon. We have forty-four souls on board. Mayday, Mayday, Mayday. This is *Deepsea Explorer. . . .*"

At that moment the radio failed, its antenna shattered by flying debris. But the message was out, and at once the Maytime sirens wailed into the night.

One second asleep in her hammock, the next second Lieutenant Bethany Ferret tumbled to the deck, coming awake as she raced to *Resolute*'s bridge. Snapping the interphone on, she paused to calm her voice, then spoke as though this were just another practice.

To the engine room she called, "Boa, start Engine One, start Engine Two." She did not inquire whether the chief engine ferret was awake or ready with a quarter-minute warning from the sirens.

She switched to the ship's loudspeaker. "Topside crew, paws on deck. We have a vessel in distress, this is not a drill." Her words amplified, echoed below, and the crew burst down the companionway to their posts.

"Chloe Ferret, ashore at once, please; Chloe, get ashore now, please!"

With the first siren, the rock star woke in a haze of confusion; now the loudspeaker called her name. They can't be launching the boat! She dropped from her hammock, unbelieving. No ferret in her right mind would even *think* of . . .

Already engines shuddered to life beneath her.

"Stand by to cast off," said the loudspeaker. Then: "Cast off the bow line."

Chloe staggered up the companionway.

"Cast off the stern line."

The journalist stopped, clung to the pawrail. She was still asleep, too frightened to move. Storm season's past. Practice is nearly always in quiet water.

The loudspeaker continued, insistent. "Chloe Ferret, ashore at once, please." Then, sharply: "*Clo, get ashore!*"

She froze on the steps. This has to be a dream.

"All engines back one-quarter."

Resolute began to move, Chloe could feel it beneath her. In this storm, the boat was going to sea!

"Cast off the spring lines."

She listened to it all, her paws clenched, saw herself in the companionway as though she were an observer far away, watching her own life as it happened.

"Engines ahead one-quarter. Crew to stations, jackets and harness. Forward lookout, give me a searchlight, please. All engines ahead one-half . . . all engines ahead three-quarters."

Resolute began to pitch on the waves, gathering speed, though she had barely left dockside.

Chloe staggered back to the survivors' quarters, found her life jacket, slipped it on. Then she stopped, and began to tremble.

On the bridge, Bethany felt the keen edge of the storm, the edge of the wildest weather she had known, and she pressed into it nearly at top speed.

"Starboard High, Port High, give me main searchlights on the jetty forward. All lookouts, your station checks, please."

Practice, practice, practice, Dhimine had said. Now it was her voice on the interphone, calm and even to her captain. "Main searchlight, on. Secondary is on . . . and off. Smoke flares, parachute flares, dye-markers and line-launchers are loaded and safe, circuit lights are green . . ."

The captain listened to the checks, marked the position of the distress vessel on her chart, guessed her compass course to the site, set the autopilot to Heading Hold but did not engage it, preferring to steer *Resolute* by paw.

With the sound of pebbles on steel, rain fired against the topsides and armor glass. Under the searchlights, the downwind side of the channel was white water, breakers nearly burying the rocks as J-101 raced seaward.

This is going to be interesting, Bethany thought. Already she was planning her approach to the distress vessel, visualizing the positions ahead. If we hold station on the leeward side, forward if possible, she thought, that will leave room for the Coast Guard cutters to work the midships and aft sections, but it will put us between the ship and the shore, not much time for us to search for animals. If we hold station to windward, it'll give us more time to work, but the seas will be rougher. . . .

"Hello, *Resolute*, this is *Strongpaw*. We're in the channel outward bound. We do not have your lights in sight. Say your position."

Bethany spoke to the interphone, "High lookouts, give me your secondary lights aft, down the channel."

The two searchlights blazed over the wake as the boat flew between the jetties.

The captain lifted the interphone, spoke to Captain Chester Ferret, a Canadian animal on exchange duty at Maytime. "Hello, *Strongpaw*. *Resolute* is at Marker Four, we've got lights aft for you."

A long silence. "Nothing in sight, Bethany. What's your speed?"

"We're ahead full. Forty knots."

Another silence, longer still. "See you at the rescue site, hey?"

For a second, as *Resolute* cleared the end of the jetties, Bethany thought the boat had run aground. The sea was a cratered moonscape, sudden cliffs high above her radio mast, yawning caverns under her keel. Breakers sledged against the bow as though they would hammer it flat. She couldn't force her way through this sea at high speed.

"All engines ahead standard," she called to the engine room.

"Ahead standard, aye," Boa replied, easing the throttles back. At once the boat slowed, the pounding not so vicious as it had been.

"How are you doing, Forward?" she called.

"No problem, ma'am," said her brother, watching the dark at the tops of the seas through night-vision lenses. "Distress vessel is not in sight."

I love you, Vink, the captain thought.

"Hello, lookouts, we are three miles from the last reported position. Our time en route is twelve minutes, could be less if she's drifting downwind. We have no radar contact and we may not get it for a while. Look sharp."

8

Aboard *Deepsea Explorer*, the mice and ship's rats watched the known world slant downward. Jasper Rat, though not the eldest, had spent more time at sea than anyone, and the others turned to him, eyes wide. What did it mean, the terrible screeching noise, this vast tilting of the deck, salt water flooding where water had never been?

"We're going to be all right," he said. "We're close to shore, and if the ship is in danger we can hope for rescue. They'll take us under tow to port." He looked at the anxious faces about him, more than a hundred rodents, the mice already trembling. "If the water reaches B deck, we may lose the ship, and I want you all to get forward to the chain locker, up the anchor chain to the hawsehole, and hold on tight. I'll take Sammy with me, and we'll go there now ourselves. The rescue ferrets will need all the help we can give, to get us out of here."

"What if the ferrets don't come, Jasper?"

"The ferrets always come."

The mouse shuddered. "If they don't?"

"Then we jump from the hawsehole and we swim for it."

"Jasper, I can't swim!"

"Then you hold my paw and we jump together."

Another voice from the back. "I can't swim, either. . . ."

"When a ship is in trouble, the ferrets will come," said the sea rat firmly. "And when they hoist the rescue cage up to us, I don't want any me-first and I don't want any panic. I want the youngest animals on the first load down to the ferrets, and I expect the rest of you to stay calm. The mice, all other animals next, sea rats last. Nobody jumps from this ship unless I tell them to jump."

"Will they rescue the cat?"

"They'll rescue all of us. The cat won't hurt us when the ship is in danger. It's the law of the sea." He did not wait for further questions. "Sammy, let's go."

⌢
• •

Belowdecks on *Resolute*, Chloe Ferret was wide-awake. Ferrets are not often seasick but they can be frightened. She knew it was worse for her, that every other animal on board had a job to do, they could cling to their duty. She could only cling to her hammock support and wait it out.

She had taken Harley's storm stories for fiction. How grateful she was now, in the midst of the storm, for Vincent's patient lessons about the strength of the J-boats, how few were lost at sea. Vincent had shown her with drawings and equations that it was nearly impossible for surface water to crush a hull of *Resolute*'s size and design. There was little danger so long as they kept clear of rocks and shoals and sinking ships. All she had to do, she thought, was hang on.

Chloe decided that she could at least watch the action from a better place, and stumbled down the tossing deck toward the companionway and up the ladder, gripping the pawrails. Before she opened the hatch to the deck, she grasped the safety hook of her harness tightly in one paw. There was a steel cable on the bulkhead aft of the entrance, she knew, and she'd snap the hook fast the instant she was out the hatch, just as Boa had taught her in practice.

As the boat rolled starboard, she pressed the handle and pushed hard on the door. At once she was thrown nearly overboard. Black water surged about her knees, her hat disappeared in a half second. But she was ready and she knew where the line waited. By the time the sea swept her off her paws, she was fastened secure, harness to cable, and the ride was a one-way express toward the ladder at the foot of the bridge.

Thrown helpless by the seas pouring by, her safety line humming like a harp string, she opened her eyes and looked forward. For one crazy moment she enjoyed the sight, the bow an express elevator up the side of a massive breaker curling as if to smother the ferret boat. Yet in a flash *Resolute* rode high above the seas, searchlight beams chalk white into the raging dark.

Chloe heard herself scream, half terror, half wild delight at the chaos ahead, until the bow dropped into the bottom of the next wave and a wall of foaming black toppled aft to crush her against the bulkhead. So this is their job, she thought, that dispassionate observer in her mind. I thought I knew them . . . I thought . . . even little Dhimine, she *asked* for this! *Who are these animals?*

Eyes wide, she leaped to the bridge ladder, her paws tight on the rails. The sea swept over her from head to tail, and she was surprised that it felt no colder than ice.

The instant the sea passed, she unsnapped her safety hook and bolted up the ladder to the bridge, wrenched the door open and hurled herself inside.

The captain turned, startled at the crash inside the bridge, saw the journalist gasp in the crimson glow of the night-lights.

"*Clo!* Hold tight!" Bethany spun the wheel to drive *Resolute* directly into the next sea, which would have tumbled the boat had it caught her broadside.

Glad to be alive, Chloe Ferret clung to the pawholds inside the bridge as the J-boat shuddered and righted, the wave sweeping over the ferret craft from deck to lookout stations. Through the armor glass she could see Harley's silhouette in the ruby glow of the Port High's night-lights, his muscled body braced against his harness, leaning into the storm as though he could sight the distress vessel by sheer force of will.

"I told you to get off the boat!" Bethany spun the wheel back to course, moving ahead wave by wave, turning directly into seas only when the safety of her ship depended on it. "I gave you an order!"

The rock star shivered. She couldn't remember the last time anyone had shouted at her. "I'm sorry, Captain! I was scared!"

"Stay right where you are, Chloe . . ." Bethany's voice was lost over the crash of the sea against the armor glass. ". . . not go back to your quarters, do not even move until we make it through . . ."

A crash of static, and Dhimine's voice came over the interphone and the bridge loudspeakers. "Starboard High has the vessel in sight, ma'am."

Stunned at the call, Bethany shot a glance to Dhimine's pelorus repeater. It was pointing nearly abeam on the starboard side. At the peak of the next wave, for just a moment, a radar return, some giant structure between her boat and the shore.

"Oh, come on!" she said. "Not possible!" But she knew it was. Without its rudder, *Deepsea Explorer* drifted broad abeam, its tall steel side to the storm, wind and sea pushing it helpless toward Moray Reef.

"What's happened?" said Chloe.

Bethany spun the wheel hard to starboard, turning downwind directly toward the ship. "She's going on the rocks, Clo."

The captain selected Rescue Frequency and pressed her microphone button. "Maytime Rescue," she called, "J-101 has the distress vessel in sight. She has broached to, point seven miles west of Moray Reef. We are commencing an upwind approach to the bow of the vessel, we have lights above."

Then to the interphone: "Port High, give us a flare, please, Harley."

A trail of sparks shot upward from the lookout station, turning the scene to daylight: the vast low bulk of *Deepsea Explorer* tilting downwind, seas bursting alongside, spray flying high over her decks.

"Attention, all paws," called Bethany. "This is a survivor rescue mission. We cannot save the distress vessel, she will be on the rocks within the hour. We are on a standard upwind approach to the bow section. All ahead one-third, please, Boa."

Below, the chief engine ferret reached his paw to the throttles and smoothly brought the power back to a steady purr. "Ahead one-third, aye."

"Highs," Bethany called, "give me searchlights astern, please."

Chloe glanced behind, caught her breath at the height of water rising there, threatening to engulf *Resolute* as the boat lost headway.

The captain struggled with the wheel, balancing them all on wind and wave. Even slowing, *Resolute* closed the distance to the giant hull in minutes. At close range Bethany could see the anchor chains from the hawseholes plunging straight down into the sea. The captain had tried to anchor, she thought, though the water offshore was too deep. The anchors wouldn't touch bottom until too late, until the vessel was over the shelf, and by then the ship would be lost.

"Bethany," said Chloe, "if the boat goes onshore, they'll be safe, won't they? I mean . . ."

The captain's voice came tonelessly, dispassionate, while her mind calculated wind and wave and distance. "No, Chloe. No, they will not be safe, they will be dead." She pressed the interphone button. "Sequential flares, please."

Just before Harley's flare was swallowed in the sea, Dhimine's was launched, a rocket trail upward, and daylight returned.

Looking astern over her shoulder in absolute concentration, picking the moment as one monster wave surged beneath them and before the next could rise, the captain turned the helm hard into the wind and *Resolute* spun like a weather vane seaward. "Stand by for ahead standard, Boa . . . stand by . . . *Now!*"

An instant calm response: "Ahead standard, aye."

Engines surging to halt her drift downwind, J-101 pressed ahead into the seas just enough to hold a position close to windward of *Deepsea Explorer*. In the giant ship's starboard hawsehole the captain saw two ship's rats, soaked in rain and seawater, waiting. Their lives depended now on *Resolute*.

"Dhimine, Harley, we'll need lines to the ship for the rescue cage. Lay them on the hawsehole, forward, by the sea rats. Take your time. Don't miss."

The captain looked ahead to the bow station, clenched her jaw. "Vink, I want you to take the cage up the lines as soon as they're fast."

Her brother's voice came back, expecting the order, no fear at what she had asked. "Cage is ready, ma'am. On your command . . ."

Dhimine fired her rescue line toward the stricken ship; an instant later Harley fired his to the same target.

The sea rats ducked inside the hawse tunnel as the lines shot toward them, but the second the ropes slapped home, they grabbed the ends and made them fast to the anchor chain.

Bethany pressed the interphone button. "Go, Vink!"

From the bridge, she watched her brother dash from his station with an awkward bundle of nylon web, snap his harness to the safety cable. Straightaway he was thrown by a sea bursting over the bows, tumbling him aft to the bridge. One paw clenched tight on the webbing, the other released the safety harness. Instantly the young ferret darted up the ladder to the Starboard High lookout station and reached for Dhimine's rescue line, stretched over the water to *Deepsea Explorer*.

The two sea rats cheered at the sight. "I told you they'd come!" shouted Jasper over the wind. "I *told* you the ferrets would come!"

Harley Ferret fired another parachute flare upwind, wishing it were he, not the ensign, taking the cage aboard. Yet he tended his duty, reloading the line launcher, setting another flare cartridge into its firing tube.

Cage slung like a backpack over his shoulders, the ensign darted out the rescue line toward *Deepsea Explorer*.

Harley watched, tense as iron, unsnapped his safety harness. If that animal goes into the water, he thought, I'm going after him.

Bethany didn't watch, intent on holding *Resolute* as steady as she could. Though they had practiced it over and again, running the cage in a force-eight gale was no easy task. One moment slack, the next hauling taut with a snap that would have hurled an untrained animal into the sea, the line was a living, writhing creature that did not allow a single misstep.

But like a circus ferret on the high wire, in the glare of searchlights and rocket flares, her brother darted ahead, stopped, darted ahead again, until he reached the hawsehole and the sea rats hauled him inside.

"Welcome to the ship," said Jasper to the dripping ferret. "How long do we have?"

Sammy looked at his friend, startled by the question.

"Maybe an hour, maybe not," said Vincent. "The anchor chains will slow us when they hit the shelf, but your ship's not going to make it." He brushed the water from his eyes with one soaking paw, unsnapped the rescue cage and assembled it, sliding the main pulley over one rescue line to *Resolute*. "How many animals aboard?"

"Over a hundred. They're most of 'em here," said the sea rat, turning to look down the hawse pipe, now a tunnel of frightened rodents. "Little guys first," he called. "Come on, you mice! Don't be afraid, it's the Rescue Ferrets!"

9

"Hello, *Resolute*, this is *Strongpaw*. We've got your lights in sight, we're taking station midships, with your permission."

The first cage of survivors loading, Bethany felt comfortable and in charge. A dangerous feeling, she knew, and summoned back anxiety. Complacency she would not allow.

"Welcome, *Strongpaw*, permission granted. We've got a cage on the line, we're taking off survivors forward. You might send a search team across, bring survivors up to the deck midships and run your cage from there. She'll be on the rocks before long."

"Aye, aye, Captain. What's your power to hold station?"

Bethany smiled in spite of herself. She was still unaccustomed to other commanders calling her *Captain*. "Ahead standard is working for us, Chet. It's a bit of a breeze out there."

"Busy night, hey?"

Bethany clicked her microphone button twice to agree.

On the bridge, Chloe Ferret seethed at her own inactivity. "I've got to do something, Bethany! Let me do something to help!"

The captain had every right to lock her below; any help the journalist knew how to give would only put her in harm's way. To lose the rock star at sea, for some, would be a greater disaster than losing *Deepsea Explorer*. Still, Chloe had trained earnestly with her crew, the captain thought, she was no cream puff. . . .

Now the first cage of survivors was on its way, twenty mice peering down in terror at the sea a-rage beneath them.

"You can help, Clo."

Chloe turned, watched her friend. "Tell me what I can do. Anything!"

"Harley's going to open the cage at the main companionway. The survivors won't know what to do or where to go. They'll be awfully scared. Meet them at the ladder belowdecks, tell them they're safe, take them to the survivors' quarters, put them in rescue blankets and hammocks. That'll help a lot!"

"Aye, aye, ma'am." She moved at once to the door, filled with purpose.

"*Your safety harness, Clo!* Keep your harness on, keep your harness snapped to that cable until you are belowdecks!"

"Aye, aye, Cap'n!"

Bethany shook her head. I must be crazy, she thought. But her order had been given. No sooner was her celebrity friend out the doorway than another towering sea thundered aboard, washing the decks shoulder high. Her paws torn from the cable by the force of it, Chloe was swept helplessly away for the length of her safety line, smashed to a wrenching stop. Drenched in seawater, the animal found her footing the second the sea was gone, darted to the main companionway, unsnapped her safety line and disappeared below.

The captain breathed a sigh of relief.

Topside, the cage and its survivors settled on deck, where Harley stood, securely fastened to his own safety cable.

Between waves he dragged the cage to the companionway, opened the webbing and cascaded the rodents below.

For a flash he caught Chloe's eyes as she waited, tossed her a salute. "First of your guests, ma'am!" he shouted.

She smiled to him and saluted back, in what he found a most attractive way. Then the door slammed shut and he was signaling Vincent to haul the empty webbing back to *Explorer*.

The Coast Guard arrived in their massive cutter, secured rescue lines to the stern of the vessel and, with the same practiced efficiency as the sea ferrets, began taking human survivors from the stricken ship. Before long, almost uneventfully, all were aboard, and the cutter cast off for home, shuttering a searchlight "Good luck" to the ferret J-boats.

For this they pay me, thought Bethany, taking a split second to enjoy the challenge and the danger of her job. Then she was back to work, the last of the mice, the parrot, the Sheltie and a stoic dripping calico cat in the next cage sliding down to *Resolute*. Only the ship's rats were still aboard, trusting the ferrets to lift them off.

Deepsea Explorer was sluggish and heavy now in the water, filling from the ragged hole that had been her starboard propeller-shaft tunnel and the seams that had failed forward. The more water poured inside, the faster the ship sank. The captain knew that she would not have much longer to bring aboard those brave rats.

☁

Belowdecks, Chloe was an angel of calm for the survivors. Everywhere at once, she opened the bright yellow and orange rescue blankets, strung hammocks for the exhausted mice, comforted as best she could.

One mouse, mahogany brown with a blaze of white at her nose and chest, cried inconsolably, "They're gone, they're gone!"

Chloe tucked the blanket tighter around its shoulders. "The ship is lost," she soothed, "but you're safe, and your friends. Ships can be replaced."

"You don't understand," said the mouse. "The disks! Everything we went to find, everything we learned, it's all on board, it'll go down with the ship!"

"There will be other voyages," said Chloe, kneeling at her side.

"No! From all the data we gathered, we thought it was too late, we thought it was the end, *but we found how to reverse it!* The ocean does not have to die! It's all in the disks and the disks are going down!"

☁

Ever so slightly, Bethany Ferret relaxed. There's time, she thought, there's time and a little to spare, to get all off.

Each storm has a personality, and in the course of the rescue *Resolute*'s captain had come to know the ways of this one. Turning the helm to let the wind take her boat backward, just a little, when the line went tight, then straight again into the seas to gain head-way before it sagged. She found the rhythms of its waves and its cross-swells, learned with practice just how to counter the force of the gale, hold the cage line nearly steady against the wind and all but the most powerful seas. With those, the line dipped to the water or whipped tight as iron, no matter what she did with rudder or engine.

Her paws easy on the helm, she watched the last cage of survivors slide down the rescue line. The mission was nearly finished.

Then she saw something that she could barely believe. She whipped her head so fast that her rescue cap fell to the deck of the bridge. She saw a blur against the storm: there was an animal climbing the ladder to Starboard High, there was Chloe Ferret, grasping the rescue line and running, four paws top speed, no safety cable, above the knife-edge seas to the hulk of the near-sunken ship.

"CHLOE!"

Bethany pressed the interphone button. *"Starboard High, report to the bridge now! Dhimine, you have command of the boat!"*

There was a startled squeak in response, but immediately the littlest ferret dropped from her station to the bridge companionway, raced up the ladder.

Harley, waiting on deck for the cage, looked up, thunderstruck, saw the rock star on the high rope. Only years of Rescue Service discipline kept him from following her at once. There were survivors in the cage, and they'd be swept away if he did not take them below.

The lean young ferret leaped into the air a second before the cage arrived on deck, caught it and shoved it forward to the companionway, dumped the animals below and shut the door tight.

Harley looked to the bridge at the instant its door slammed open, saw Dhimine take the helm, watched Bethany fly in one bound to the deck, another to the Starboard High lookout ladder, then out the rescue line after Chloe Ferret.

Vincent met his sister at the hawsehole, astonished that she would leave the bridge in the midst of . . .

"Where'd she go, Vink?"

"The computer room aft!" her brother told her. "Said she had to get the data! What data? Why—"

"Clo's gone crazy!" said the captain. "Get back to the boat, I'll find her and drag her out!"

"Bethany, let me get her."

"No! She's my responsibility! Go, Vink! That is an order!"

He stiffened. "Aye, aye, ma'am!"

"And stand by to take us aboard before this thing goes down!" She cuffed him gently with her paw, then disappeared aft at a run.

Her brother snapped his safety harness to the lifeline, stepped out of the hawsehole and ran down the slope of the rescue line toward *Resolute*. At that moment, though, a giant sea lifted *Resolute* like a toy, the rope went bar-tight, spray flying from the fibers, then it snapped and Ensign Vincent Ferret tumbled headlong into the sea.

At once he inflated his life vest, at once his strobe light began flashing, but he was adrift in the very waves that pounded the humans' ship toward the rocks. The tiny, tenth-of-a-second flash of his light fired more often than not underwater, hidden by the fury of the storm.

For Harley Ferret, it all happened softly. He watched Vincent begin his run down the rescue line as though in some terrible slow-honey nightmare, watched the line stretch and part, watched his friend tumble dreamlike through the air—a colored pinwheel of scarf and life vest and sable fur—and fall, ever so slowly, into the sea.

Dhimine watched, too, from the bridge. Trembling uncontrollably, she saw Harley, no thought for his own life and apparently with no plan to return to *Resolute*, leap straightaway into the sea toward Vincent's beacon flash.

Just then *Strongpaw* slipped its lines and cleared the *Explorer*. "We've got 'em, *Resolute*! We've run a Lost Mouse, there are no animals belowdecks. Take it easy going back, hey?"

Dhimine did not hear. She touched the interphone button, amazed at how cool her voice sounded from the captain's station, no matter how her paws and body shook. "Boa, engines ahead one-third and on deck now! Vincent's in the water, Harley's overboard after him. Get to Starboard High and lay a line on them now, please!"

She planned to drift backward toward the hulk, saving distance for the rescue, though it brought *Resolute* perilously close to the iron cliff of the vessel. She trusted Boa to find the two in the water, to fire a rescue line as accurately in wind and sea as she could do it herself. If the line did not touch the ferrets in the water, if it did not wrap itself around them, they'd have no way of knowing it had even been fired. They'd be gone.

The best she could do for now was to steer the boat, and that is what she did.

Increasing pressure belowdecks detonated *Deepsea Explorer*'s forward hatch cover away as though by dynamite, seas flooding in, and still Dhimine held *Resolute* directly into the storm. She could hope to rescue Vincent and Harley; she had no idea what had happened to Chloe and the captain.

10

B ETHANY FERRET threw open the door to the computer data room, now barely above the waves thundering aboard, steadily swallowing *Deepsea Explorer* into the abyss off Moray Reef.

Burrowing behind the shelf of boxed computer disks, tumbling them to the deck, Chloe Ferret jumped down and began dragging the boxes into a large orange-colored bag, white letters: *Intership Delivery.*

"The mouse told me, Bethany! It's research! The animals, the oceans, the future, it took them years, they have the answer at last! It's all here! It can't go down with the boat!"

For an irrational second, the captain wanted to explain the difference between a boat and a ship. "We're sinking, Clo! When this thing goes under we're going with it unless we get off *now!*"

The other wasn't hearing. "Then get off, Bethany! I won't go unless the disks go with me!"

The captain grabbed the bag, dragged it to the disks, pushed sealed boxes inside with all paws. Blue plastic boxes, white labels: *Ozone Depletion and Recovery, Coral Regrowth Statistics, Ocean Temperature Soundings, Data Correlation Curves.*

"Chloe, I swear I am going to lock you below, I'm going to put you on ferret food and water, I'm going to hang your hat so high . . ."

11

In the water, Harley found, it was not just difficult, it was impossible to see the flash of Vincent's rescue beacon. Now and then he thought he saw the dimmest of flickers, and he swam toward them. He trusted his life and the first officer's to Dhimine. Somehow he knew the little ferret would . . . somehow, she would find them before the giant alongside went to the bottom.

He heard Vincent's voice, faintly over the roar of water. *"Harley! Don't . . . you can't be here . . . get back to the boat!"*

A dim, wet flash, not five paws away, the glow of a colored scarf in the flarelight.

"AYE, AYE, SIR!" he shouted. *"LET'S BOTH OF US . . . BACK TO THE BOAT, SIR!"*

⸚

Drifting astern at low power, the seas still raked *Resolute*'s deck. On Dhimine's command, Boa clambered from below to the main deck, then up the ladder directly to the Starboard High lookout station. He saw nothing in the water between *Resolute* and the sinking hulk. Nothing but seas, their tops blown away like shrapnel in the gale.

The chief engine ferret grabbed binoculars in the very moment the parachute flare sank to the water and went out; the world turned to black, split only by *Resolute*'s twin searchlights. Then, outside the shafts of those lights, came a tiny flash in the ebony sea. Another flash, alongside the first, swept by currents away from the ferret vessel.

Boa's huge paw grasped the rescue-line gun, spun it aft on its pivot. He judged the wind, aimed to windward of the twin sparkles in the dark, squeezed the trigger.

At once, he reached to the flare launcher, hoping it was loaded, and fired. Sparks shot up, the darkest of pauses, then noon hung once again over the site. He followed the lay of the line on the water, saw two yellow life jackets directly down the center of the line.

"Yes!" he shouted in the storm. "*Got 'em both!*" Now you guys hang on, he thought. All you have to do is hang on and Boa's gonna haul you in.

Awash in the seas, the black iron of *Deepsea Explorer* had become a reef itself, as dangerous as any rocks ashore. *Resolute*, drifting backward, was two giant waves from tearing her propellers against the wreck. It was all Dhimine could do to steer the boat, and the moment Boa had fired the lifeline she pressed the interphone. "All ahead two-thirds, Boa! We're drifting into the ship!"

The big ferret tumbled down the ladder from the lookout station, no safety harness. A wave swept aboard as his paws touched the deck, and only his great weight kept him upright. He staggered in the surge, then threw himself at the engine-room companionway, caught the rail with one paw, wrenched the door open, dropped down the ladder. Before he recovered his balance from the drop, he pushed both throttles forward.

His interphone headset lay on the deck, but he spoke aloud nevertheless. "Ahead two-thirds, aye!"

White water burst from the propellers, a few paws from the steel that would bend them useless.

Love you! Boa thought to his engines. Never did he doubt that they would answer their throttles.

On the bridge, Dhimine held her breath and watched while *Resolute* crept away from the black steel.

Boa heaved himself up the ladder to the rescue line. He wrapped it about his massive paws and hauled. It felt in the storm and seas as though the line were fast to the wreck itself.

"*Ha-ha!*" he shouted, an animal gone mad in the tempest. "*Gotcha both!*"

The big ferret hauled as he never had in his life, lower paws braced against *Resolute*'s stern rail, the steel bending ever so slightly. He growled, powerful shoulders trembling, pulling in the rescue line, paw over paw, the storm raging seas against him, from time to time swirling him out of sight in black water.

"*No, you don't!*" he snarled, teeth clenched, into the fury. "*Nobody takes these animals from Boa!*"

12

B**ETWEEN THE TWO** of them, Bethany and Chloe stuffed the orange bag half-full of computer disks, all the boxes from the shelf marked *Expedition Records*. Chloe threw three lightning half-hitches around the throat of the bag, the extra one for luck, snapped a bowline on the end for a handle.

"Let's take more!" she said, reaching for another bag. "Just in case. *Expedition Video* sounds important!"

"*No!*" shouted Bethany. She felt the ship groan underpaw, giant pressures building within as it settled. "*Chloe*, no! *No! No!*"

The two animals dragged the bag from the computer room onto the bridge, a task made easier now by deeper water over the deck—the bag floated more than it dragged.

They splashed toward the bridge railing in the instant the mid-ships hatch cover exploded in a fountain of salt spray, the sound of near-miss dynamite.

Seconds, thought Bethany. We have seconds before she goes down. Chloe pulled for the windward side, till the captain shouted, "Lee side! *Lee side!*"

Chloe was not certain which was the lee side, then remembered. Of course, she thought. The water's too wild to windward, we'd be gone.

At once she turned back toward Bethany. The sight would stay with her for the rest of her life: the trim officer silhouetted in the stark light of a parachute flare, the whole scene in blacks and whites, save for that cherry-lemon scarf proud at her throat.

Too late, Bethany thought. Looking into the storm, even Chloe knew they were doomed. There was no time for fear, no time for regrets.

Abruptly, faster than the ferret officer thought possible, *Deepsea Explorer* sank. One second the forward half of the ship was awash, the next it was gone in foam and spray, the ship turning nearly straight down, the deck under the two animals suddenly became a wall down which they slid, dropping heavily onto the bridge railing now a floor over the abyss, the entire vessel lifting, then dropping like stone into the sea.

"Hang on, Clo!" Bethany shouted, though she knew nothing could help them now. Whether they hung on or let go, the great ship would drag them under; either *Explorer* would take them, or the whirlpools that would follow her to the bottom.

In that moment the lieutenant felt a strange and perfect peace. Nothing else mattered. Not the data, not the storm, not their adventure on this minor planet of a minor sun in a minor galaxy of stars flung across space and time. Everything was just as it should be. She was about to give her life that others would live, and it was proper that she should. It was as though the storm had ended, the wind and seas turned calm.

She smiled at her friend. "Take my paw, Clo."

Chloe, feeling the same lovely peace, reached her paw to her friend's. "It's all right, isn't it, Bethany?" she said quietly. The black hull slipped down.

In that peace, a broad, warm light spread across the sea. An arc of color, a giant rainbow, shimmered about them, lofting up, perfect gentle lights, away into the sky.

Before them, as softly as though they had simply not noticed, stood a small, sable-color ferret, looking upon them with the most exquisite knowing love. Every shred of fear and doubt vanished in the presence of this creature.

"Bethany," it said, a voice they heard in their mind more than in their ears. "Chloe."

Then it was silent for a time that could have been an age. They beheld that creature uncaring of time. In that forever-second, the two of them remembered who they were, where they had come from, why they had wanted these lifetimes on earth.

Of course, thought Bethany. How could I have forgotten? So much she yearned to go with the lovely animal, how ready she was to follow wherever it might show the way to walk.

"This is not your time to cross the bridge," said the ferret. "You have much yet to learn and to do in the places and times you have chosen to express yourselves, you have many adventures ahead." The two ferrets looked into those dark eyes, unable to move or speak. "You've followed your highest sense of right, so far, through all your tests. Well done."

The creature came near, lifted its paw, touched their shoulders. "Here's the reminder you wished." It looked deep into Chloe's eyes. "Express beauty."

Slowly, evenly, it turned to gaze upon Bethany. "Express love."

It stayed with them, timeless, surrounding them with joy.

Then it slipped away, dissolving into a place more real than the ferrets' here and now, and was gone. Gone, too, the arc of color, the light fading away.

Standing together, swept in happiness, the two animals were all at once knocked from their paws by a bone-jarring, dragging thunder. In a flash the storm raged around them as it had before, seas breaking and churning below.

Instead of sinking, *Deepsea Explorer* shuddered to rest at an angle nearly vertical, her anchors and chains into the abyss, her bow stuck fast on the granite shelf.

Bethany blinked. They had just been given the minutes they needed to live.

"Now, Clo!"

The ferrets dragged the bag between them to the railing's end, overlooking a lake of calm protected from storm by the hulk of *Deepsea Explorer*.

The ship was lost, Bethany knew, but with the bow stuck on the rocks below, it would take a few seconds longer for the stern to follow. There would be suctions and down-currents, but death was no longer certain.

"Jump!"

They threw the bag overboard and followed it into the dark, into the water between the wreck and the breakers downwind.

Their life-jacket beacons flashed, bright and clear in the smooth icy water.

"Swim, Clo! Away from the wreck!" It had been drilled into the rescue ferret: never let it happen, survivors in the water near a ship going down.

Like two sudden otters, the ferrets swam as hard as they could, towing the bag behind them.

"Bethany . . ." her voice faded.

"Are you all right, Clo?"

"Did you see . . . ?"

"Later, Clo! We'll think about it later!" said the sea ferret. "Now we swim!"

Then the sky broke open over them in a blaze of light. Slicing like an arrow across the calm water came *Resolute* and her glare of searchlights, turning hard to port, sliding broadside to halt ahead of the two animals in the water.

Harley Ferret didn't stop with the boat. He flew over the side, together with Ensign Vincent Ferret, diving to his sister.

"Get aboard!" shouted Bethany to her brother as he surfaced, frightened they could all be lost in the currents. "I can swim faster than you can!"

Vincent reached a paw to the bag of disks. "Then I'll race you, Sis."

Chloe called from the dark, "Harley!"

By then the lean ferret was at her side, his paw reaching for hers. "You're safe, Miss Chloe," he said. "We're almost there."

From deck, Boa reached down and hauled the animals from the water two at a time in his great paws, first the captain and her brother, then the rock star and her rescuer.

There came a last explosion from the hulk, the stern hatch blowing away from pressures it could no longer resist. The towering steel mass groaned in the night, leaned ponderously toward the ferret rescue boat.

Boa shouted to the bridge, Harley and Chloe still hanging from his arms as the hulk grew over them, toppling down in slow motion. "Got 'em, Dhimine! *Get us out of here!*"

"Power, Boa! I need all ahead flank!"

In a miracle, before the chief could move, *Resolute*'s engines burst into life, cracking full-throttle thunders. Dhimine was nearly yanked off her paws by the acceleration, but she steered the boat, raced it from beneath the falling disaster and back into the storm.

"Ahead standard!" she called as *Resolute* struck the first of the wild seas once again.

A monster fountain of flying water, and *Deepsea Explorer* went down, in her place a vast slick of violent suctions and whirlpools. The storm swept in, raging to the rocks as though the giant had never floated there.

"Ahead standard, aye," said Bethany from the engine room, the throttles under her paws. "Good save, Captain!"

Trembling, the little ferret at the helm touched the interphone button. "Thank you, ma'am," she said, flooded in relief, turning *Resolute* head-on into the seas.

Harley Ferret saw Chloe safely belowdecks, then scrambled aloft to Port High.

Bethany turned the engine room back to Boa, climbed the ladder to the bridge, opened the door.

Dhimine saluted, relinquishing the helm. "Your boat, Captain."

Bethany touched her paw to her brow. "Thank you, Dhimine. Give me a station check when you can, please."

With a nod the exhausted little ferret was out the door and up the ladder to her post.

Then came her voice on the interphone: "Starboard High, main searchlight, on. Secondary is on . . . and off. Smoke flares, parachute flares . . ."

"All searchlights off," called the captain when the checks were finished. "Look sharp for the Maytime jetty light!"

Resolute plunged through the seas on her return a little more slowly, a little less violently than she had on her race to the disaster. The captain steered well to windward of the jetty, those dark rocks waiting in the night.

"All lookouts," she called, "I have intermittent radar on the buoy, no returns from the jetty." Odd, she thought. The radar reflectors on the jetty carried away? Careful, Bethany!

Now the screen showed a clear return from the radar buoy. It was safe to turn, whether she could see or not, into the channel to her left.

"Breakers on the port side!" called Harley, and at once his searchlight stabbed into the black.

At the limit of the light, through the swirling veils of seawater, Bethany saw the faint surging glow of seas on rocks.

"Not again!" she said aloud. *"Be careful, Captain!"*

The radar buoy, chained to its concrete block at the bottom of the channel, had once more been dragged from its position in a storm. A shock of cold went through her.

"All stations," she called, "the buoy's dragged! We need a visual on the jetties!"

For a long minute there was silence on the interphone, night-vision binoculars from three stations straining for some glimpse . . .

"The port-side jetty's in sight," came Vincent's voice, calm and even. The center pelorus repeater above Bethany's armor glass swung thirty degrees to port, the forward searchlight flashing out, catching a single green reflector set above the rocks.

Came Harley's voice: "Port High's got the jetty."

"Starboard High's got the starboard jetty," called Dhimine. Her searchlight caught a red reflector through the storm, held it fast.

Bethany guided *Resolute* carefully downwind, the vessel feeling its way on the beams of its searchlights like some seagoing rock climber through a wind-whipped crevasse. Heavy rollers swept between the jetties, smothering the rocks in foam, last chance to crush J-101 as they had before.

That will not be, thought Bethany, her paws firmly on the helm, her rescue cap pushed to the back of her head. *That will not be!*

13

DOCKSIDE, ALL survivors stayed for a while on deck, the mice nearly invisible under their bright FRS rescue blankets. "Of course you can keep the blankets," Chloe told each one. "Take them home, courtesy of the Ferret Rescue Service!"

The gifts were unauthorized, Bethany later explained to the base commander, though it might be a thoughtful policy to consider for the future.

Then the bedraggled creatures shuttled off in buses to hot meals and warm beds. *Deepsea Explorer*'s computer disks, neatly boxed, were driven away in a van to the Maytime Coast Guard station.

As her crew secured *Resolute* after the mission, Bethany touched the button for the ship's speakers. "Attention, all paws."

They stopped and listened from on deck and belowdecks, swells rocking the boat even in its berth.

"I cannot tell you," came the captain's voice, "how proud I am . . . how proud *Resolute* must be, of her crew this night." She took the rescue cap from her head, wiped tears away, unashamed.

Rain pelted down as they listened in silence.

"Well done, Boa."

The big ferret stood in the engine room, a rag in his paw. He had been wiping down his gleaming diesels, thanking them for the work they had done. She's a good captain, he thought.

"Well done, Harley."

Doin' my job, Skipper, he thought, just doin' my job.

"Well done, Dhimine."

The littlest ferret shook her head. If you only knew how frightened I was . . .

"Well done, Vink."

He nodded, at his station. Mom's proud of you, Sis.

"And you, Chloe . . . well done!"

In the survivors' quarters, folding hammocks and returning them to lockers, the rock star felt sudden, hot tears in her eyes. She had come for a story. How much more she had found!

"With the crew's permission, from all of us . . ." Bethany's voice echoed across J-101, and through the rain-slick docks. "Well done, *Resolute*. You saved lives. Theirs and ours."

The captain put down the microphone and let relief wash over her. Alone on the bridge, she sobbed as though her heart would break, as though it could not contain the love she felt for all ferrets, for all the animals she had ever known.

14

F OR TWO DAYS the storm raged on, till finally the third dawned in sunlight and a breezy, blue sky. At noon, Chloe's silver limousine whispered to a stop alongside *Resolute*'s berth. The driver, impeccably groomed, waited patiently at the rear door.

Bethany stood by the helm, Harley curled on the storm-shield above the Port High lookout, the two ferrets working to install a night-vision repeater link to the bridge.

"I'm getting hash on the screen, Harley. We've got a loose connection. "

Looking up, the captain saw Chloe emerge from belowdecks, carrying her notebooks. She walked slowly, thoughtfully, toward the bridge, touching good-bye to J-101's familiar pawrails and safety cables.

"Stand by, Harley," said Bethany.

She heard the knock on the bridge entry door. "Come in, Clo."

There were tears in the rock star's eyes. "I'm going back, Bethany, and I don't want to go!"

The officer hugged her friend. "Some of us serve on boats, Clo, some of us don't. Some behind the spotlights, some in front." Bethany watched the lovely ferret's eyes. "That doesn't matter. *Express beauty* does."

Chloe blinked, startled. "You saw it! The most beautiful, loving . . . it wasn't a dream?"

"Maybe. But I'll never forget." There was a long silence, the two remembering. "And the Rainbow Bridge, we dreamed that together."

"No!" said Chloe. "You and me, we weren't asleep!" She was still for a time, then brushed her eye with her paw. "I saw it." She turned to Bethany, her voice a whisper. "My mother said I would, someday, when my life was done."

Bethany nodded. "Mine, too."

Katrinka Ferret hadn't been dreaming when she died. She had told her eldest kit what she saw as she saw it, and she had been filled with joy. What Bethany remembered most about that night was how happy her mother had been, the dazzling colors of love that had filled the room.

The Rainbow Bridge may not be of this world, Bethany thought, but it's somewhere, waiting. It's real.

The two talked for a while about what had happened, what they had seen at the railing of *Deepsea Explorer*, how they had changed because of it. Near-death vision of the ferrets' way to heaven or a gentle hallucination they had shared, they would tell no other animal of that scene for years to come.

In time, the captain touched the loudspeaker button. "All paws on deck midships," she said quietly into the microphone, and followed her friend down the bridge ladder to the main deck.

Chloe Ferret was surrounded by the ship's crew, by the family she had joined when she risked her life to save others from harm.

"We know you have to go," said Bethany. "We wish you didn't. You'll always be part of *Resolute*."

Harley nodded, a bold smile. "You can sing for me anytime, Clo. Anytime you want."

The rock star embraced him, rubbed his muscled back. "Dear brave Harley," she whispered, "I'll always sing for you."

The littlest ferret, down from her station and smelling of brass polish, hid her face in her paws, her hat askew. "Oh, Clo . . ."

"Hey, Dhimine," Chloe whispered through her tears, embracing the sea ferret who seemed no older than a kit. "Chin up. Friends forever, okay?"

The lookout nodded bravely.

"You'd best remember your knots," said Boa gruff big oil-stained creature. "They'll save your life, you know, someday. They could."

Chloe declined to shake his paw, chose a hug in which she nearly disappeared from sight. "I'll not forget!"

"There's my shipmate," he said, releasing her.

Before she quite left his embrace, she kissed his cheek, surprised them both. "Write to me, Boa!"

The first officer stood nearby. "A privilege to sail with you, Miss Chloe."

"Oh, Vincent!" She shook her head at his formality, hugging him till he laughed and backed away.

At the gangway, she paused, turned to face the flag of the FRS. "If I hadn't lost my hat, I'd salute the ship."

"You didn't lose your hat, Clo," said the captain, "you found it."

Bethany lifted her battered rescue-cap and placed it on the star's sleek head. Then she slipped the knot of her cherry-lemon crew-scarf and drew it around the neck of her friend. "You are loved."

Chloe Ferret's eyes filled once again with tears. She stood erect and saluted the ship's pennant, torn and frayed, fluttering from its halyard aloft. Then she ducked into her limousine and the driver shut the door.

Resolute's crew watched the wave of her paw behind charcoal glass, and she was gone.

"That," said Bethany, "is one beautiful ferret."

"Aye, aye," said her crew quietly.

The captain straightened, took control of her feelings. "I believe we have a practice at fifteen thirty hours," she said briskly. "We stand alert tomorrow from oh six hundred hours. Everybody ready?"

"I miss her," said Dhimine.

Boa patted her shoulder. "We all do."

Bethany squared her shoulders. "I doubt that's the last we'll see of Chloe Ferret," she said. "She's got work to do, and so do we. Harley, I'd like to finish the night cam before practice."

15

RESCUES COME IN threes, the sea ferrets believed, and it was so. The first day *Resolute* stood alert after the *Deepsea Explorer* storm, the siren went off for the trawler *Libby J. Haines*, capsized from overload.

She was keel-up when they arrived, the ship turned lifeboat for the human crew and a dozen shivering mice. *Mild seas, easy rescue,* wrote Bethany in the ship's log. *Twelve lives.*

So it went, from rescue to rescue. Hours and hours of boredom, they say in the FRS, punctuated by moments of stark terror. Yet that was the life that each of them had chosen, and not one would trade it for another.

In July, Chloe's story made the cover of *Mustelid* magazine, a striking sunset photo of *Resolute* off the Maytime jetties, flying seaward in a cloud of golden spray, her lookouts silhouetted at their posts, her skipper on the bridge, wearing the sky like a scarf.

Copies were everywhere: in offices on the Maytime station, in crews' quarters, even in the mess hall, open on the dining tables. Sea and shore ferrets alike read and stared, finding their own image now and then in the photo backgrounds. They thrust pens and magazines at Bethany and her crew for autographs.

In August the posters went up for the rock concert, *Zsa-Zsa and the Show Ferrets*, in benefit for the Ferret Rescue Service at Maytime.

A day before the event, the three stars arrived at the dock in a white limousine, Chloe wearing her battered rescue-cap and crewscarf, Zsa-Zsa and Mistinguette in large dark sunglasses. For the afternoon they met and talked with the rescue ferrets, toured *Resolute*. Chloe showed Boa that she could still tie a bowline with the snap of her paw, at least on the second attempt, and no one thought it strange that the two talked privately for quite some time.

The visitors crowded onto the bridge for a practice run during which Dhimine found the Lost Mouse in just under forty seconds.

⌢⌣

What happened at the concert is not part of this tale, though it must be said that Zsa-Zsa opened with "Wild Ferret." The three performed "Just Close Your Eyes" as purely as ever they had, and their friend Whitepaw appeared from a blast of smoke and flame to join "If I Could Fly," a number that brought every ferret in the audience to its paws in delight.

At the end of the evening, Chloe took the stage in her *Resolute* scarf and cap, Misty and Zsa-Zsa backing her so gently on "Night Rescue" that there were tears in all their eyes before the last chord haunted into silence and the lights cut to black.

An hour after the concert the Show Ferrets were still swamped by autograph seekers, unwilling to break away from the animals they had charmed.

Yet this time the crew of *Resolute* blinked as long into flash cameras as the rock stars, signed their names for fans awed by the presence of real-life rescue ferrets, close enough to touch.

In the midst of pandemonium, Dhimine looked up, suddenly realizing, to Bethany.

"Captain," she asked, "are we famous?"

The words were caught in a firework of photoflash, and her picture appeared on the cover of *Celebrity Ferrets*, her question turned large type below.

16

CELEBRITY FADES, character doesn't.

Bethany and Vincent, Boa and Harley and Dhimine and the J-boat crews of Ferret Rescue Station Maytime are no longer in the spotlights. They are still behind them, however, still on duty at the edge of the sea.

Not long after the *Deepsea Explorer* rescue, Dhimine applied for Sea Ferret Officers' School, and on her service record and the recommendations of her captain and the Maytime base commander, she was accepted.

The competition for Dhimine's position at *Resolute's* Starboard High lookout was intense. In one afternoon Bethany had fourteen interviews from highly qualified applicants.

The last was her second meeting with one Kimiko Ferret, who had impressed Bethany not so much by her lofty marks in training as by what seemed to be an inborn knowledge of J-boats and by a certain awareness of her mission, a quality Bethany sensed more than saw.

The young animal came from a family of sea ferrets and watched the captain with absolute confidence at the end of the interview. "I promise you, ma'am," she said, "that you have found the best look-out in the service, save for one since promoted."

"Save for one?"

"Do I look familiar to you, ma'am? Have you seen me before?"

"I expect I have," said Bethany, "or you wouldn't have asked."

The sea ferret's gaze never wavered. "Don't you remember, Captain? Survivor number eight? You came back down the line and found me in the sail locker."

Where do these animals come from? her friend Chloe once had asked. Now Bethany accepted a fact, no more questions. We come for love, we come for beauty, we come because it is our destiny to serve.

"So you're back," she said to the youngster. She watched her applicant for a long moment, and at last she shook her head. "The best save one, Kimiko? No. I need the best sea ferrets on my boat, the best but none, and I'll have nothing less." Bethany stood. The interview was over.

The applicant rose at once. "Yes, ma'am. Thank you, ma'am!"

So confident, Bethany thought. "We launch at dawn. We'll use no radar. Distress ship unknown, position unknown. I'll expect you on duty at Starboard High, and I'll expect you to sight the vessel first."

"I will, ma'am!"

As the sea ferret saluted and turned to leave, the captain saw herself in the young animal, she saw Dhimine and Harley and Vincent and Boa, she saw the spirit of all the rescue ferrets at Maytime.

"A minute," she said.

"Yes, ma'am?"

On the captain's desk lay a narrow wooden box. She opened it, drew forth a long fold of silk, bright angled stripes of cherry-lemon. She slipped it about Kimiko's neck, fastened it with a square knot.

"From your boat," she said, "from *Resolute*. Welcome aboard."

— end —

BOOK 4

Monty and Cheyenne

The Ferrets, the Mountain, and the Sea

ONCE THERE WERE *two ferrets who lived by a country lane.*

The lane led one way toward a dawn mountain, the other to a twilight sea. The two were friends, but the mountain called to him and the sea to her, called so strongly that neither could turn aside.

"I am sad," he told her, "that our paths must take us in such different directions."

"And I," she said, "that we cannot go our ways together."

The two held their love warmly in their hearts, but listened to their highest right and walked the lane toward its opposite ends.

After many adventures, they discovered that the path toward the dawn led over the mountain to the sea, and the path toward the twilight led across the sea to the mountain.

On the other side of the mountain, on the other side of the sea, the lovers met again, and their paths were one.

Our highest right knows all futures. As we listen to its whisper, we find that the prize ahead is our own greatest happiness.

—Antonius Ferret, *Fables*

1

"I NEVER SAW A ranchpaw ever wore a *blue* hat . . ."

She was just a kit, and truth to tell so was he, when he taught the silver-fur Cheyenne Jasmine Ferret to ride delphins.

She adjusted the sky-color brim lower over her eyes, hint of a smile. "I'm not a ranchpaw, Montgomery Ferret, and it'll do you well to remember that. You teach me everything you know, please, and leave my hat out of it!"

They lived near the end of the river road, their parents' ranches side by side, sheltered from the west by the lofty Sweetroot Mountains, from the north and east by wide Montana wilderness. Before school and after, before chores and after, they rode together.

Now Monty Ferret sat relaxed upon Boffin, his gray delphin, paws crossed easily atop the animal's mane, and watched his lovely friend. "When you're asking her to jump, you want to get your weight back, Cheye, you want to shift your weight off your front paws, let Starlet get her head up to jump."

"She doesn't want to jump, Monty." Cheyenne cantered the delphin to her friend, slowed to a walk close by, a tight circle around the unruffled Boffin. "I move back and she still doesn't want to jump. She stops."

"So what do you think is wrong?"

"She doesn't want to jump."

"If that doesn't beat everything," said her instructor. "She wants to jump when I ride her. Why is that, do you suppose?"

"She likes you. All the delphins like you." The kit burst with frustration. "She doesn't want to jump because I'm not *you!*"

"Now you're stubborn again, and that's likely not going to be much help," said Monty, a picture of calm. "So let me ask again. What's she *thinking*? Ever you find an animal does something you don't understand, ask yourself: *What's it thinking*?"

Contrite, determined to learn: "How?"

"Go into her mind! Pretend you're Starlet right now. Now you're coming round the turn, you see the fence, you're thinking *I want to jump, for Cheyenne!* Why don't you do it?"

A long silence, his student nearly in a trance, imagining. "I can't jump."

"Good. Why can't you jump?"

The kit considered, her mind in the delphin's, all at once realizing. *"I'm not running fast enough! Cheyenne's holding me back!"*

Her teacher smiled. "Now that's interesting, isn't it? Do you think that's true? Are you going to try that jump again?"

Her fur a radiant fall of light, her head low over the delphin's mane, pastel hat barely showing above Starlet's ears, Cheyenne wheeled without a word, urged her mount topspeed around the turn toward the jump. Drumbeat hooves pounded from the earth, echoed from stone-canyon walls. Sand kicked into the air behind the two, pebbles flying.

Monty watched. "Go, Cheye," he murmured.

The silver kit lifted her weight, whispered to her delphin, *"Fly!"*

A flick of Starlet's tail, the two launched into silence, slow-motion airborne on the wind, no hoofbeats for a long pause, the low fence rail blurring beneath them.

Then ground thudded and trembled, the echoes again, Starlet swerving at the touch of Cheyenne's paw, cutting a half-circle to stop, breathing hard, by Monty and Boffin.

The kit's eyes sparkled. "It works!"

Her burly little trainer nodded.

"What did I do?" She was breathless with excitement and victory.

He said nothing. Tilted his head, listened.

"I was in her mind! I wanted to jump . . . *she* wanted to jump!"

"I reckon so."

"Again?"

"Does she want to jump again, Cheye, or does she want to rest, now?"

The delphin's ears tilted ahead, she shook the wind from her mane.

Cheyenne flashed a smile, eyes darker than midnight. "She wants to jump!"

"You show her how . . ."

Then his friend was off again at a gallop.

Montgomery Ferret practiced watching with his ears, with his body, eyes closed. Out near the border-fence, here comes the turn. He felt the hoofbeats. A little slow.

Cheyenne urged her delphin one beat faster toward the fence, shifted her weight and called the animal into the air. Silence . . . two . . . three . . . hoofbeats pounding again, slowing, turning.

Finally Monty could stand it no more. He leaned forward, whispered, "Let's show 'em, Boffers. The high fence, now . . ."

The kits were ever together, Monty and Cheyenne growing up inseparable: out riding, exploring, noses in field guides about wild plants and animals and stars in the sky. From time to time, the two would excuse themselves from table, ask to be off for a sunrise ride before one family or the other had finished breakfast. "Your juice, at least," parents would say.

Monty's brother Zander watched and said it for them all: "Born for each other, those two. Different as rock and water, alike as birds on a branch!"

Cousin Jupe had looked up at this, nodded *well said*. Everyone knew, he thought, no one noticed.

Monty's gift with animals he vowed to pass along to his friend, and nearly did. Yet while butterflies would land at once upon his upturned paw, they flew cautious near Cheyenne, waiting a more formal invitation.

I'm not as gentle as Monty, she thought, I'm not as peaceful, inside.

He taught her patience, sprinkling seeds on the wide brim of that powder-blue hat, bid her stand motionless till the chickadees came to breakfast. Patience she learned, and the delight of their tiny weight, trusting, on the edge.

She considered that, and told him, one day. "I trust you with my life," she said, the two and their delphins far up Sable Canyon. "I never thought about it, but all of a sudden, Monty, it's always been true." She said the words as though she had never thought them before. "*I trust you.*"

He nodded, matter-of-fact. "I'll be here for you, Cheye. Long as I live. No matter what."

☉

If the world outdoors was Monty's first love, the world indoors, of images on-screen, was Cheyenne's. Weekends, after they explored the countryside, the two ferrets rode to Little Paw and the gilt-and-scarlet middle-row seats at CineMustelid.

"This one you will love, kitlets." Alexopoulos Ferret passed torn ticket stubs back through the window of his last-century box office, shipped board by gilded board across the sea from the island of Chios. "He is a young director, this Heshsty Ferret, but watch what he does with the light, the way he lets the light tell his story!"

Soon Cheyenne inquired of Alexopoulos whether she might help at the theater, sell tickets and popcorn, change posters and marquee, clean and polish—anything to find how magic projects to the heart from images on-screen.

"I can pay only a little," he said, "but the movies will be free."

Every showing of every film, Cheyenne Ferret learned. The more she cared, the more she noticed the power of the slightest motion, how actors can show a story's crisis, close up, as simply as shifting their thought behind an unchanging expression.

Alexopoulos answered her questions, tested her with questions of his own, filled her with the lore of film. He watched her closely, saw a quality grow about her, in time, that made other animals turn their heads to see.

Only in part is it her beauty that attracts them, he thought. It is more than beauty. Cheyenne Ferret has a certain . . . she has a transparency to others. He nodded, for that was it. Within herself lay the magic that she felt from the screen.

Times the lessons she set were hard, to act every scene without a sound, standing alone in the dark at the back of the theater. One matinee, missing a line for the third time, she whispered despair as he passed, "I'll never learn it, Mr. Alexopoulos!"

"Probably not," he whispered back. "It takes a great heart, this work."

With Monty she would watch each film through yet again, her eyes on his face more than the screen. How does this scene touch him? Can I sense what he feels?

Actors move their spirit into fiction's mind, she thought, as Monty moves his into delphins'. In film, spirit and technique need each other. Should either fail, a story is lost, an audience unchanged.

Time and again tears streaked her fur as the friends emerged from the dark, untied their delphins and rode home together.

"It's so beautiful, Monty!" she told him once, riding home from *Desperate Voyage*. "Laura Ferret loved him all along, didn't she? And she never told him till the end! All that time, and poor Stefan never knew."

"Beats me why she didn't tell him up front!" He lifted his hat, ran a paw to smooth his fur. "If I would've been her, I would've told him. He still could make his choice, he'd just have had more information to work with if he knew, seems to me."

"No, you silly!" Cheyenne leaned toward her friend in the sunset, Starlet and Boffin side by side. *"I couldn't tell you, Stefan. I wanted, but I couldn't. Love isn't love, when it's asked . . ."*

The way she said the words they came softer, more intimate than they had from the screen itself. It was as though she were speaking not to some distant Stefan but to Montgomery Ferret, close enough to touch.

Instead of fading as she learned, her fascination with the pictures grew. An actor can let us share a life, she saw, let us *live* a life that we could never touch, otherwise. An actor can show what it is to make different decisions, become a wiser, deeper animal. How would it feel, she wondered, to give such a gift?

She thought about this for a long time, the friends talked, and one day she decided.

"I'm going to Hollywood," she told him, their picnic spread on red-check gingham, crisp wild plants they had gathered: greens, nuts, berries. A canteen of mountain water hung from a pine branch nearby. In the grass about them drifts of pale blue mountain daisies listened, nodded agreement.

Monty was silent. It has to be, he thought, and that's all right. She's studied hard, she's got the mind for it, the love for it. She's so pretty, a ferret can't help but watch what she'll do.

"Mr. Alexopoulos told me it's a hard business, acting," he said. "And a lot of it's indoors. Start early, work late. Over and over, the same scenes. That wouldn't get old for you, Cheye, that wouldn't get . . . ordinary?"

"*It's okay to do ordinary, so long as you don't* feel *ordinary*," she quoted. "Monty, I want to be part of something that changes animals' lives. It would be worth the indoors, and the over-and-over." She looked to her friend, trusted him to know. "I need to try."

He felt his life shifting, turning around the gingham upon the grass. He waited in the silence, finally asked that which matters, to ferrets, more than any other. "It's your highest right?"

Shadows lengthened a fraction till she answered. She touched the dust-blue brim of her hat lower over her eyes. "Yes."

"Big changes coming."

She nodded.

The two friends looked at each other for a long time.

The evening before Cheyenne left for Hollywood was the Harvest Dance, at the Village Hall in Little Paw. Monty and Cheyenne were there, their parents, their friends, Alexopoulos himself, CineMustelid closed for this night, animals from all the countryside round. Ferrets in their best scarves and hats came to dance to the music of fiddle and guitar, lively tunes to make them merry, and fleet of paw.

Arms linked, lithe bodies and graceful tails spun in reels and squares and lines and quarter-dances on a floor carpeted in forest leaves. The friends saw each other flashing by on one star or another. Cheyenne in her blue hat, Monty in his dusted-off brown one, they caught paws and glances for an instant and let go again, they turned with the music and the scents of winter ahead. Of change, ahead.

After a while, Monty disappeared. Cheyenne noticed, whirled herself away from the dance and out the open door from the light of the hall into darkness. She found him sitting on the hitching post by the board sidewalk, leaning against the night.

"Where's my handsome ranchpaw?"

"Hi, Cheye. Just wanted a little quiet."

"It's a wonderful dance."

He nodded.

"Come on," she said, teasing him in the moonlight. "Out with it."

"I like the quiet."

"So what did you learn in your quiet, Monty?"

He thought carefully, his last chance, decided yes. "I learned this."

In his paw, a single mountain daisy, the color of daylight and sky, chosen that afternoon, carried down from their picnic-place in the high country.

"Oh . . ."

"I'm not much on good-byes."

"I know." She watched him under the moon, studying that broad strong face, his mask and whiskers, as though to hold the moment forever.

Time curled and softened about the two like a warm blanket neither wanted to lift. So long had they been friends that they had taken it for granted: we'll never be apart.

At last Monty stood, slipped Boffin's reins from the hitching post. "You have a good trip to California, now . . ."

"Unless I do my best, Monty, I'll never know."

The minutes slowed, but didn't stop for the two ferrets.

He touched the brim of his hat, watching her eyes, a silent good-bye.

She stepped toward him, kissed his cheek. At the very last, her voice a whisper in the dark: "Bye, Monty . . ."

He swung easily up into his saddle, the night closed in, her friend was gone.

In the morning Cheyenne Jasmine Ferret took the train from Little Paw, Montana, destination Hollywood.

One way, no return.

2

B\ EFORE THE TRAIN had chuffed past the Little Paw town limits, before even the rooftop of the Village Hall was out of sight, Cheyenne Ferret knew she was making the biggest mistake of her life.

Her whiskers pressed against the glass of the train window, she looked back at the only familiar land in the world.

So easy to say, "Off to Hollywood!" or even, "Unless I try I'll never know." Now the unknown had changed from a reversible maybe to a certainty ahead.

Her last sight of the peaks above Sable Canyon, did she imagine a silhouette there, a lone delphin and rider, watching her go? She forced herself to look away before the train took the scene from her, blocked it from sight.

The other ferrets in the coach that morning saw her a composed and lovely creature, sitting paws folded, still and straight. They did not see a ferret fighting for her life in deep-water rapids of change.

I don't know where I'll sleep tonight. I don't know where I'll go when I get off the train in Hollywood. I don't know whom I'll meet, what work I'll do to survive, I don't know if I'll ever see a studio lot or a movie set.

I know Montana. I know Mom and Dad and Monty and his folks. I know my bedroom, I know Starlet and Boffin, I know my friends and their delphins. And all of them—*all of them!*—are sliding behind me this moment, rolling away. A tear fell upon her paw. *How can I be such a fool?*

"Ticket, ma'am?" The conductor ferret looked upon her as he would upon his own young sister, but she didn't see, didn't meet his eyes. She looked away, brushed her tears, handed the folded slip: *Little Paw–Denver, Denver–Hollywood.*

She heard the click of his ticket-punch, and when he gave it back there was a hole in the paper, the shape of a heart.

Now she looked up, wondering, and the conductor leaned down, spoke softly to the traveler. "You don't have to know what's waiting. You're guided by your highest right, Cheyenne Jasmine Ferret, and you will be always!"

Eyes wide, she did not respond.

The conductor touched his cap to her and moved toward the next car: "Tickets, please."

How could he know her name? How could he know her future?

Cheyenne melted in mystery. For answer came only muffled steel rhythms beneath her, wheels on track; gentle swaying of coach; golden Montana rolling swiftly past her window.

She held her ticket, the punched hole casting a heart of sunlight upon her fur.

⌣

Hollywood, for Cheyenne Jasmine Ferret, was not what she had expected.

She had walked but a few steps from the Sunset Express when she saw a handsome ferret holding a sign to the debarking passengers: *ACTOR?*

Puzzled, she stopped and asked.

"It means if you're an actor," he said, "it's your first time in town, we can help. Do you need a place to stay, do you need a portfolio, do you need to know who's shooting what and where's the audition? We can help."

Cheyenne smiled. "I need all the help I can get."

The Young Actors' Home, Cheyenne found, was a well-kept mansion not far from Wilshire Boulevard, a place of many rooms maintained in the old style. It had belonged to silent-film star Beastil Ferret, bequeathed in perpetuity to actors of new generations. Dark-paneled halls swirled with ingenues and character players, comedians and dancers and stunt ferrets. At the first-floor kitchen they took turns cooking meals and being house-parent.

Welcome at once, others remembering their own arrivals, Cheyenne heard it over and again: "You're so pretty!" "Glad you're here!" "You're going to do just fine."

All the ferrets confident, each convinced that no other could fill a role meant for himself, they felt no competition. They loaned each other hats and scarves for auditions, even read for the same roles, persuaded that the right animal will always find the part for which she or he was destined.

"Cheyenne?" asked Jerica Ferret, a petite sable, tasting the name. She scanned the room list, found one at the top of the stairs, led the way. "Westerns only, Cheyenne?"

"I hope not westerns only!" The stairs were flowered in carpet the color of forest moss. The walls were flocked scarlet and gold, hint of CineMustelid. "I love the West, but I'm hoping for period pieces, too; drama, comedy, mystery, action."

"Cheyenne's a beautiful name. It may be a little Western for this business, though. See what happens, but if you've got another name you love, or one you've always wanted, now would be a good time to try it on."

Before her portfolio was finished, she sent one of the photos to Monty Ferret, back home. *For my handsome ranchpaw, with me always . . . With love from your Cheyenne.* It would be the last she would sign that name for a very long time.

One day she auditioned for a small role in *The Lady Speaks*, a film about the past century, for the part of the stage manager, a single line: "*We're ready for you now, Placidia.*"

Jasmine practiced the words over and again, roommates offering advice and commentary on her delivery.

"We're ready for you now, Placidia." Not authoritative, she

decided, not cold, but warm and welcoming, as though she had come to Placidia expecting a gift.

At the audition, the casting director watched her carefully, listened once to the line, no change in her expression, handed Jasmine a card. *Wednesday at six on B.*

The young actress said thank you too late, after the director had moved on to the choice of twin kits from four sets of cute little faces.

She dashed home, throwing open the walnut-and-glass doors of the old mansion.

"I got it! I got the part!"

Others glad, they gathered round, asked her to read the line again just as she had at audition. Six meant 6 A.M., they told her, B was the second giant soundstage at Silver Mask Studios.

⌢

Wednesday at 5:30 A.M. Jasmine arrived combed and brushed, Stage B, Silver Mask, having presented her card at the gate.

"Good luck, Miss Jasmine," the gateferret had said, and waved her through.

She slipped in the door with the makeup artists.

"You're Jasmine," said one with a smile.

She nodded, a-tremble with butterflies.

"You come with us, sweetheart, and we'll get you all ready for the camera. I'm Mollie, here's Penta and Glorielle."

"This is my first shoot . . ."

"Don't worry," said Glorielle.

Heavy black cables snaked the floor, drops and half-curtains sectioned off the soundstage, video monitors displaying distant sets, empty of action, no one watching. Overhead, a forest of massive floodlights high in the scaffolding, more of them set on great lifts and tripods.

Can I learn this? Will this become my home?

The three sat her down in the makeup room, walls of lights and mirrors, counters for colors and brushes and sponges, they studied her from many angles.

"What do you think, Penta?" asked Mollie. "What a beautiful face! I'd say a light pan, a touch of liner."

"She's got the bones, all right," said Glorielle. "Lovely. And something more . . ."

Penta watched as though Jasmine were a sculpture from a land far over the rainbow.

Finally she shook her head. "A dust of chalk. That's all."

With this, the others looked at the young animal anew, nodding agreement. No pan, no liner for this lovely dark-eyed snow with the indefinable aura. Only a sift of matte, enough to keep the highlights in her coat from strobing on film. Nothing more.

For the first time, Jasmine Ferret felt the pouf of chalk, sniffed its cool fragrance.

One day, thought Penta, watching the mirror, she's going to own this town.

She was pronounced perfect and released. "Don't stand on the red mats, dear, they're setting up the big lights this morning," called Mollie. "Relax! Enjoy!"

The chalk seems to work, thought Jasmine. Heads turned her way on the set, eyes appraising. Whispers.

"Look!"

"*Oh, my . . .*"

The assistant director was there, the camera operator, the sound crew, crane and dolly operators, electricians moving floods and spots in the catwalks overhead. No one was unaware that somebody new was on the set, and word filtered around that the somebody was named Jasmine.

At last the director arrived, an easy-spoken, toffee-color animal, black mask speckled silver. About his neck Heshsty Ferret had thrown a worn silk scarf, his casual trademark.

He nodded to all, for the set had gone quiet when he appeared. "Good morning, everyone. A few pages, today. Anybody see anything that is *not* going to be fun?"

He looked up, and scanning his colleagues he caught sight of Jasmine, standing alone outside the group. His expression did not change, he said no word. Silent, everyone watching him watching her, he remembered to nod hello to the newcomer.

Politely, she nodded back.

Jasmine had heard the rumor, as had all Hollywood, that Heshsty Ferret was finishing a screenplay so secret that only the title was known. Some claimed that *First Light* would take three films to tell, others thought five. Some knew that Part 1 was titled *Origin*, others had heard *Home Planet*. Beyond that, it was speculation; the tightest-security project in Silver Mask's history centered on this modest director's vision of the far beginnings of his own race.

Jasmine stood twenty paws distant, that morning on the sound-stage, listened to Heshsty's outline of the day's shooting.

"As you've seen from the dailies, *The Lady Speaks* is beginning to work rather well. Everybody keep doing today what we did yesterday . . ." He smiled, scanning the shooting script. ". . . keep loving that camera."

He turned to two ferrets standing together in period scarves and hats.

"Millisa and Nolan, you're leading the way for us, this morning. Hold that wonderful tension please, you two, just the way you are. Millisa gets her big scene today, and what we'r . . ."

In the midst of the word, Jasmine heard a snap overhead, a rush and hiss through the air, a blur of a floodlight plummeting to the floor not five paws away, an explosion of blue voltage, blinding, glass and sheet-iron caught in the light's safety shroud.

"*Fang!*" Jasmine ducked, brought her paws up to protect.

Echoes from the shattered light subsided, every eye riveted speechless upon Jasmine Ferret, hearing not the crash but the echo of her sudden oath. No one moved.

"Miss Jasmine," said Heshsty Ferret, his voice level and calm, "this is a soundstage, at a motion picture studio. All of us are happy you're here, we look forward to working with you. Yet we'd appreciate not hearing such language in our workplace, if you don't mind."

She was mortified. Her first day on set, and she had *cursed!* She hoped to say "I'm sorry, sir," but her whiskers quivered, the words stuck in her throat. The best she could do was to shake her head no.

"Thank you," said the director, looking away, back again briefly to Jasmine, then to his leading lady. "Now. Millisa gets her big scene today . . ."

Jasmine didn't shoot her own scene until nearly noon, watched the others, learning fast. She knew her marks and she hit them, stopped a few paws from the leading lady, a look of warm anticipation. "We're ready for you now, Placidia."

Silence. Then five words from Heshsty Ferret: "Cut. Print. Thank you, Jasmine."

No suggestions, no cover-shots, no let's try for one better. She left uncaring even to see the dailies of her scene, convinced that she would never again work in Hollywood.

She could not believe what she had done. *I cursed!* she thought. *On a soundstage!*

She was the only animal in the building who hadn't noticed her eyes, her own luminous vulnerability during her moment on camera, the only one not aware that Heshsty Ferret watched her leave, watched every step she took, all the way off the set.

Such was the intensity of the moment that their names were linked next day in the tabloids. *HESHSTY FERRET SAVES INGENUE'S LIFE* went the headline in *Possibly So* magazine.

Somewhat more accurately, in the "Hollywood" column of *Maybe*: "There was electricity on the set of Heshsty Ferret's *The Lady Speaks* yesterday as the director made the acquaintance of Jasmine Ferret, newly arrived at Silver Mask from Texas."

3

MONTY FERRET missed Cheyenne more than he would admit. Yet ferrets do not complain, nor do they seek to change the choices of others after a decision's made.

She disappeared west, he stayed at Little Paw. Devoted to delphins, determined to know their language, gradually he came to understand that Boffin's parents had been wild creatures, as fast as the wind. *Monty,* his delphin told him, as best the ferret could sense, *the time's come! I need to race!*

Testing what he heard, Monty turned Boffin loose down a measured prairie straightaway, timed the runs along the thousand- and the ten-thousand-thousand-paw courses. His delphin's race times made Monty blink. To Boffin's delight, they entered nearly every event statewide, the two unbeatable, the talk of delphin-loving ferrets all the way across Montana.

Boffin whickered, turned his head, moved his whiskers just so: *I told you I could run!*

With their winnings, Monty bought Old Gramp Weasel's spread by the Little Paw River, restoring the pine-branch cabin, adding a bunkhouse and tack room. Working alone, he rebuilt the corral, smoothed a racing track on level ground, added a barn.

Came a day just after dawn, as he strained with scaffold and tackle to hoist the key-branch ridge-post aloft:

"Need a paw?"

The visitor had approached so near and quietly before she spoke that Monty startled, nearly let go the rope of his block and tackle. The ridge-beam jerked downward under the scaffold, swayed overhead.

He turned his head as best he could while he hauled, and there to his right stood a small ferret, an animal the color of nutmeg, her mask in shades of clove.

"Thanks," he replied through gritted teeth, creaking the weight of the great branch upward again, a decipaw at a time. "Be with you in a bit." He took a great breath, hauled again.

"Looks heavy," said his visitor.

"Yep." He considered belaying the rope to rest for a while, declined the thought. He would stop hauling when the pole was where it needed to be.

"Can I help?"

Monty smiled, his paws trembling on the rope. Throw her entire weight on the tackle, wouldn't move a straw.

"Yes, you can," he grunted. "Make me stronger!"

"How much stronger?"

At that, Monty began to laugh, the ridge-beam creaking downward as he did. It was all he could do to hold the tension while he forced the rope into a jam-cleat. Its fall arrested, the branch swung ponderously forth and back overhead.

He turned. "Excuse me?"

"How much stronger do you want to be?" The little ferret watched him unsmiling, solemn as a woodchuck.

"Why, strong enough to meet my need."

The stranger nodded approval. "Well said!" She took a step toward him, as though to introduce herself, but instead murmured a quiet comment: "And it's done."

He offered his paw. "Monty Ferret," he said. "What's done?"

"Call me Kinnie. Try your rope."

"In a minute. That's the heavy one, the ridge-beam. The others won't be so bad."

"Try it now."

Why does she insist? Yet he remembered his Courtesies: Respect for elders, respect for peers, respect for kits.

Odd, he couldn't tell which she was, his forthright little visitor, for she seemed both wise and young, other and intimate. He honored her nevertheless and did as she asked.

Both paws on the tackle, he took a breath and bore down upon the rope, pulled it free of its cleat. The line was as tight in his paws as had been before, yet barely did he strain to hold the great wooden beam aloft.

Strong enough to meet my need, he had asked, and suddenly it was so. Who is this creature?

Not without effort, but neither with much of it did Monty gather the rope to himself, paw over paw, the monster branch wheeling slowly upward.

Now it swung just above the slots he had cut at the center of the roof-support posts. He eased the rope and one end settled into place, the ridge-beam pivoting about the post till the other end hovered over the notch at the opposite side. Then it dropped home, an echoing thud when Monty slacked the line. Tackle now loose in his paws, the beam required nothing more than a tap of setting-pegs to secure it in place.

"Good barn," said his visitor.

"Thank you. A little stouter than need be."

"No. You'll be glad, this winter."

Monty studied his visitor in silence. How could she know about a winter yet to come? A philosopher ferret, he concluded. Rare animals, mystical and strange, they say. Now here one stands.

"Welcome," he said.

"Thank you for inviting me."

Don't remember inviting, he thought. But I'm curious, of course. Maybe curiosity's the invitation. "I get three wishes?"

"No. One. All else follows."

"I want to know."

"That's your wish?"

He nodded.

"And it's done."

That phrase again, he thought, like a sorcerer's incantation. "What's done?"

"Your wish. It's done. You know."

"I don't feel any different."

"Nothing's changed, but different you are."

"Why?"

She explained, as to a kit, "I give you permission to become aware of what you know."

"Show me."

"Show yourself. I ask, you answer." The little animal moved, now, just a few steps in the dust of the morning, backing away from him as though she planned to become the size of a house. "Who am I, Montgomery Ferret?"

"I'm not sure . . ."

"Wrong. You are sure. You are absolutely certain. But you lack courage to say the unusual." She sighed. "I give you permission to be courageous." Then, patiently: "Who am I, Montgomery Ferret?"

"You're a philosopher ferret."

"Was that so hard? I am, in your terms, a philosopher ferret. *How do you know that?*"

He reached for his truth. "I know." Would she understand?

A smile for the bravery of his answer. From courage, she thought, does wisdom spring.

The nutmeg creature rubbed her paws together, delighted that Monty had allowed her to appear at last. So much to say! "Where do I come from?"

Habit told Monty, *I don't know.* Fear said, *How could I know?* Yet like all ferrets, he tested choices every day against his highest right, and thus had he been led, so far, along his way. His highest right had chosen Montana for his home, had chosen to meet his friend Cheyenne when both were kits. His highest right had let her go toward her destiny as hers had let him go to his. His highest right had lifted a roof beam this morning, and his highest right would find a way to teach his gift to others who cared.

Yet never had he asked for more than guidance, never had he asked his highest self to light those darks unlit by others. Now a lightning bolt: *How can it answer if I don't ask?*

"I'm a philosopher ferret," Kinnie said, quiet patience. "Where do I come from?"

Highest self, he asked silently, where do philosopher ferrets come from?

He didn't have to wait, or to think. "Not from a place." Of course. So simple: "From a direction of spirit," he said, "a direction of caring."

"Yes. Can you come from there?"

"Of course I can," he said. Anyone can.

"Now a quiz. You know that I am a philosopher ferret because . . ." She hinted, expecting a certain answer, "Because I leave no . . ."

She wants me to give her words, not mine? Monty tilted his head, puzzled. ". . . stone unturned?"

She frowned. "*Pawprints!* I leave no pawprints!"

Be patient when she veers, he told himself. She wants me to notice.

He looked, and sure enough. In the fine powder-dust, the floor of Monty's barn-to-be, not a mark where she had stepped.

"I leave no pawprints because . . ."

Trusting, accepting her permission to be brave: ". . . because I watch your image within and project it where I will. You leave no pawprints because you are not of my outer world but my inner."

Kinnie inclined her head, almost a bow to him. "Good! Not '*the* outer world,' you said, '*my* outer world'!" She stepped to one side, looked down. "Of course I *could* leave pawprints . . ."

It felt like puzzle pieces falling into place, for Monty, permissions like snowflakes, gentle, unique. He could have explained everything about her that instant, about her and about himself. Of course she could leave pawprints, if she wanted to.

How strange, he thought. Find the greatest teachers, ask the hardest questions, they never say, *Study philosophy*, or, *Get your degree*. They say, *You already know*.

The little ferret watched this in Monty's eyes. "Then where's the school for philosopher ferrets?"

"On the corner," he replied, a smile for the picture he saw, one room in a forest glade, bright curtains at the window, a little chimney. "The school's on the corner of the trail where I ask what I need to know and the road where I realize the answer."

"I like the 'realize' part, Monty. That's the place, all right. And I'm your teacher."

Monty laughed. "No, ma'am. You're the same as me."

"Oh? Indeed." She frowned again, paws akimbo, clove-color fists at her waist. "Don't you mean I am like you, I am similar to you? Not the same as you."

"You're the same as me."

Kinnie was quiet, studying him. When they get the idea, she thought, they get it fast. "And who, then, are your fellow philosopher ferrets?"

Once the answer would have been impossible. "Every creature who cares to ask, find their own answers."

"Every creature? You mean every *ferret* who cares to ask. Otherwise, philosopher ants? Philosopher humans? Philosopher elephants?"

"No," said Monty. "What's real for elephants is real for ants."

All at once she approached, looked up to him, touched his shoulder. "Not bad, Monty Ferret. It took you a lifetime, but you've got the idea. The fun begins!"

As though she had expected it, a sound behind them. With a jaunty wave the nutmeg ferret vanished. No pawprints.

Hoofbeats approaching, a delphin whinny, glad to find Monty.

"Whoa down, Lightning," said Jupe Ferret, slowing from a trot around the corner of the ranch house. "He's squared a ridge-beam that'll stand forever, but the kit's gonna need some help to raise her up."

The delphin stopped close enough for Monty to produce a carrot cube from the bag in his tool kit, crunched it happily.

Then Jupe leaned back in his saddle, stared at the great branch set in place above. His whiskers tilted forward. "Well, I declare! Good mornin', Monty."

His cousin touched the brim of his hat. "Jupe."

The rider's eyes did not waver from the beam at the roof peak. "Before dawn, you moved that piece up there? On your own?"

"Nope," said Monty. "Had some help."

From his flood of learning had bobbed a caution: sometimes we'd best keep quiet about what we know. Fast as light within, he thought, but outside, let's take her one step at a time.

So it was, that summer, that Monty Ferret opened his own Western riding and racing school, mostly for kits but grown-ups welcome.

Alonetimes, he practiced asking questions of his higher self, came to realize, day by day, what he had long believed was true—ferrets have powers they haven't begun to touch. Other times he taught riding, and the language of delphins.

"First thing," he told each new class, gathered round the starting line, "you're going to learn how to lose a delphin race."

And they did. They practiced all ways to be graceful in defeat, invented new ones, how to honor those delphins and ferrets who rode faster than they, to cherish challenge and strategies well planned. Monty Ferret taught them to ask winners for advice with such open sincerity that advice was freely given.

Last and least, he taught them to race and win.

Hidden within were the greater lessons: animals are equals; how to meet with them in places of the mind; to link spirits toward ends mutually wished.

Others came to listen, asked for more. Finally Monty took time to record what he had learned and how he had learned it, his calm, earnest voice telling stories to a microphone.

With *Secrets of the Delphins*, the tapes released, it turned out that it didn't matter whether his listeners rode delphins or not. It was Monty's adventure that mattered, his humor, his homespun common sense. His stories entertained ferrets who would never touch a delphin or even see one.

Softly, then, began a snow of listener mail to Little Paw from around the world, and in it, one day, a heavy envelope postmarked Loch Y'ar, Scotland.

Dear Brother, wrote Zander Ferret. *What grand discoveries, Monty, congratulations!* Secrets of the Delphins *is unique, original, fascinating to hear. You're changing the way we think about delphins, the way we treat animals everywhere.*

Zander told of his own adventures, too, a zoologist abroad.

It is the most wonderful news. We have managed to clone a new type of miniature sheepling, less than a quarter the size of your smallest delphin. Of warm and dear disposition, their minds link as one when they wish. They are intelligent, thoughtful, reflective. Their wool is long-strand, in colors to rival the purest of nature every shade of the rainbow, pastels to brights, and absolutely fast.

We've applied your principles, Monty, about listening to our little sheep. At first we were amazed, but although they are romantics, we've found that they are shrewd business animals as well.

In short, the Rainbows have agreed to contract for their wool, on condition that they find suitable accommodations at a resort in the high country of the Wild West, as they describe it, Wyoming or Montana. They prefer open lands with weathers and views conducive to abstract thought and light exercise, in the care of ferret guides. Their outdoor skills are poor.

They would require accommodations for two thousand sheep, along with a few pipers and drummers of whom they've become quite fond, Scottish ferrets skilled at Highland airs.

Your work has convinced us that my own brother is the one ferret to establish and operate a top-quality ranch, catering to the needs and wishes of this unique culture. Of course the ranch would include expanded facilities for your racing schools and delphin studies, at whatever level you wish.

After several pages of a careful business and financial analysis, his brother concluded:

In short, dear Monty, you'll be fascinated with the character and qualities of the Rainbows. I wonder if you might respond as soon as you receive this letter, that you will travel to meet the sheep and discuss their offer and ours in person.

Ever your affectionate,

Zander

Montgomery Ferret put the letter down on his barn-wood desktop, ran his paws slowly over his muzzle and ears, creaked back in his chair, closed his eyes.

Highest right, he asked, what to choose? I'm no sophisticated businessferret, I'm a ranchpaw, I love Montana. If I say yes to Zander, will I enrich lives or disappoint them? If I say no, will I be dashing hopes or shifting them toward a better path? How is it that I can meet their needs and mine, too?

His highest right responded at once, four words:

Will it be fun?

⌣

The storm of his choice overwhelmed Montgomery Ferret almost but not quite.

It rose up from a thousand megapaws of prairie and forest and river and mountainside, in the wilderness to the north and east of Little Paw, by the village of Northstar. The entrance was marked with a heavy arch of curved timber across the road, letters carved into black pine, filled with white clay:

MONTY FERRET'S RAINBOW SHEEP RESORT
AND
RANCHPAW TRAINING CENTER

The land swarmed with construction ferrets, rang with the sound of hammers and saws, the grate of stone on stone as chimneys rose from ground to sky, the creak and thud of fine straight branches becoming walls, the clank of chinking irons, the scrape of wooden furniture on wide-plank floors.

Then it was finished, no longer a model landscape in the trailer office but full-size to the horizon. Here the staff quarters and ranchkit training grounds, bunkhouses and barns, corrals and racing tracks and dining hall. A distance away nestled cluster on cluster of rustic branch cabins for the Rainbows, meditation centers, hot tubs and picnic spots, towers for pipes and drums to call the sunset.

The higher delight for the little sheep, however, the dream that had called them here, was the wilderness of untamed Montana.

He had hoped to share his joy of the land with one other, but destiny had taken her from his sight. Now he would share that country with thousands.

4

BLUE FLAMES ERUPTED near table seven, swirled at the edge of a party of twelve. Masks and whiskers at other tables turned to watch, celebrities from the highest tiers of the land murmured to each other, every entrée a performance.

Gerhardt-Grenoble Ferret lofted his grand Midnight Omelet in the fire, called down a meteor shower, dust of saffron and coriander through the flames, deftly slipped his creation, still afire, to all. Fragrance irresistible.

"*Voilà*," he said. "*Bon appétit, mesdames et messieurs.*" A sad smile, a bow and wave to the cultured applause, a nod, as he left, to personal friends among the dazzling guests. No one noticed, as he walked away, that the chef seemed lost in thought, as if behind the smile he were saying good-bye.

It could not be said that Manhattan's La Mer des Étoiles was Gerhardt-Grenoble's flagship restaurant. They were all flagships, those haute-dining spots in Paris, in Beverly Hills, in Tokyo and Buenos Aires and Nuku Hiva. When ferrets play at high society, they do so with perspective and delight, and they found in the wonder-chef a superstar the equal of his patrons.

"Magic," whispered the waiter at table seven. "Here is no cook, here is the magician, no?"

👀

Early mornings, before dawn, no matter where he was in the world, it was the habit of Gerhardt-Grenoble to don scarf and cap, visit the finest markets of the city; to sniff and touch the freshest fruits and vegetables, through all the raucous bustle of the morning. He did so this day in Manhattan with his oldest friend and partner, the two nodding to proprietors for this carton or that tray, newly picked, to be shipped to La Mer. They moved from stand to stand through the stalls, noses twitching in currents of fragrance. The world is a kitchen, he thought, a chef's at home anywhere on the planet.

"*Hup, hup, hya*," called the banana ferrets, tossing the heavy fruits one to another from cargo container to display. "*Hup, hup, hya!*"

"*La belle cuisine,*" said the chef, gentle Swiss accent over the noise. "It has brought us a long way together, Armond."

"A long way, indeed, from your first kitchen," replied his partner. "It will bring us a long way yet." Armond sniffed a tomato the color of deep-sky sunset, put it down, chose from another tray, sniffed again, nodded to the watchful merchant ferret.

The merchant saw the nod, noted the carton number on his order form.

"You'll do well," said the chef.

Armond turned to his friend, lifted his chin a fraction, listening. "Gren?"

From a scarf pocket Gerhardt-Grenoble drew forth a newspaper story, folded in half, offered it without comment.

His partner opened the clipping and read. THE WOOLLY WEST: MONTGOMERY FERRET'S RAINBOW SHEEP RESORT ONLY SOURCE OF FABULOUS FLEECE.

A few lines down, a photo of Monty holding a Rainbow lamb, then the story from the newspaper torn through, as though the reader hadn't cared what followed the headline.

Armond looked from the clipping to Gerhardt-Grenoble, expressionless. "You're leaving."

"Yes. Our agreement."

"I haven't forgotten. Either one of us. For any reason."

"La Mer is yours. Worldwide."

"Gren, you are at the top of your powers! This is what you want?"

The chef nodded. The proprietor, watching, saw the nod, made note to deliver two dozen red zucchini to La Mer.

"It will happen to you, Armond. There comes a time when we are called to surpass technique. And technique can only be surpassed by . . . what?"

"Warmth? Style? That certain *la*?"

"No. *Simplicity!*"

"Simplicity. Of course. But for simplicity you do not have to leave all that you have created. You go where? To . . ." Armond glanced at the clipping . . . "Montgomery?"

A smile. "To Montana."

"Your fame will follow you. Your reputation."

"No. Gerhardt-Grenoble was last seen . . . come to think of it, Armond, you yourself were the last animal to see him. Promise that you shall never tell where he went."

"How long? Will you return?"

"Enjoy La Mer."

There's an old ferret proverb: *Having climbed certain peaks we descend no more, but spread our wings and fly beyond.*

The two animals were quiet amid the *hup-hup-hya*'s, the callings and tumults of the market. Then the chef turned, nodded good-bye to his friend and disappeared into the crowd.

When one is a genius, thought Armond, one is often a little crazy.

5

"*H*UP . . . *HUP* . . . *hya!*"

At the command, a line of ranchkits hurled their soft Rainbow-wool lassos at a row of wooden sheep, fluffed out with hay. Every noose amiss, bounced off targets or fallen short in the dust.

The ranchpaw instructor shrugged good-naturedly, the ferret kits pulling in their colorful lariats, turning to listen.

Gerhardt-Grenoble Ferret noticed this, stepped from the ranch taxi into Montana summer, sniffed the sage and pine and wildflowers.

"When you hear *hya*," said the instructor, lean and prairie-wise, "the lasso wants to fly *over* the sheep. It wants to go over your sheep's neck instead of onto a nearby rock or bush. Someday, that saw-sheep could be a Rainbow wandered to the edge of a ravine or a gorge, your lasso's going to save its life. So we need to practice, don't we?" He showed them, backing away and away, an impossible distance, the kits thought, from his target.

"*Not too far, Dakota!*" one ranchkit cried, the others hushing her at once.

"Now make sure to carry the fall of the lariat a good way round from the slip to your paw," he called, whirling his azure lasso overhead, "so it'll snake on out after you let 'er go. Like . . . so . . . !"

The chef found the ranch office, a door marked *Monty Ferret*, and knocked.

"It's open."

He entered. The rancher looked younger than his photo in the newspaper. Broad of face and smoothly muscled, he was leaning over a ledger on his desk, at which sat a businessferret, her back to the door.

Gerhardt-Grenoble blinked. On the desk was a photo of Jasmine Ferret, an inscription he couldn't quite read.

Monty looked up from the ledger. "Howdy."

What was a photo of his celebrity friend doing in the wilderness of Montana? The chef blinked again, recovered his composure. "Howty." The word came out more Swiss than Western.

"How can we help you, today?"

"I'm your new chef."

The rancher smiled. "That's very nice, Mister . . ."

"Call me Cookie."

"That's very nice, Cookie, and I thank you for the thought, but we've already got a chef."

"Good. He'll want to be my assistant."

Monty laughed, ran a paw back from his forehead, smoothing the fur. "Bud's going to want to be your assistant?"

Cookie nodded.

"And maybe you want to tell me why Bud's going to want to be your assistant when he's already head cook, has been since we built the ranch?"

"I'll show you why."

Monty Ferret stroked his whiskers with a paw. "You'll show me."

"Yes."

Monty smiled again. "How are you going to show me?"

Cookie raised his eyebrows. "I will need three eggs."

Now the businessferret turned, amused at his words. Her dark mask delicately chiseled, eyes like cool ebony, missing nothing.

"This is Adrienne," said Monty, "our business manager." He laid a pencil for a bookmark in the ledger. "As a matter of fact, I believe we may have some eggs. Maybe Bud will lend a few."

Adrienne, still smiling, offered her paw.

6

MONTGOMERY FERRET rode Ladyhawke slowly and quietly in the dawn toward the high range, black woolen lariat coiled by his saddle horn, bedroll behind. Silent paints splashed the sky eastward, the air cold and sharp. He breathed deep.

It was breathing light itself, light and the cool saps of pine and sage and fir, of earth and grass mixed with the scents of pure river, of wildflower touched by the gentlest breeze.

Love it, he thought. Never get tired of this, never will.

He breathed again. He smelled distance in the air, the fragrance now of meadow grass as he rode to the Halfway Meadows, then the hint of Strawberry, now Citron and Peach, Tangerine and Blueberry and Licorice and Apricot.

Apricot ran to meet him, a sheep just a few paws high, bright color of fresh fruit and tantalizing fragrance to match.

Let's see what he wants, Ladyhawke, thought Monty. His delphin stopped, no word or touch. The rancher dismounted, reached a paw to the little clone. "Hi, Apricot! You're havin' a good time, are you?"

The Rainbow edged forward, a small Scottish reply in the rancher's mind: Monty, *we're lost!*

The ferret rubbed the sheep behind its ears. "How about that. You're lost again, are you?"

Apricot nodded. Aye.

"Ranchpaws been giving the classes, have they, on your outdoor savvy? *Orientation and Landmarks? Reading the Trail?*"

Aye.

"And we haven't been paying too much attention, have we?"

There were bonny wee blooms by the tarn, Monty, we could n'a pay attention!

Came the sound of tiny hooves, the fragrance of Lime and Plum and Cherry, then the animals themselves, pure colors to match.

Following them their guide, a ranchkit upon a delphin considerably smaller than Ladyhawke, bandanna tied about his neck, an earth-color wide-brim hat.

"Good morning, sir," said the kit.

"'Morning, Budgeron. How're your Rainbows doing?"

"Fine, sir. Everyone was up to watch the sunrise, today. After a bit we'll be moving down to the lower meadows, then back to the ranch."

Monty eased up into his saddle. "Everybody's happy?"

"Yes, sir, they seem to be. We'll have a little skip rope this morning, sir. And they'd like to splash in the river a bit."

"You'll be careful for the cold."

"Yes, sir. We've got towels and robes for them in the wagon, they can ride back to the ranch, if they want. But with their wool getting as long as it is, and being Rainbows, they'll stay warm. I don't suspect we'll have many riders, sir."

"I'd reckon not." Monty smiled for the youngster's grown-up talk, for his earnest responsibility. Budgeron Ferret was a city kit, but had taken to the land and its challenges. He had an ear for language and a way with words, an easy grace with them that required only vision and practice to perfect.

"You're taking notes, are you, Budgeron?"

"Notes, sir?"

"Montana. The sky, the rivers. What everyone says when they're talking. What you think about it. You're taking it all down."

The kit tilted his hat back, looked up at the rancher. "Why, yes, sir, I am."

"Do you know who you are, Budgeron?"

The kit looked away, thoughtful, back again. "I've got my hopes, sir . . ."

"You don't mind work, if it's hard enough?"

The kit shook his head. Was Monty Ferret reading his future?

"Then chances are, those hopes will be coming true. Not words, are going to lead you, as much as *ideas*, wouldn't you think?"

"I don't know, sir."

"You know, Budgeron. You may not be aware, *but you know.*"

Monty gave no command that the ranchkit could discern, but Ladyhawke began to walk away, and her rider didn't look back.

Left alone, the sheep turned to the kit as though to ask where are we, Budgeron? Where are we going now?

The young rider shook his head, touched the coil of his crimson lariat, a gift of wool from Strawberry. I know my own future? Why not? If Monty Ferret says so, why not?

"This way, please," he said to the Rainbows. They were enjoying the scenery. "Tangerine? Apricot? Come on, everybody. This way."

"Noodles 'n Sauce! Hear, you ranchpaws, ranchkits . . . Noodles 'n Sauce!"

Cookie's ferret-metal triangle clanged from his chuckwagon through the last of the afternoon as the kits finished rounding the Rainbows, gentling them into their camp for a night unseasonably cold, setting oat treats in bowls by their bedrolls.

Nearby, big Jupe Ferret finished writing for the day, closed his notebook, tucked it into his saddlebag by a paperback classic worn nearly through: Avedoi Merek's *The Ferret Way*. He rode the short distance to the chuckwagon, dismounted near the waterhole, let loose his delphin, Lightning, to drink.

"Noodles 'n Sauce is it again?" He enjoyed Cookie's humor. No matter the entrée, no matter the exquisite fragrance or exotic taste conjured from the simplest ingredients, the chef's blackboard menu read the same.

"Every day's not too often for Noodles 'n Sauce." Then the chef looked at him, testing, refining his Western accent with Swiss precision. "Should I be saying *ever* day, Jupe? Must I drop the terminal y?"

"*Every* day's just fine, you're doin' fine, Cookie." A rare smile, and a question never answered twice the same: "Where *do* you come from, by the way?"

Now the first of the ranchpaws arrived, and the chef served their meals smoothly, expertly, on tin plates. He grinned at the big ferret. "East Montana."

Jupe shook his head, muttered, "Yep. About Zurich east, I'd wager." Cook's got a right to his secrets, he thought.

This evening, Noodles 'n Sauce was forest-mushroom *soufflé à la*

Niçoise, light as fair-weather cloud, surrounded by fresh-roasted vegetables upon a bed of wild rice. A barrel of mountain-water stood on the chuckwagon, and dippers to refill the brimming cups.

Soon dozens of kits and 'paws converged from the cold about the chuckwagon, their delphins free to graze, stories of the day flying above the blue gingham cloth Cookie had spread near the campfire. Plates in paw, cups on the ground, the clink of forks and wonder at the tastes. A chorus of "Mmm" and "Delicious!" and "Well done, Cookie!" rang out, as ever it did, come mealtimes.

Sunset a final glow in the air, ranchkits circled the fire to hear the old-timers tell what they had seen in the wild, some of the stories true.

One ranchpaw, Dakota Ferret, stayed out upon his delphin, Shadow, awake in the near-freezing dark, standing guard in case a night-walking Rainbow should wander near the cliffs. He'd take his supper later.

From the busy day and crisp prairie air, the Rainbows were clustered and asleep save Violet, whose habit it was to contemplate long into the night.

Cookie stood quietly by his wagon sideboard, testing the soufflé, testing his assistant, Bud: would the tiniest pinch of saffron have improved the work?

Bud was a changed ferret from not so long ago. Cooking, once his job, had become his passion.

"I'd choose no for the saffron. However, do you think a trace of *cumin,* Chef?"

Cookie smiled. There is promise, here.

Jupe fetched his verse book from his saddlebag, plied on with pencil in the firelight, half-listening to the stories, writing slowly, verse after verse of epic rhyme. The day that Monty married, if ever that day would come, this rare-spoken 'paw planned to recite for the bride a firsthand history of his cousin.

Old Barclay Ferret finished his tale "The Last Lion in Great Falls County," calculated that the kits were properly amazed. He could see their breath in the chill, as they looked this way and that for great cats in the dark. The story was a little scary, he had to admit.

"Well, what're we here for, kits?" he asked, by way of restoring their mettle. "We're here for . . ."

"Action!" called the youngsters together.

"We're here for . . ."

"*Adventure!*"

"We're here for . . ."

"*Romance on the high plains!*"

"And as you seek," said the ranchpaw, finishing the ritual, "so shall you find."

He tilted his head toward Jupe. "Go on . . . ask," he said, and at last the ranchkit Alla called across the campfire, a little voice, "Will you read to us, Jupe? Will you read what you've written so far?"

The ferret looked up from his bent pages. "The whole of it?"

"If you would."

"Nope. I'd rather not."

The other ranchkits asked, Percifal and Boa, Budgeron and Kayla and Strobe, one after the other. "Will you read to us, Jupe?"

Patiently, his reply to each: "Thank you, no." "Poem's not for kits."

Then Cookie, from the chuckwagon, while Bud ground seeds of cumin: "Monty's with the flocks on the south range tonight, Jupe. You can read your story. They won't make a word of it to him. Will you, kits?"

The bulky ranchpaw looked up from his verse book to the young ferrets, narrowed his eyes. "You'll tell no one? Not a word? I'll not have anyone giving away that Jupe's doing a poem to surprise him, someday. That's a promise?"

The kits looked at each other; Strobe spoke for them all: "Promise."

"Well, then . . ." Jupe shifted his bandanna, turned it so that the faded flower-pattern rag hung at the back of his neck instead of the front, the better for reading. He turned the battered pages to the beginning, glinted at the kits suspiciously. "You sure you want to hear this . . ."

The kits nodded solemnly. Ranchpaws shared secret smiles. Nothing Jupe liked better than to read his rhymes to the young ones.

Cookie brought the kitchen lantern nearby, brighter than the light of embers, and Jupe Ferret began to read the history of his cousin Montgomery. If asked, he'd allow it might have been maybe a little romanticized, but mostly the poem was the way he had watched it happen.

He took a sip of mountain-water, looked one more time to the kits. They nodded. Go ahead, Jupe.

He began in a deep slow voice under the stars, a voice like woodsmoke, as seasoned by weathers as was the animal himself. Off in the distance a nighthawk whirred in the sky.

> "Now Monty was born with the wind in his fur," he read,
> "And a taste of the wild in his eyes.
> If you knew him back then, you'd have thought right away
> Here's a kit who's uncommonly wise."

He looked up, saw masks and whiskers pointed to him, rapt attention.

> "His dad was a rancher, his mom was a muse,
> Expect an unusual kin.
> A wonder with delphins, at home on the plains
> And knowing The Way from within.
>
> "He grew up a-ridin', a-ropin' an' such
> He grew up a-teachin' it, too.
> And one of his students her name was Cheyenne,
> The most beautiful ferret he knew."

The kits stirred. Monty had been in *love?*
Jupe cleared his throat.

> "The two they were friends from the start, don't you see,
> Two kits of the forest and streams.
> The boy with the wisdom of nature inside,
> The girl with her Hollywood dreams.

"They thought right at first that together they'd stay,
Two pals, all that fun—they would share it!
But it happened in time, for some reason and rhyme,
They'd part for a while, and they'd bear it.

"So Monty went off to his delphins and range,
Cheyenne to her cameras and stages,
He gave of his heart to perfect what he knew,
She gave of her soul to the ages.

"As Miss Jasmine Ferret she won all our hopes,
In her eyes we saw our own yearnings.
We saw her, we loved her—as simple as that,
On the screen we shared her bright learnings."

The ranchkits stared at each other. Jasmine Ferret!

"Now many a kit took wings from her scenes,
Many a high dream was founded
On Jasmine's pure vision of what we become
When we know that our spirit's unbounded.

"The price that she paid to deliver her gift
The price that she paid for her glory
Was loneliness, wishing that Monty were there
To be a dear part of her story."

Oh, my, thought the kits. *Monty and Jasmine Ferret!*

"And as for that ferret adrift on the plains?
As for Monty himself t'was decreed
He'd give to young ferrets all that he knew
Of endurance and power and speed.

"Of how to bear up when the going gets hard,
Of how to hang on when it's tough,

To care for the ones who're depending on you
To know when enough is enough.

"Then one day it happened, a letter from far,
Request that he'd take a strange mission.
The Rainbows from Scotland's chilly Loch Y'ar
All had the same odd ambition:

"To live in Montana, they said, to a one,
To see the Wild West and its wonder
To camp out in starlight and moonlight and plain,
To camp out in lightning and thunder.

"'Twas adventure they sought, those flocks from the Loch,
The wilderness to them was calling,
They offered to trade their fine wool—give it free
In return for a life so enthralling.

"So a bargain was struck, 'tween Monty and they,
Since they so wished for the sport,
He'd show them the life they dreamed of and more,
He'd open a Rainbow Resort!

"And open it did, the following June,
Surrounded by high-plain serenity,
With ranchkits to guide them, and ranchpaws to trust,
And every sheep-wished amenity.

"Now Rainbows are different, they tend to drift off,
Follow philosophy's quest,
But dangers there are on the plains, in the hills,
They need to be careful, lest:

"Off the cliffs they tumble and fall,
Off in the rivers they sweep,
Off in the desert they wander at all
Off into caverns, no peep

"To be heard, again from those Scots
Who chose high adventure that day,
Who trusted their Monty and threw in their lots
Thinking it all to be play.

"So safety's the foremost concern of their host,
Safety and sheep-lovin' fun.
Those ranchkits and ranchpaws they prize that bright wool,
But know commerce is only but one

"Of the elements, part of the deal
They entered with Monty that day,
The others were learning, adventure, and growth,
For sheep now embarked on The Way."

From the icy dark, a low thunder.

"Sheep-whisperer, they called him, because of the sense
Monty had, his knowledge of animals' thought . . ."

Jupe looked up; the thunder came louder now, approaching. Cookie and Bud looked northward, the chuckwagon's pots and pans trembling, tins against coppers and steels. Earthquake?

All were on their paws, their delphins whiffering, moving toward the safety of the campfire.

Jupe dropped the verse book: "*Stampede!*"

The ground was thundering steadily now, louder.

"Rainbows?" said Cookie. "*Stampede?*"

There was no place to run. The great flock poured out of the night, a tidal wave of woolly bodies, pounding across the plains, a cloud of dust behind them in the dark, up the rise toward the ranchpaws.

Tending the gentle animals, no ferret had thought of rainbow sheep as a force of nature, yet now they raced south, unstoppable in a tempest of hooves.

The ferrets stood and watched dumbfounded in frosty moonlight. Rainbows gone mad? But we *love* them! They won't trample us down!

To the youngest kit, they believed, and trusted. Each stood quietly, watched the cascade of animals approaching high speed in the dark.

At the instant the stampede would engulf the camp and their guides, not ten paws from the chuckwagon, the stampede stopped, Violet in the lead, breathing hard.

Behind her were Apricot and Blueberry, Citron, Peach, Orange and Huckleberry, the scents of flower and spice and fruit around them in a sea of fragrance all at odds with the urgency of the animals. The Rainbows halted, the cloud of dust did not, rolling past to fog them all and dim the moon.

Big Jupe strode forward. "What's on? What's the matter, Rainbows?"

No answer. Danger, Jupe sensed, or tragedy. If Monty were here, he'd have known the matter in an instant. As it was, the sheep stood a panting multicolor mass, fixing the ferrets with their gaze. Then all at once they turned right about, broke into a run, reverse-stampeding north down the slopes, the way they had come.

Jupe whistled for Lightning. "C'mon, 'paws!" he cried to the others as he mounted. "They need us to follow them back!"

A flurry of whistles and cries, ranchpaws and kits mounting up, all the ferrets flying northward, a stampede of their own after the ground-shaking herd.

Wild riding it was under the moon, delphins topspeed over broken ground, leaping rocks and fissures they wouldn't dare in daylight, spray flying as they galloped through the Oat Creek shallows. Yet so tuned to the moment were the ferrets that even ranchkits rode sure and straight through the dark. Something was terribly wrong, and their job was to make it right, not to stumble and be lost themselves.

Jupe rode hard through the midst of that tossing sea of sheep, fleet Lightning passing them left and right. *They're going for the cliffs!*

The herd thundered past its sleeping-meadow straight toward the rock falls beyond. Where's the cliff-watch? *Where's Dakota?*

The rider was nowhere in sight, and without him . . .

"Hyo! Rainbows!" Jupe bellowed. "*Cliffs! Cliffs! You Rainbows hold up now! Hyo! Whoa down!"* There was no response, not a sheep slowed.

Got to get ahead of the stampede, he thought. *Go, Lightning!* Get ahead, get the leaders stopped . . .

Jupe did not consider that if he succeeded, if he outraced the stampede but could not stop the Rainbows, he and his delphin would go first over the cliffs.

Now he was nearly to the front rank of the stampede; there was Violet, bounding, racing.

Too late. The cliffs yawned black ahead. He needed seconds more.

In that instant Violet—in that instant the entire herd of Rainbows stopped, all at once, before the cliff. Abruptly Lightning broke through the first line of sheep, all she could do to keep herself from falling. But stop she did, rocks and pebbles from her four-hoof slide tumbling on over the edge.

Jupe swung down. *"Violet!* What's goin' on, honey?"

The Rainbow looked at him, panting heavily, took a step forward, her nose pointing into the dark, looked back to Jupe. Swiftly arrived the other ferrets, off their delphins to the ground.

Violet took another step toward the cliff, fixed the ranchpaw with her eyes, blinked again beyond.

Jupe followed her gaze. The earth at the cliff was razor-sharp, fresh and new. The noose of a blue woolen lasso lay on the ground, its line trailing over the edge.

"Dakota!"

Jupe spun into action, called the nearest ferrets. "Barclay! Strobe! Boa! The cliff's caved, Dakota and Shadow's gone over the edge! We're going to need some lines to hold, goin' down. Alla, Budgeron, you come with me. Let's go!"

At once Jupe disappeared over the sharp break of the rock, his lariat hitched to Barclay's delphin, the ranchkit Alla following. Down the steep rubble they slid in the moonlight, rocks bounding and falling around them, each of the ferrets with a lariat cinched about their shoulders, lines straining upward.

At the end of the slide they found Shadow, nearly covered in rock and sand. A few paws beyond, protected by the body of his delphin, lay Dakota Ferret, thrown clear, unmoving. Alla ran to the ranchpaw, touched his head, put her ear to his chest.

"He's alive, Jupe. His head's cut, he's awfully cold, but he's got a heartbeat."

"Take your bandanna . . ." said Jupe, but Alla had already done so, whipped the cloth from about her neck, doubled it twice, placed it gently over the wound, tied it tight.

"How's Shadow?" she asked.

Jupe and Budgeron heaved themselves against the rubble over the fallen delphin, sweeping it away layers at a time. Shadow blinked awake as the weight came off, gasped for air, lifted his head toward Dakota.

"He'll be fine," said Jupe to the delphin. "So'll be you. Just lay still, let us get this stuff off you, here . . ."

The delphin breathed quick, shallow breaths, obeyed the ranch-paw, lay quiet.

Dakota Ferret moved his head. "Alla . . . Jupe. The cliff . . ."

"Shhh," said Alla. "Not now. Be still."

"I'm all right."

"Yes. Just be still."

As the rocks lifted from the delphin he twisted, found his feet, rose abruptly, shaking his mane in a cloud of pebbles and sand.

"Wind knocked out of you, Shadow . . ."

A step or two toward his rider, the animal wobbled but did not fall. He breathed deep, exhaled dust.

"May I at least sit up, ma'am?" Dakota reached to his head, touched the bandage.

"No," said Alla. "In a minute. Not now. Don't move."

The ranchpaw smiled at that, this kit ordering him about. But he lay where he was, near frozen but glad to be alive.

At the top of the cliff, young Boa had fashioned a knotted-loop bosun's chair from a doubled lariat, passed its lines to the rescue team over the saddle of his delphin braced at the clifftop. Without proper sheerlegs and tackle, he knew, his harness couldn't hoist the injured creatures clear, but the rig provided a near-weightless lift for what would have been a hard climb up the wall of rock.

By dawn the two animals had been made as comfortable as possible, shivering under blankets, warming near the campfire. Cookie fixed a steaming broth of whole-grain-and-vegetable ratatouille for Dakota, Bud made a bowl of hot dandelion oats and sprouted wheatgrass for Shadow. Circling the camp ranged the Rainbows, their own sunrise in the early light, concerned for the welfare of the watch ferret and his delphin.

No sooner had the two ceased to shiver than came a sound of hooves from the trail south, and before long a quiet word. "H'lo, all. How're we doing?"

Monty Ferret dismounted, raised a paw to Dakota and to Shadow, stay still. He looked to the ranchpaw's wound, blood soaking through the proper bandage Alla had placed there.

Instead of inspecting the damage, however, Monty closed his eyes for half a minute, knelt there unmoving. There's nothing here but perfect, he thought. Perfect expression of perfect life: can't be changed, no different truth. Then he turned to the delphin and knew the same, though it seemed to the others as if he preferred to examine the trouble with eyes closed than open.

Jupe shot a glance to Cookie, to see if he noticed the strange action.

The chef caught his eye, raised his brow, nodded slowly. Interesting, he thought. Montgomery Ferret is more than he appears.

Monty rose. "Reckon you two may pull through all right," he said. "How'd you come to think that hoppin' off cliffs would be a good idea?" He had no way of knowing, but he knew.

Dakota had opened his mouth to explain, but Violet pushed forward to stand by Monty. He nodded to her, reached down to stroke her twilight wool.

"I suspect this one had something to do with it? She was walking in the dark, maybe, thinking about the universe, not watching too well where she was going?"

"I'm sorry, Monty," said Dakota. "She got past before I saw her. She was nigh the edge when I got m' lasso on her, pulled her away.

Thought the incident was all over, started to go to her when the ground plumb went out from under us, Shadow and me, in a sudden th' air was full o' rocks. Next I knew I woke up powerful cold and pained and here was little Alla, tyin' up m' head and . . ." he smiled at the kit ". . . and givin' me orders."

The Rainbow stepped to the injured ranchpaw, brought her face close to his.

"Violet's awful sorry, Dakota," said Monty. "She wishes for all the world she'd have gone off some other direction."

"Sorry for nothin', Violet." The ranchpaw rubbed the sheep behind her ears. "We're both of us just doin' our job, and we best both be careful, 'round those edges!"

The fluffy animal looked to Monty.

"Violet appreciates your greatness of heart. She thanks you kindly for saving her life."

"'S nothin'," said the ranchpaw. "If she hadn't run for the camp, run back and brought the 'paws along, we'd be lying out there still, me and Shadow, gone to ice by now." He breathed her fragrance. "We saved each other's lives, Violet. That's always a pleasure."

Later, the Rainbows crowded together in the sunlight to see the collapsed earth, staying behind ropes the ferrets had laid on the ground a safe distance from the edge. They remarked to each other in their silent language about the excitement in the night, peril and adventure in the dark, just as they had known the Wild West would be. What a life!

Thought flashed in kaleidoscopic patterns through the little clones, relief that Violet and Dakota and his delphin had survived, that the adventure had all worked out for the best. The horror of the earth opening up, their run for help, the thunder of their hooves over sand and rock. They had never run so before, and the sound of it, *the sound of it!*

Away from the camp, standing upon a rock outcrop, Apricot relived that desperate wonderful stampede, the wind of it beginning in her mind, moving her hooves in slow-time to match. The rhythm echoed to the others: *clak-clak!* clik, clik, clik . . . *clak-clak!* clik, clik, clik . . .

The other clones felt it too, knowing her thoughts. They moved to bare rock places, augmenting with their own hooves Apricot's earthy dance. They joined in, following her lead on the first two beats only, the little sheep herself following with a solo triple-beat:

Clak-clak! stamped the first few Rainbows.

clik, clik, clik . . . Apricot tapped on the rock.

CLAK-CLAK!! Other sheep ran to join, more on more.

clik, clik, clik . . .

CLAK-CLAK!!!

The sheep were absorbed, watching the sound in their linked minds as well as hearing it over the rocks, through the earth itself. Then, as Rainbows do, they began to innovate:

clik-ity-clik-ity-clik . . . tapped Apricot.

CLAK-ITY-CLAK-ITY, CLAK, CLAK-CLAK!!! stamped the flock.

clikity-clikity clik, clik-clik!

CLAKITY-CLAKITY CLAKITY-CLAKITY CLAKITY-CLAKITY CLAKITY-CLAK!!!!

clikity-clikity, clikity-clikity, clikity-clikity, clikity-clik!

Then Apricot and flock began weaving their parts together, solo and chorus intermingled: *CLAKITY* clikity *CLAKITY!* clikity *CLAK-ITY!!* clikity *CLAKITY-CLAKITY, CLAKITY-CLAKITY*, clikity-clikity-clik: *CLAKCLAK!!!*

With the last beat the Rainbows stood still as noon, listened to the sound of their hooves echoing up the canyons. It sounded like applause, from the hills. When the sheep looked up, they saw it was: a ring of ranchpaws and ranchkits clapping and whistling, tingling with the rhythm, yearning to be Rainbows themselves, and join the dance.

The little animals looked at each other, silent pleasure. What fun! If we sort ourselves now by colors, they thought, then wheel the colors in squares and lines and angles . . .

Thus from tragedy averted was born the Montana Rainbow Zouave Rhythm March Corps and Scottish Dance Company.

The cliffs haunted Monty. Not for their danger, for all would be more careful in rugged country than ever before. The cliffs haunted into a mirror of a different time, slipped loose from where he had tucked it away to forget.

That evening Monty Ferret rode Ladyhawke from the campfire into the open country, lost in memory.

7

THE DRIVER HAD stopped, climbed down from the stagecoach to pick up the mail from the trail-box for Fort Laramie. One letter slipped from his glove, cartwheeled away in the wind. Before he could catch it, the snow-flash envelope fluttered at the hooves of the skittish creatures hitched to the Rock Springs–Denver *Comet*.

Rondo, the lead delphin, whinnied and reared from the flash, then he bolted and the animals ran for their lives. The stagecoach leaped away, driverless, pounding down the narrow desert trail, sagebrush blurring by, the six runaway delphins not pulling the *Comet* so much as frantic to get out of its way.

The clank and jangle of the harness disappeared in a storm of high wheels spinning, iron rims crashing through sand and rock, the coach tilting, swerving.

Tumbled from the velveteen seat within, the beautiful Dulcimer Ferret gasped but did not cry out. Sole passenger, top-level courier for the governor of Wyoming Territory, she knew the West. Those delphins were far more frightened than she, and they'd drag a capsized coach nonstop, drag it to a trail of kindling in the desert.

She leaped for the hatch overhead, forced it open, fought to climb through and catch the reins loose-tied at the driver's seat.

The coach flew over a rise, crashed to earth in a cloud of spraying rock and dust, a snap of breaking springs, Dulcimer slammed from the hatch against the wooden armrest to the tilting floor.

At once she was on her paws, blood streaming from a gash on her head, the coach careening downhill toward the edge at Laramie Rim.

She threw herself again at the hatch, this time struggled through, caught the seat midjounce with one paw, grabbed the bundle of reins with the other, pulled hard.

Paws braced on the topping-rail, she strained against the tall brake handle, smoke streamed from the wheels. Still the delphins galloped for the cliffs, uncaring, desperate to escape the coach.

Mindless of disaster ahead, Dulcimer Ferret snapped the reins an expert turn around the gully-head, hauled back with all her might.

"There we go," she cried, the coach thundering, crashing on. "It's all right, you delphins, everything's all right!"

Heads high against the tension bar-tight on their reins, hooves sliding against the weight behind them, hearing her voice soothing, calling, the delphins slowed, ever so slightly, cliffs stark and close.

"Whoa down, now! Whoa down, little ones."

Gallop to canter went the delphin team, then trot to walk and finally to stand, sides heaving, heads turning toward the driver as Dulcimer eased the reins.

The lovely ferret slipped from the high seat, ran at once to the lead delphin, held his neck, stroked his nose. The cliff dropped sheer, less than a hundred paws distant.

"There now, there's my good delph. We had a nice run, didn't we?"

She ruffled the satin mane, softly, as though time had stopped. In a moment it did.

"*CUT! And print! Spectacular shot, Jasmine!*" Gemini Ferret released the bullhorn trigger. He looked to the camera operator perched behind the eyepiece, location baseball cap turned backward, embroidered silver on black, sweeping letters: *Dulcimer Ferret.*

The C.O. nodded. "Got it, G.F."

The director trembled, deep to his bones. He lifted the bullhorn once more. "*Terrifying, Jasmine,*" he called to his leading lady, "*but spectacular!*"

He didn't care if his star had grown up a ranchkit in Montana, he didn't care she was an expert rider. That shot was too close to the edge for Jasmine Ferret, megafilm or not.

"We won't need to cover that, will we, Streak?"

"No, sir. It's safe."

The director glanced at the clock, squinted to the angle of the sun. "A break, gentleferrets, then let's set scene ninety-one."

In the desert by the stagecoach, Montgomery Ferret shrugged out of his hidden harness on the down-camera side of the lead delphin and grinned at the actress.

"You had me goin', Cheyenne. Another second or so, I was about to ask Rondo to haul up pretty short." He patted the lead delphin, offered a carrot-cube the animal quickly accepted.

Jasmine smiled back. "Another second or so, Monty, I'd have been hoping you would!" She touched the syrup blood with her paw. "Am I a mess?"

"You could never be that, Cheye. I swear, the world's the richer for getting to watch you on-screen!"

She touched his shoulder. "Thanks for being here, Monty. I wouldn't have done the film without you to back me up."

The ranchpaw nodded. "You're doing fine, kit, I haven't had to step in once. But I'm happy to ride around and watch."

All the fame, he thought, and she hasn't changed. Not toward me, nor anybody. She's still the kit next door, loves the movies.

The script ferret approached, delicate, courteous. "We're setting up for ninety-one, Miss Jasmine. Makeup is going to want you to stop by, when you can . . ."

"You mean they want me right now, don't you, Jessie?"

A quick smile. "Sooner's probably better than later, Miss Jasmine."

"On my way." But she tarried.

"Monty . . ."

"Yes, ma'am."

"I know we wanted our dinner tonight . . ."

Monty gathered the tangled reins, fastened them neatly at the topping-rail, "That's no problem, Cheye. You've got to be tired, this close to wrap. We'll have it some other time."

"Oh, no! I mean, could we meet earlier? We've been so rushed, we haven't talked, there's so much to say."

There was no hiding his pleasure. "You name the minute."

"After the dailies this evening, come by my trailer. We'll have our dinner in, if you want, a little more time to talk."

"You don't need to rest?"

"You are my rest, Monty." Then she turned and hurried off to makeup.

The burly ranchpaw felt like a kit again, slipping out his window to ride in the moonlight with his friend.

Monty turned away, back to the team of stunt delphins.

"That was a good job, guys and gals." More carrot-cubes appeared for all, and from the hackamore at Rondo's muzzle he led them, a slow walk, back to the trail. "You are a team of one-take delphins, if ever there was. You are professionals." He winked at the leader. "And you did have me goin', Rondo. That was right down to the edge."

The delphin nodded, satisfied. But then he nudged the wrangler, as much as to change the subject, *Does that sound right to you, Monty, that my character would bolt and run away from a letter blowing in the wind? The script says it's supposed to look like a bat. Couldn't we have a real bat, a big one? Then I agree, my character would bolt!*

Monty smiled. "We don't write the script, Rondo. We just make it come alive."

The delphin sighed. *All the same, between you and me . . .*

"Between you and me? A big white bat coming at me, I'd be a lot more likely to bolt than he drops a letter . . ."

"Monty," came the voice of the assistant director on the bullhorn, "would you check the coach, please? We'll need another shot if we can, Lyndelle doubles for Jasmine, this time the close shot on the delphins, and we don't need to take it so near the Rim."

Monty called back. "Coach is fine, sir." Special-built, steel-reinforced, it could take ten runaways between repairs.

"Ready for close-ups, Rondo, everybody! Thirty minutes!"

The silence of agreement.

"All right," said Monty, "let's bring her back up on the road."

The delphins clambered up the loose-rock slope at the edge of the trail, empty stage clattering behind.

A few steps, and the leader nudged Monty once more.

"What's on your mind, Rondo?"

The delphin tossed his head, *If you get a chance, could you talk to G.F.? Tell him about the bat? I'm sure he'd agree: a big white bat, a delphin-eater. Else he's going to lose the audience—"What kind of delphin runs away, somebody drops a letter?"*

Monty patted the animal. "I just work here, same as you, Rondo," he said, "but I'll ask."

Later, stroking his black whiskers, Gemini Ferret listened to Monty, nodded. "A fine idea. Your delphin's right. That's the better shot."

In the final cut of *Dulcimer Ferret*, the letter dropped, it blew in the wind, billowed into a death-color bat near the size of Rondo himself. Test audiences were hypnotized by Jasmine Ferret, but when asked about the runaway scene, not a single viewer blamed the delphins for bolting.

⌢

Monty looked at her in the candlelight, the rush and dust of the day settled and gone. She wore a sheer sky scarf and a locket: a silver heart.

"You ought to know I'm happy for you, Cheyenne," he said at last. "You're good at this business. I'm proud of you."

"Thanks, Monty." She smiled at the strong steadfast ferret her young riding teacher had become. "We have a good script, don't we?"

He looked at her, level dark eyes. "It's not the script. Do you know they cried, the crew, watching the dailies yesterday? They watched you on the screen and they had tears in their eyes. I'm talking about the crew!"

"Monty, I'm doing what I dreamed I could do. It's hard, sometimes. There's a price, but . . ."

She fell quiet, shifted her talk to telepathy and knew he could understand her wordless, how she felt, what she missed.

He missed it too, and knowing her sad beyond his means to comfort, he spoke again. "Pretty locket."

She brushed a tear, thanked him silently for changing the mood. "Want to see?" She slipped it from her neck, placed it before him.

"I'd best not."

"Oh, go ahead, ranchpaw. It won't bite you. Open it."

He touched the clasp and the silver heart sprang open. Inside, a single blue mountain daisy. He blinked, looked at her. "I remember."

That was dangerous, too. She turned the talk yet again.

"CineMustelid?"

"Still there in Little Paw," he said. "Alexopoulos doesn't brag about you, but he lets it be known that Jasmine Ferret sold tickets from this very booth, and she sat in this seat, and that one, and that one . . . He loves you, Cheye."

"I love him, too. I owe him."

Meals barely touched, they talked that evening about the days when they were kits together, the rides they took, she yearning to know that Sable Canyon was safe, their secret meadows, their old friends.

"Tell me, Monty. The most important event for you since . . . since we were together."

That would have to be his wild delphin encounter, what they did at the pond when they found the ferret was not just listening, he was understanding most of what they said.

"That big guy!" Monty shook his head. "Cheyenne, after all my guessing, clue by clue, I knew their language. It's not words, it's . . . I had followed them all the way to Button Water, up the draw from Johnny Polecat's old cabin, and the Alpha, the leader, I watched him say to the others, *Our ferret friend thinks he knows what we're saying!*"

Monty took a sip of mountain-water from the glass in front of him. "Then he angled to my left, as if I were a delphin myself, and he said, *If this kit can understand me, he'll wade out till his nose is just above water. And if he does that, we'll show him what no ferret has ever seen. I want you all to form a circle around the edge, and then real slowly, every one of us, we'll bow to him. But nobody move yet, he's got to wade in the water to his nose.*"

Monty's eyes were bright, remembering. "Now this is a bond of twenty-four wild delphins, Cheyenne, they're going to make a circle and they're going to bow to me! I watched the Alpha say that." He stopped, tried again to explain. "It's not words, they use. It's not even sounds, all the time. It's little movements, they shift their weight, shake their mane, flick an ear or an eyelash. And it's in their minds. There's nothing they can't say!"

She watched her old friend, the story gentled in his love for the animals.

"If I walked into the pond, now, they were all to circle and bow. So I showed 'em. I walked straight out into that water." He laughed at himself. "Mind, it was springtime, the snow melting. But I was so excited, Cheye, I can't tell you. I was going to say I understood! So out into that . . . well, it was liquid ice. I walked until just my nose was above the water, nose and whiskers and my eyes, I was willing to freeze to death, looking for what they were going to do. And do you know what they did, do you know what those delphins did?"

"They spread out around the pond," she said, charmed by his tale, "left and right, and they formed a circle . . ."

He shook his head, a grin to melt her heart. "Nothing! They did *nothing!* They looked at me as though I was gone crazy, some ferret fell into the pond!"

"Not even one little bow?"

"Oh! that was a cold ride home! They were whinnying and laughing, behind me."

"Monty! That was cruel of them!"

He held up a paw in the delphins' defense. "They didn't push me, Cheye. They didn't force me. You've got to love an animal's got a sense of humor." He touched his glass, too happy to drink. "Next time I found them, the Alpha came over and he said he was sorry for their little joke, that I nearly froze. But his ears were way forward and his nose was twitching, the way they do when they laugh."

He went on for a while about the delphins. Never did he tell her that he had framed the photograph she had sent from the Young Actors' Home, that he kept it on the rough wooden desk of his cabin, that he talked to her picture every day, that he loved her still.

He told his stories and he listened to hers, about her first days in a strange city, jammed with auditions, with disappointment, triumph, with acting classes. About her discovery as an actress, in spite of her comment when the floodlight fell. The screen test for *First Light*, the leading role, how lucky she had been . . .

"Not lucky, Cheyenne," he said.

"There are lots of kits in Hollywood, Monty. Looking for a break. Not many of them ever . . . there's a lot of support, but it's really hard . . ."

He lifted his water glass, watched her in a quiet toast over the rim. "'*She's magic in the camera!*' Gemini Ferret said that, yesterday. He said everybody knows it: Jasmine Ferret's one of the greatest stars in the history of film. '*She's not her character, Monty, she's the soul of her character!*'"

"He said that?"

Monty nodded.

"How . . ." She reached for her glass. "How very kind . . ." Then she turned the conversation back to Montana. "Trish and Zander?"

He smiled. "Zander's in Scotland."

"Scotland!"

"So much I haven't told you. Zander cloned what they call rainbow sheep. There's thousands of them now, they all want to see the Wild West. I'll be working with him, a little, on that. And Trish found her mate, she's married, moved to West Palm Beach, plays her harp still, recitals. Nakayama Ferret's a CPA, his own accounting firm."

"Trish loved her music and her numbers."

"So does Nakayama. He plays the flute, they do quadratic equations, for fun." Monty ran his paw over his forehead. "I'm an uncle, Cheye! Little Chloe. As cute a kit as you ever did see . . ."

His voice trailed off, lost in how swiftly the old days had passed. He hadn't known so many choices had gone by till this moment with his friend.

"And Monty?" she said.

He paused, decided not to burden her with his feelings. "Monty's doing fine. I'll probably never see the sights, like you and Zander and

Trish. Don't really much want to. I'm happy in Montana. That's my home, Cheyenne. Montana and the delphins, ranchkits come learn to be 'paws. Pretty soon a fair-size flock of sheep coming to visit. I guess I love animals." He wondered, do I sound like a failure, explaining?

He knows himself, she thought. What a success he's become! She smiled, shy. "Is there somebody in your life?"

She thought he hadn't heard, her friend studying his water glass. Then he raised his eyes, looked directly into hers. "Why, yes, Cheyenne. There is somebody in my life."

She pushed his meaning away. "That's good to hear. I'm happy for you, Monty."

"Thank you. I hope there's somebody in your life, too."

Since she had become the world's Jasmine Ferret, since her first role in *The Lady Speaks*, the match-loving tabloid press had pondered who should be her mate. Her name had appeared a dozen times in the "Wouldn't It Be Nice?" column of *Celebrity Ferrets Today*, linked with Heshsty, with most of her leading actors. Once there had been rumors of Jasmine and Stilton Ferret, when she and the billionaire had passed through Los Angeles International Airport on the same day.

She thought about his question, wondered how to answer. "There is someone," she said.

"If you have any trouble with this animal," said Monty, "you tell him you've got a friend back home, he's a wild ferret and he fancies he's looking out for Cheyenne."

"You don't want to believe the press too much," she said. "The tabs mean well, but how they carry on! Heshsty's a dear, he's my pal, we love to work together. I'd like you to meet him, someday." She sighed. "No, the somebody I care about, I don't have any trouble with him, Monty." A trace of sorrow in her voice.

And there they left it. The hours weren't enough for what they needed to say, but neither would the day have been enough, or the week. Meal finished, candle burned low, Monty rose. "It's late. I'd best be on my way."

They stepped from her trailer into the cool air, her silver fur turned bright as snow in the moonlight. "You're glad, too, Monty? You're happy being a ranchpaw?"

He smiled. "I get kidded sometimes, I don't mind. I like being the ferret who talks to delphins, I like being a sheep-whisperer. There's a lot to learn that nobody knows, or probably much cares. I care. That's enough."

"I care, too." She hugged him gently, kissed his cheek the way she had when they had parted in Little Paw, so long ago.

They stood close in the quiet. If I tell her how I feel, he thought, and if she told me the same, what of her career? I'll not say a word to change her future.

"Well," he said, finally. "G'night, Cheyenne. You don't know how much . . ."

"I know." She leaned her head against his shoulder. If she told him how she felt, and if he felt the same, might it turn his destiny, might it stop a gift he would otherwise give to the world? She watched him for the longest seconds, considering. "I miss you, Monty. I miss home."

"I miss you too, Cheye. Someday maybe you'll come home. Not now. Not for a while. But . . ."

She warmed in his reminder that she had a choice. "Sometimes I forget I have a home. But I love my work."

He said nothing.

At last she let him go. "Night, Monty. Thanks. So much . . ." She returned to the trailer, forced herself not to look back. She so missed him, the quality of him, his confidence. She missed the home she saw, shimmering there in the window of her friend. Had Montgomery Ferret lifted a paw or said a word, she would have stayed with him for the rest of her life.

He did not. Quietly, the door between them closed.

Shooting on *Dulcimer* wrapped the next day. A chartered helicopter arrived for Jasmine, she was off to the starring role in *West from Home*, Taminder Ferret's towering novel of a single-minded independent animal, her beauty, her determination, her rise to stardom. Heshsty Ferret had chosen her for the role, the tabloids would suggest, for the pleasure of fiction become fact, scenes a mirror of the movie star's life.

For Monty, it was that sudden. Coaxing delphins into trailers, he glanced to watch the rotorcraft hovering down, glanced again to see it lift off a few minutes later, tilt forward and disappear to the east. He didn't know it had come for Jasmine till the A.D. mentioned she was gone.

8

"Monty Ferret's Rainbow Sheep Resort and Ranchpaw Training Center, this is Sophia how may I help you?"

Jupe Ferret shook his head. Telephones, he thought.

He didn't spend much time in the office; came now in need of notepads for his saga. Why a ranch needs an office, or a telephone, he wasn't sure. Though the ranchpaw allowed that the world had changed since he and Monty were kits in bandannas and hand-me-down Western hats, one doesn't require a telephone in the high country to get along.

He listened with half an ear while the bright young office manager explained what he had heard more than once: We're sorry, but Rainbow wool may not be purchased outright. The sheep have the right of approval over every use of their product. Approval will not be granted without a meeting between the designer and the Rainbows themselves. The schedule is not difficult but the travel may be; our nearest airport is Helena, Montana, and the drive to the ranch will take nearly two hours. Thank you for calling . . .

The ranchpaw searched through the supply cabinets, found the clothbound tablets, wrote an IOU: *Two of these. Jupe.*

An automobile arrived outside, and shortly a knock on the counter, an executive inquiring. "Is this the office?"

"Yes, ma'am," said Sophia, rising to help, "you've come to the right place."

The telephone rang again. "Could you get that, Jupe?" the receptionist asked, sweetly.

Nearly to the door, holding his notebooks, the ranchpaw stepped back inside. He reached over the counter between a pair of city plants that would have been in real trouble if ever they had to live on the range, lifted the receiver.

"Sheep farm."

A soft French accent. "This is Monty Ferret's Rainbow Sheep Resort?"

"Yep."

"Last week I called. Could you tell me, now, a time to visit?"

"Friday," said Jupe. The day of the Canyon Performance, they'd be all brushed up.

"For approval? We can meet . . . ?"

"Yep."

"At . . . ah . . . three o'clock?"

"Yep."

"My name is"—the caller paused, understanding—"not necessary, is it?"

"Nope."

"Friday at three."

A crisp nod from Jupe, and he hung up the receiver. Then he left the office, headed toward the barn.

9

Budgeron Ferret was up early, out in the predawn frost of the empty corral, writing pad on the middle rail, words by moonlight.

I'm scared, he wrote. *Tomorrow's the big ride, we're on our own, all the way to the high range, Thunder Mountain. Rainbows don't care, for them it's a picnic.* He paused, chewed on the end of his pencil. *Scares me most are the cliffs. Me and Strobe, we've got to keep them away from the edges. Cookie tells me be careful, there's places the trail's hard to find. Boa and Alla right behind us, don't let me lose the way. . . .*

There was a sound, the scrape of a match behind him in the barn, so sudden in the stillness that he spun around, dropped his pencil.

"Up early, Budgeron." Monty Ferret's mask and whiskers glowed in the light of flame touching lantern wick, sunrise not a hint in the east. He held the match upright, flicked the stem of it so quickly that the fire disappeared, held it for a while to cool, stuck it into his hatband.

"Yes, sir." Budgie stooped to recover his pencil.

The sheep-whisperer hung the lantern from a spike in the barn wall, leaned against the top rail of the corral, looked toward the mountain's ghost in the moonlight, nearly to the horizon. "Tomorrow's the big one."

"Yes, sir."

"Worried about the cliffs?"

"Yes, sir, I am."

"Good."

Budgie thought about that.

"It's the dangers you don't worry about that'll get you." Monty touched the wood of the rail. "When you're surprised, you're in trouble."

Then he turned, lifted the lamp, walked toward the ranch house. "Different from writing, I'll bet."

The ranchkit followed. "I wouldn't know, sir."

"You will." They walked in silence for a while. "The kits that come here, Budgeron, I can tell the ones going to change the world."

After a while Budgie found the courage to ask. "How do you tell that, sir?"

"They're the ones who know what they want." Monty ambled toward the dining hall, no hurry, lantern casting a sphere of golden light about the two animals. "You take Boa, he's brought his tool bag to a ranchpaw summer. No question that kit's going to be some master mechanic, one day. I don't know what kind of machine, but Boa's your animal makes engines run. Lives are going to depend on that kit, someday."

"So why is he here, sir? You don't need engines on a sheep ranch."

"Don't need writers, either." Monty opened the door to the building, washing in the first glow of sunrise. "Boa's here the same reason you are."

Budgie looked up, confident. "To prove we can do it."

The rancher led the way to a private wing of the dining hall, arches facing west, tiled path terminating in the white stucco of a walled patio: green plants potted close, a table, chairs, an adobe fireplace, coals sending a blanket of warmth near the table.

Monty pulled a chair out for Budgeron, seated himself opposite, set the lantern on the floor.

"You ever read Taminder Ferret?" he asked. *"Sea and Stars?"*

Budgie opened his mouth, closed it. *"Sea and Stars,* yes, sir! How did you know? *Winter Fire!* And *West from Home!* Those books, sir, he showed me what can happen! It stops being a page of print, the words they melt and they change into colors, into places, into animals, there's this *adventure,* sir, that the world disappears clear till the end and you're *gone,* and finally you wake up and somehow . . . somehow *all this came out of a book,* a book that you can hold in your paws but if you open it anywhere you're all tumbled back again into his world and *he's the only one can take you there!"*

It was more than he had said in one burst all summer.

The rancher listened, watched. "Want to talk about writing?"

Sunrise finally balanced on the hills toward Devil's Fork, Cookie appeared, rolling a polished wooden cart of ingredients before him. This morning he was respectfully silent, save for a subtle wink of recognition to Monty's guest. On the dining-hall blackboard, under *Monty's Private Breakfast This Morning With*: he had chalked *Budgeron Ferret.*

On the coolest spot of the grill he set his copper omelet pan, frothed and spiced *oeufs à l'orange* cooked slow and paper-thin, then deftly rolled for the two, the kit talking earnestly, the rancher listening, nodding now and then. Meanwhile, paws like an illusionist's, Cookie prepared *riz espagnol flambé* to half-circle the omelet, a splash of watercress, a meteor of Montana salsa. The meal he set before the two was lighter than morning air, wafting the colors of the day beginning.

"Thank you, Cookie," said Monty.

"Very much," said the kit. It felt odd to Budgeron, that today he was special, for once he couldn't chat and laugh with Cookie over the morning's exotic entrée.

The chef nodded to them both, a quiet smile, rolled his cart softly away, leaving coals simmering to themselves behind him.

The two talked on, until the ranch stirred awake an hour later to the enchanted clang of Cookie's triangle.

Monty rose. "I guess you've got a day ahead of you."

"Yes, sir. Thank you for your time and the breakfast!"

The kit was a few steps down the hallway when the rancher called after him, "Oh, Budgeron! For you."

Budgie turned back, blinked at Monty, holding out a book. "It's yours. It's for you."

"Thank you, sir!"

It wasn't till he was back in the bunkhouse, the others gone to breakfast, that he examined the gift.

White letters angling on a night-blue jacket: *West from Home*. The ranchkit opened the cover, his paws trembling. Opposite the title page, an inscription:

Whoever you are, young writer, bold dark sweeps of the pen, *Now that Monty Ferret has given this book to you, my torch is yours to light with your own flame, and one day to pass along.*

It was signed in a flourish: *Taminder Ferret.*

10

JASMINE FERRET sat erect on the ruffles of her dressing-table chair, refused to be exhausted. Tuesday she had wrapped on *Pheretima*, an extravagant shoot in Venezuela. Wednesday a jet to the south of France for the Boxxes Film Festival, Thursday another round of interviews with news and magazine ferrets, last night the College of Actors Awards, evening swiftly turned to morning, no chance to rest, today a flight with an old friend to his mystery destination.

She leaned toward her mirror, ran an ebony brush through her fur, lifting and turning, leaving it tousled behind in what the world had come to call the Jasmine Look. At the edge of the mirror, an old railroad ticket, punched with a hole in the shape of a heart. Adjoining, a snapshot of a handsome young ferret in bandanna and hat.

Two crystal cubes were placed at the rear of the dressing table, each mounted on a silver spire, inscriptions illegible in the mirror. In front of them, hastily set down, two Whiskers, streamlined ferret sculptures, each quite heavy and gold. Engraved on the first, *COAA Best Actress: Jasmine Ferret.* On the other, the evening's highest award. *Kits' Choice: Jasmine Ferret.*

From her armoire she chose a filmy scarf by Donatien Ferret, cobalt and foam silver, to match her locket. The touch of a discreetly monogrammed whisker-comb, the lightest dust of chalk, she was ready a few minutes early.

Her face had changed, but she hadn't noticed. There was wisdom now, with the luminous beauty.

By the mirror a great round window framed her Malibu beachfront, ocean stretching beyond. Stark and sharp, that horizon. Not since she was a kit had she lived with the green fields and mountains of Montana. She missed the sound of the river, she missed still clear air.

She reached to the locket, opened it, watched an old scene conjure itself once more from that high mountain daisy, caught in time. She had been called to the stage, and she did not regret it. The price, though, the price! To live alone is to live without intimacy, a price that can turn one to stone.

I miss home, she thought, I miss it so much. And now . . . do I even have a home, anymore?

A soft knock. "Monsieur Donatien Ferret to see you, ma'am."

"Thank you, Gweneth." Jasmine did not bother to glance at the delicate clock on her dresser, for it would be precisely 1 P.M. The designer had a sense of business unsurpassed in the industry, and that sense began with punctuality.

The actress rose, followed the balcony of her dressing room to a sunlit living space, glass and polished wood and silk velvets, overlooking the sea.

A cosmopolitan animal, perfectly groomed, turned at her entry, a sand-color gift box near him on the table. His soft French accent: "Hallo, Jasmine. Congratulations once more. First your Ice-Cubes from Boxxes, last night Whiskers twice over! *Magnifique*, as always."

"Hello, Donatien. Thank you."

"This is not the best time? You're a little tired, a little sad."

The actress smiled. "I was, a while ago. You brighten my day."

"It is my happy spirit which does this for you. You have changes coming, Jasmine?"

One goes nowhere in business, Jasmine thought, without being sensitive to others.

"I'll tell you later." She noticed the box on the table, did not inquire.

"You promised to come with me, no questions," he said. "But a later day will also be fine . . ."

Jasmine smiled, shrugged away fatigue. "No questions. When do we leave?"

"Now." The designer lifted the gift box. "For you."

"Thank you. You're so kind." She untied the ribbon, lifted the lid. Within, under a veil of tissue paper, a wide-brim Western hat. Not a hat that a ranchpaw would wear, for it was blue, the color of Montana sky.

She looked up, startled, eyes wide to Donatien. *How could you know?*

As she seemed stunned at the sight, her friend lifted the hat from its box, set it back on her head. "Tsk," he murmured. He shook his head no, reset the hat, tilting it low over her eyes. He brightened. "*Voilà! C'est parfait!* Jasmine, not a word."

He turned her to the mirror, saw the look in her eyes. "Not a word! I know! *You love it!*"

☺

The two arrived at the Van Nuys airport, the actress and the designer, that glamorous pair from the white limousine, up the stairs of a business jet, *Donatien* lettered on its fuselage, gold against black. No one knew what Jasmine thought, dozing through the flight, the dust-blue Western hat pulled to shade her eyes, although a glimpse of the two would be reported next day in *Who's Together?* magazine.

They landed that afternoon at Helena Municipal Airport, stepped into a dark limousine and set off southward.

Jasmine listened as they drove, the designer stitching in a fabric of coincidence the depth of which he did not know.

For his new scarfwear, Donatien told her, he needed Rainbow wool and none other, and do you believe that in only one place can it be found? Calls to Montana, an appointment made for a touch of business, a minute for the canny Rainbows to agree that a line of haute-couture scarves in such exquisite taste was proper use of those rare colors.

The perfect day, he told her—Jasmine to join him for a rest, a grounding she could not help but enjoy, a visit to the hills and plains of which she had so often spoken, not far from her kithood home.

She nodded, a smile for her friend. "You're an angel, Donatien!"

He could not have known, nor did she wish to tell him just now. If such loving coincidence brought her here, would it not find Monty home, could their paths touch again?

She felt her heart beating. There's order in the world, she thought, there's a beautiful order in the world.

11

Monty Ferret had ridden Ladyhawke the back way, following the streambed to Northstar, a town that now, with the success of the sheep resort, called itself Gateway to the Rainbows. By the road stood a sign painted by kits, depicting a countryside amok with fluffy colors.

He rode slowly, watched the hillsides, listened to the stream, the birds, to his own heart speaking.

Everything I wanted, he thought, everything I hoped for, it's come true. I'm just a country ferret, loved my mountains, the outdoors, Montana, and here I live. I loved my delphins, wanted to understand all the animals around me, now I do, pretty well, and we all get along just fine. I wanted to make their dreams come true, the little Scots, and the ranchkits, too. He smiled. We show 'em Action, Adventure, Romance on the High Plains! and sure enough, the sheep are happy and the kits go home strong and wise and kind, they earn their own respect. That's what I wanted for them, and that's what I got.

I've had a few questions of my own, he thought, found a few answers that work for me.

He lifted his hat and ran a paw over his forehead, smoothing the fur. A soul can learn a lot, in one lifetime, but even so . . .

Ladyhawke huffed, stopped, blinked to watch a small ferret, appeared from empty air.

On the middle of the stream, a shimmering nutmeg coat, a clove-color mask, solemn amusement.

"Hello, Monty." The ferret's dark eyes locked on his. "Need some help?"

The rancher smiled down at her, nodded at the current splashing over her paws. "Counts as pawprints, does it?"

"It does, thank you," she said. "Need some help?"

"I miss her, Kinnie. I miss Cheyenne."

"She's—"

"I know she's got her destiny, I know I've got mine. I ask within, and the answer comes back that everything's okay, it's just the way we meant it to be. I've done mostly what I came here to do, seems to me. Maybe she has, too, maybe not. But when I ask why did we want to be born in Little Paw, why did we become such good friends if all we were going to do was part forever"—he touched his hat lower—"what I get is *there's a reason*, and I'm not sure that's what I want to hear."

"It won't be—"

"Is there something we have to do that we haven't done? You got some sort of cosmic agenda for us, Kinnie, or is this what it feels like, to know everything and still be sad? Missing her, that's a sign I'm not a finished philosopher ferret, I guess."

"Could be." The little animal took a small step upward, to the top of the wavelets. No more splashing about her ankles, no more paw-prints in the water. "And it could be that missing her's a sign of another destiny between you. Could be a sign that you haven't done everything you came to do, after all."

"You can tell me what's going to happen, can't you?"

She shook her head. "Sorry. I can tell you a rule of space-time: *What's going to happen has already happened.* I can tell you a rule of consciousness: *What you perceive is up to you.*"

"And you're going to tell me I'm a fool, feeling sad when always and everywhere I'm surrounded by love?"

The dark eyes twinkled. "No. I'll let you say that yourself."

He smiled at her. "Did I ask you to come find me here, talk to me this way?"

As though she hadn't heard, Kinnie looked to the horizon, to Northstar Mountain. Then she turned back and nodded brightly. "You're a dear ferret, Monty. You've learned much. You are greatly loved."

Ladyhawke blinked at where her rider's other-level friend had stood, the stream chuckling over empty stones. The delphin tossed her head, *Wouldn't hurt to listen, Monty Ferret.*

I listen, Lady-H, he said to her in his mind. Takes me a while, sometimes, but I listen.

•••

Delphin and rider came over the rise south of town, on a trail lifted from stream to pine needles underhoof, now and then a glimpse of buildings beyond the trees.

"Your big day, Monty!" The café door hadn't closed behind the rancher when Quill raised a glass of mountain-water, a toast. The other ferrets turned: "H'lo, Monty."

"Not my big day," he said, "it's theirs. Those sheep are good lit-tle hoof-dancers! Can't sit still, watching."

How hard they had practiced these last months, the Montana Rainbow Zouave Rhythm March Corps and Scottish Dance Company!

Wandering off had dropped to zero, the sheep who chose not to audition for the Canyon Performance mesmerized by the rehearsals.

He sat at the counter, his back to Main Street.

"What's it to be, Montgomery?" Roxy Ferret never knew what Monty would order. It was always something different, unless he was feeling lonely.

"How about a fresh strawberry?"

"One fresh strawberry, comin' up," she said. I wouldn't be lonely, the proprietress thought, if I had all that excitement going on, the Canyon Performance tonight.

"Thank you, Rox."

"I sense you feel down a little, kit," she said, serving the fruit sliced in four.

"Oh, no. I got nothin' to feel down about."

At that moment a black limousine passed the café, shadowy figures within. Roxy grinned. "There's another one!"

By the time Monty turned to see, the vehicle had disappeared, faint trail of dust filtering down.

"We are on the map, kits," said Roxy. "I can't guess how many of those, lately. Two dozen if there was one. All up to your ranch."

"They like the wool," said Monty. "Can't say as I blame 'em. It's like nothin' you've seen, is it?"

"Pricey," said Quill, "but I've got to admit it is plumb beautiful."

"Got to admit," said Monty, softly.

Jasmine Ferret suggested Donatien go alone to his meeting with the Rainbows, but the designer would have none of it.

"They are beautiful," he said. "How often does one get the chance to meet such creatures? Please come."

So Jasmine went along, quietly.

It did not go as well as Donatien had hoped. The Rainbows were distracted, the Canyon Performance just hours away, the sheep uneasy in the presence of the fashion designer. Would he find their dance boring, would he judge them harshly? The more they thought, the more the little sheep felt that it would be best not to approve a sale to Donatien Ferret. Not today.

The designer felt the animals' hesitation, discomfort. "These scarves. I've designed them so the colors themselves warm and protect."

The Rainbows looked at one another. Not today.

Jasmine rose from her place at the edge of the room. Monty had told her long ago, "Ever you find an animal you don't understand, ask yourself, *What's it thinking?*"

What were they thinking now, the Rainbows?

From old practice she sensed her way into their thought, a display of mind and spirit unanimous, for the moment, in discomfort.

Donatien is a designer, yes, the sheep were worrying, but he is a showferret as well. What if he doesn't like our performance? What then? Will he not care so much for who we are, and for our wool, and will his work not be so beautiful as it must be?

Wordless, Jasmine glided along their level of thought, a place of broad views and wide verandas. The Rainbows looked at each other. The only one who had met them here was Monty Ferret. Now this one.

In her mind, Jasmine suggested a solution. What if with every scarf might come a card telling the background of the rare sheep, photos of the Rainbows in dance? With each a testament to the Montana Rainbow Zouave Rhythm March Corps and Scottish Dance Company? Could this make a difference, that they're more than wool, they're more than the most beautiful wool in the world?

Within, the climate of thought shifted. Donatien Ferret would recognize us as artists, too?

Jasmine nodded. If he did not respect you, he would not have come.

And the card, would it be in color?

Yes.

Thank you. And a decision: Done.

The Rainbows, sensitive creatures, once ready to file from the room in a cloud of foreboding, now trotted to the written request, stamped it *Approved*, little hoofprints. And would Donatien care to join them, last rehearsal before the show?

He would be honored.

Respect and understanding go a long way, in business.

☙

Jasmine walked alone from the conference room, across the grass by the dining hall, toward the office. Alone. Jasmine Ferret the actress, she thought. So much recognition, so much isolation. So much of life alone!

But this was delicious Montana. She sniffed the mountains in the air, the forests and streams, she sniffed her past, the kit Cheyenne from Little Paw. She touched the locket on its chain around her neck, lost in thought.

"Jasmine Ferret?"

She stopped, turned at a familiar voice. By the door to the dining hall, copper pot in one paw, chef's hat askew, stood Gerhardt-Grenoble Ferret.

"Gren?" This was not possible.

The silver ferret ran to embrace her friend, his copper pot a-clang to the ground. "Gren, what happened to you? You disappeared! Armond . . . not a word, said he'd promised not to tell!"

Her fatigue vanished in discovery. "This is Montana!" she said. "This is my home! What are you doing . . ." She stood back and took in the sight of him.

"It's my home, too, Jasmine. No more Grenoble. Call me Cookie."

"Cookie!" She laughed. "But you were happy at La Mer!"

The chef looked toward the office, took Jasmine's paw and led her to the kitchen. Simple woodstoves, wooden counters, bowls and pans, utensils made by paw. About them, the room bustled quietly, Bud and his assistants preparing the chuckwagon buffet for evening concertgoers.

"I was happy, for a long time, the challenge. But after you're the best, after you're Number One, then what? I was the star, I was giving interviews, or I was traveling, some hotel room, alone. What kind of life is that, alone? There is a challenge beyond Number One."

"I didn't know, Gr—Cookie."

"You know. For that is your life, too."

He reached overhead, brought down a giant wooden salad bowl, set a dish of butter lettuce leaves in front of her on the counter, took cold-pressed virgin olive oil from the cupboard, and a bottle of balsamic vinegar, large bottles, labels in Italian. How can I get through to her?

"Wash your paws, and dry," he said. "Tear the leaves into little pieces, please. Small little pieces."

Silent, watching her friend in control of his world without a word spoken, Jasmine felt a peace about him that she had not noticed before.

"Oh you, Jasmine Ferret." He laughed. "You know what kind of life that is! No secrets from Cookie! I was Celebrity Chef, all my friends the celebrities, too . . . *Jasmine Ferret's* my friend, her picture with me, signed, on the wall at La Mer! But she didn't know: Gerhardt-Grenoble's alone! And why should she care?" He smiled, shrugged. "That's no kind of life."

She tore the lettuce very small. "We missed you."

"That's no kind of life," he repeated. From beneath the spice rack he pulled a mortar and pestle fashioned out of rock from Northstar Mountain, placed a sprig of sage on the stone. "That is no life and you know it, Jasmine Ferret." He waved to the sky, the mountains west. "*This!* This is life!"

"But you're alone, Cookie! What difference does it make, Beverly Hills or Manhattan or Northstar, Montana?"

The chef had been shaking his head all through her words.

"Not alone?" asked Jasmine.

He crushed the sage, chose and added two sprigs more, ground them together. "I was led to this place, Jasmine. Very first day, my reward, I met Adrienne. You will meet her."

"*Adrienne Ferret?* MusTelCo's CFO? She's here? When she left New York for the simple life, she came here?"

He nodded.

Guided by their highest right, she thought. "I'm . . . I'm happy for you, Cookie."

"When is Cookie going to be happy for you, Jasmine Ferret?"

"There's nobody who knows who I am. There are ferrets in the world who could love Jasmine, but I'm not . . ." Lettuce leaves unfinished, she turned to him. "Nobody knows who I am."

"Cheyenne Ferret knows." She looked up to him, startled. Before she could answer, ask how he knew that name, the chef caught her paw. "Let me show you."

He led the actress up a narrow flight of stairs, pressed open a wooden door. Before them a hallway of dark Spanish tiles, walls of rough adobe painted white, wooden beams overhead.

"Where . . . ?"

"Monty's gone. You need to see."

"These are Monty's rooms? He's not here? Cookie, this is wrong! Take me back!"

The chef stopped. No ferret leads another where it does not wish to go.

"Jasmine, listen!"

She was still. No ferret refuses when a friend asks it to hear.

"You've been invited!"

"But Monty's—"

"You've been invited since the day you left Little Paw!"

Jasmine felt a wave of shock through her, from the tip of her tail to her soft brushed whiskers. "Gren—"

"I'm not Gerhardt-Grenoble! You're not Jasmine! Not here!" His tail thrashed left-right. "Let me show you."

Cookie swept his paw toward the next door in the hallway. Another few steps . . .

The room was silent, no one there. Caution overcome by curiosity, the actress moved ahead, poked her nose around the corner, stepped into the room.

Before her lay a place from her past, not a replica but the same loving air of home in Little Paw. An open fireplace, a wide couch, its wood frame built by paw, carved relief on the back: two kits in a meadow of mountain daisies. A hat rack made from a pine branch. It felt familiar, she couldn't place it.

On the wall, a photo of young Cheyenne Ferret astride her delphin, standing at the upper ford of the Big Paw, the glint of Hidden

Lake through the trees in the background. She thought she had forgotten that photo.

She moved slowly through the room, taking it in. A red gingham picnic cloth draped from a peg on the wall, torn movie-ticket stubs: *Desperate Voy* . . . A photo unframed on the desk, taken not so long ago: the elderly Boffin and Starlet together at the corner of her parents' corral. Her paw went to the image, stroked it. A slow whisper: "My little Starlet . . ."

She did not turn to Cookie. "Would you mind if I stayed for a minute? Would Monty mind?"

"He has told me, Cheyenne," said the chef, from the doorway. "I don't know he has told anyone else. It is your place, here. Stay as long as you wish."

She didn't answer, nor meet his eyes. He closed the door.

Jasmine removed her hat, hung it gently on the branch of that familiar tree. My oldest friend, she thought. How far we've come from the days we were kits.

He had to stay in Montana, I had to go.

She curled into the couch, stared at the fireplace. *Unless I do my best, Monty, I'll never know.*

She had done her best. She had paid her price and she had made a difference. And now . . .

She closed her eyes. With Monty gone, in this place so much like home, for just a little while, she needed to rest.

Montgomery Ferret arrived home not long before the Canyon Performance was to begin. He'd watch, he decided, from the bluff above the table rock that the Rainbows had chosen for their premiere, a stage closed on three sides by cliffs, a place of echoes.

Down the hallway, he noticed that the door to Cheyenne's room was closed.

He frowned. Who's been here? No one closes that door. Cookie?

The rancher touched the wood and it swung aside. The room was empty, seemed empty.

Monty's heart stopped. For there, from the pine branch he had brought down from Sable Canyon, hung a sky-blue Western hat.

12

A<small>LL THE TOWN</small> was there, ferrets come in pickup trucks, in cars, on delphins. They rode up, hiked up the back trail to see the Rainbows' show, proud of their little Montana Scots.

The wide arc in front of the cliff was packed with concertgoers, the sun beginning to sink at the western side, toward the canyon top. High on the rim, near the edge, stood ten Scottish ferrets: five pipers, five drummers, in full-dress tartan caps and scarves. The pipers silently fingered the chanters of their instruments though they had played the marches and reels a hundred times before. It's a big crowd, down there. Two minutes to go.

Hidden in the arroyo behind the bare rock stage were the Rainbows, all the little clones feeling the same butterflies within, all moving through the march and dance routines high-speed in their collective mind. Along the steep hairpin road down the face of the cliff above the stage, a strange sight: four ranchpaw pickup trucks parked, front wheels blocked, rear axles lifted on jacks, the drivers there, waiting for the show.

The lead piper nodded to his mates, they huffed to inflate the bagpipes, the sound of drones began, frail for a moment, then all at once the chanters, a cry of eagles aloft. The crowd below went still, blood chilled in the skirl of the pipes and, long seconds later, the first beat of the drums.

The pipers' melody rang out, an ancient slow-march: "Scotland's Lambs Bid Dreams o' Flight." Slow it was, freighted with thrill tight under rein, the audience beginning to tremble.

Now another sound, though the stage remained bare—a slow stamp of hooves in unison. At last, up from behind the smooth rock, a movement, the peaks of one tam-o'-shanter, of five, of ten, of twenty, and now from each side, the Rainbow Zouaves streamed upon the stage.

Gradually did the melody of the pipes increase its tempo, faster came the march and stamp of hooves on rock, the sheep expressionless, colors brushed and matched in ranks. Some said later that it was the sound of steel hoof-taps they heard; others said no, hooves alone, but echoing like steel from that hard stage.

It was a grand start, the crowd scarcely breathing. Faster came the pipes, faster the march, hooves united thunder, then the first surprise syncopation, and the crowd burst in a cheer of uncontained delight.

Slow-time, full-time, double-time, skirled the pipes, quick-time, double-quick, triple-quick, till the storm of hooves was a giant engine spun by the Zouaves, their bright forms swaying, turning smoothly, their feet nearly invisible for the speed of the march and then in one breath, instant

Silence.

Echoes.

Echoes . . .

The crowd detonated, unable to hold its tension, a sound so sharp and affirm that several of the marchers, still breathing hard, blinked in the storm of it.

Thus began an evening that no one would forget. After the Zouave marchers came the Rainbow hoof-dancers, led at first by the pipes into wild complex rhythms and finally *a cappella*, hooves became their own hurricane melody. At one moment there were no fewer than four sheep airborne at once, launched inverted from dashes up the vertical walls of the stage. At another, one could count six separate living pinwheels a-spin, fast enough the colors began to blend.

Sun fading, the show finished to a climax that brought nearly a hundred Rainbows onstage, Zouaves and dancers together, all bodies still, all hooves flashing, the sound, despite its intricate rhythm, nearly deafening.

Sitting easily astride Ladyhawke, Monty Ferret watched from the bluff, as swept in delight as any kit from town.

Show over, stage empty in the dusk, the crowd refused to leave, applause roared out unabated, cheers cried for more.

"What do you say, Cheye? Do our little guys have a future?"

There were tears in her eyes, the excitement of the show, she thought. "They're . . . they're fabulous, they're spectacular, they're five-star, Monty, they're ten-star. I'm all Hollywood and I don't want to be."

"Then maybe you could be Montana, instead."

She watched his eyes. He did not turn away, a level gaze, not kidding at all.

In the dark, then, over unceasing applause, radiance. The four ranchpaws on the road above pulled their pickup headlight switches together, and the stage illuminated. With the light, the pipes began again. Encore!

Monty nodded to Cheyenne, touched Ladyhawke's mane. Their two delphins moved down the bluff, away from the stage and the crowd, toward the high land north of the ranch.

"My guess is that we're going to have a moonrise here pretty soon, that it's going to be near full, right about yonder, up from Northstar Mountain."

He pointed. Already the mountain glowed, backlit in moonlight.

Cheyenne Ferret laughed. "Oh? 'It's going to appear right about yonder'?"

"Now you don't like my talk, do y'?" he said, eyes twinkling. "Y' don't care for m' idiom?"

She turned to him as they rode, side by side, into the night. "I love your idiom, Monty! I love your talk. It's just, I've just been so long in a place . . . where there is no yonder."

He did not reply.

"Is it time I took the train from Hollywood, Monty? One-way ticket home, no looking back?"

"Are you asking my opinion?" He lifted his hat, ran a paw over his forehead, smoothing the fur. "You do what you know is highest for you, Cheye. If you decide to take that train, I've got no problem with you looking back at all. I suspect, by the time you get here, you'll be looking forward again."

She nodded. Having climbed certain peaks, she thought, we descend no more, but spread our wings and fly beyond. "When I come home, Monty, do I get my yonder back?"

"You do."

She smiled happily, said nothing more.

They rode toward the slopes of Northstar Mountain, the two of them together, into the moonlight.

— end —

BOOK 5

Stormy and Strobe

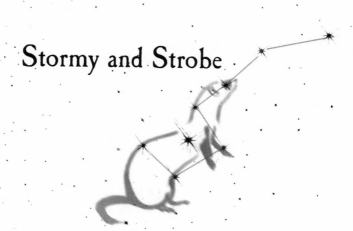

The Ferret and the Eagle

A young ferret, loving the sky, built for himself wings of cloth, stretched on a frame of bamboo. Fastening these upon his shoulders, he jumped from a high place and crashed to the ground.

Again and again he tried to fly, after each crash fashioning improved wings, risking his life to test them. In time he learned to fly and not to crash, circling high in rising airs, landing gently at the end of each flight. He was filled with delight, and taught his skills to others who loved the sky as well, who yearned to fly for themselves.

One day an eagle soared past the ferret and his students, and scoffed. "Beginners! Never will you fly so high or so fast as me!"

Hearing this, the students were discouraged, for it seemed to them that what the eagle said was true, that a ferret's place was on the ground.

"Be not dismayed by the eagle's words," their teacher told them, "for the mark of true flight is not our altitude but our attitude, not our speed but our joy in the paths we find above the earth."

The students listened, welcomed his truth to be their own. Aloft again, they treasured their adventures and skills and discoveries as *never they had before, and passed along to younger ferrets the wisdom they learned from the sky.*

We are led, when we share our loves, to an enchanted life of inner happiness, which unsharing others cannot know.

- Antonius Ferret, *Fables*

1

P̲OMPOM F̲ERRET sat in the pilot's seat, one small paw on the engine throttles, surrounded by panels of flight instruments, levers and gauges, knobs and switches.

The kit turned her powder-color mask upward, puzzled. "But what makes it fly, sir?"

Gold-stripe scarf tied neatly at his throat, captain's hat brushed and polished, Strobe Ferret was chief pilot for MusTelCo, the largest ferret corporation in the world. He had heard the question a thousand times at airshows, time and again from the young animals who came to tour the FerrJet's flight deck.

"Magic!" he said. "There, out the window, see the wing—can you see the curve on top of the wing?"

The little face turned, solemn black eyes, nodded at seamless metal, white and royal blue. Outside, a gentle crowd, ferrets of every age strolling down rows of aircraft at the Air Expo, touching wings, peering through windshields, asking questions, telling stories of flight. Pompom looked for the magic.

"When we move a wing through the air, that simple curve, it pushes air down. When we move it fast, it pushes a lot of air down. And when it pushes air down, what happens to a wing?"

Pompom turned from the sight, eyes sparkling at the captain, sudden understanding. "It goes up!"

"Magic," he said, "and it can be you, making it happen someday." He grinned at her. "Pretend we're in the air. Now show me how we make the airplane climb."

The kit reached a paw, unsure, touched the control wheel.

"That's it," said Strobe. "Ease the wheel back and we go up; forward, and we go down. Turn it left," he asked, "and . . . ?"

Floating behind them on the flight deck, at the edge of the dimension between two worlds, hovered a tiny golden helicopter, a single angel ferret fairy at the controls.

From his soap-bubble cockpit, the ghost pilot paused, warmed by the scene. Then Tech Angel Gnat turned back to his work. So long had it been since he was mortal that he had forgotten how it felt to be locked in a body reluctant to turn invisible or to pass through walls and doors.

Mortalhood is a fine state to visit, he thought, the *dook-dook-dook* of his rotor blades echoing as the helicopter slipped inside the FerrJet's cabin-pressure system, but it's no place to call home.

Gnat's passion on earth had been flight, and his death had changed nothing. Flight was his passion still.

First-rate maintenance, he frowned, inspecting the joints and seals of the system under his helicopter spotlight, checking screws and bolts and safety wires. Somewhere in this aircraft there has to be a flaw. If not maintenance overlooked, he hoped, then it'll be wear, or a tool left loose in the system, or metal fatigue.

I'll find a weakness, Gnat told himself. It's for his own good. If I have to break it myself, this aircraft will not finish the run that Captain Strobe Ferret has planned to fly tonight.

He reached the outflow valve, inspected it, moved on. Then on strange intuition, he turned back, looked closer. The smallest smile, and he pressed his microphone button, spoke softly on the angel ferret fairy communication frequency.

"Pinecone has the red light," he said. "Pinecone has the red light."

2

"THERE'S A FERRET in the sky!" From the hillside, gathering berries, the kit pointed. "See, Mom? She's reaching for something. There's her nose. See her paws, stretching up?"

The kit's mother looked heavenward. "It's a beautiful ferret, Tabitha. Let's watch her change, now . . ."

The two stopped, sat on the grass, berry basket between them, facing the tall, sleek cloud. From time to time they'd choose a blueberry, then watch the cloud once more.

After a while: "Isn't it going to melt?"

"It will. Clouds change as they blow along with the wind."

They watched. Other clouds changed, theirs didn't.

"When a ferret cloud keeps its shape, do you know what that means, Tabby?"

"No, Mother."

"They say that when ferret clouds don't swirl and tumble, it means there are angel ferret fairies inside, and the cloud won't float away till their meeting's over."

"Oh . . . ," said the kit. "That's just a story, isn't it?"

"Could be," said her mother. "But isn't it odd, the way your cloud doesn't change?"

"Order!" called Marcus Ferret, from the front of the room. "May we have a little order, please?"

Parked on the cloud outside were a dozen tiny helicopters, the colors of sunrise. Within the glowing whiteness of the briefing room ranged their pilots, ferrets no larger than a pawprint, all chattering and listening at once, none of them to Marcus.

"I'd appreciate a little order!" said the chief angel ferret fairy. He sighed. They were excellent pilots, every one of them, or they wouldn't be here. They were fearless, innovative, resourceful, every one a volunteer . . . just the animals to call upon when destinies needed to meet.

Now this elite task force was more interested in swapping old adventures than hearing about the new one to come.

"Parker Ferret was going to walk by Simoune, he was lost in thought, he was going to pass right by. You can imagine—their guardian angels were going crazy, I was the closest angel ferret fairy, and they said, 'We need help, Pavo, now!' Do you know what I did?"

"You made her sneeze," said Gawaine. "No. You made a butterfly land on her shoulder. That's what I would have done. And Parker saw the butterfly and, instead of walking past, he said, 'How do you do that?' Right?"

"No," said Pavo. "I made her sneeze."

"Oh. Did it work?"

"Of course it worked. But I like your butterfly idea . . ."

"Order, please, angel ferret fairies!"

It didn't go quiet in the briefing room, but the noise dropped a little. Marcus nodded toward the cloud wall, and at once appeared the image of a young ferret, her fur the color of snow, streaked with night. She wore the cap and scarf of a pilot. From the scene, one could hear a muffled thunder of engines.

For a long moment he stood uncaring of the fairies' chatter, watching the image. It had been so long, he thought, she had come so far.

At last he realized that the room was still.

"Thank you," said Marcus. "Her name is Janine, they call her Stormy."

"She's pretty!"

Marcus considered before confirming the comment. He hadn't thought of her beauty before. "Yes, she is a pretty ferret." He cleared his throat. "This is not a practice, gentle fairies, this is a Class Three intervention. Code name: Operation Midnight Snack."

There was a murmur in the room, pilots wrote the words on their kneeboards.

"The others *failed*?"

"Every one."

Had a snowflake fallen upon the cloud floor, it would have been heard by all. What they heard instead was the *dook-dook-dook-dook-dook* of tiny rotor blades, outside. The sound faded and an angel ferret fairy entered, a newcomer, not long ago a mortal himself.

"Sorry I'm late."

"Welcome to our meeting, Baxter," said Marcus.

"Wrong cloud," the angel muttered, seating himself with the other pilots upon the misty floor.

"Operation Midnight Snack," the chief fairy repeated, for Baxter's benefit. "Her name is Stormy."

An image appeared alongside the first, another aviator, older than the female, his fur the color of walnut. Like her, he was seated at the controls of an airplane.

"This is Strobe," said Marcus. "I must tell you first of all that these are determined mortals."

He watched the pictures, then turned and faced the angel ferret fairy pilots. "Strobe and Stormy have high ideals, of course; we all do. But these two are particularly rigorous in their devotion to the mission—one might say stubborn, one might say headstrong, one might say inflexible."

The pilots shifted uneasily. More than one had ignored their own destiny's subtle hints.

Baxter, just arrived from Angel Ferret Fairy School, was unaffected. What happens, happens, he thought. There's no such thing as a big deal. Everything, always, works out for the best.

"They must meet," said Marcus.

The newcomer raised his paw.

"Yes, Baxter."

"Aren't there alternate worlds, sir? So even if Stormy and Strobe don't meet in this one, they will in . . . ?"

"Of course there are alternate worlds," said Marcus. It was a fair question for someone new to ask. "But our highest sense of right is to express the most possible love in this world, and to help others do so. Alternate worlds can handle their affairs as they wish."

Baxter nodded, satisfied, turned back to the images. Strobe was a handsome animal, one that he hadn't met. There was something about Stormy, however, that was intensely familiar. He couldn't place her. A good memory for faces, he'd had that on earth, he had it now. He knew that look, but he couldn't place her at all.

"Their guardian angels have asked us to help," said Marcus. "Strobe and Stormy Ferret, if they meet, there will be . . . they'll change the world for a lot of animals. But this is the last chance, on our time line, to make it happen." He paused, reached for his light-pointer. "If I may have the chart, please."

An aeronautical chart flashed on the wall of cloud. Marcus lifted the pointer and a glowing red arrow slid along the colored airways.

"Stormy will be heading south, here, down airway Victor Two-Three. She's a pilot for Air Ferrets, flying an FDC-4 out of Seattle for Salinas."

A low chatter once again, this time glad recognition. The four-engine Ferret DC-4 is a favorite cargo plane. A number of the fairies present had flown the aircraft when they were mortals, and once one has flown an honest lovely airplane, one never forgets.

The pointer moved. "Northbound up Victor Two-Three will come Strobe."

The fairies leaned forward, watching the plot thicken, beginning to see their part in the drama to come.

"He's MusTelCo's chief pilot. That's Stilton Ferret's company, of course. He'd trust Strobe with his life. They're old friends. Strobe's the pilot in command wherever Stilton flies. There's no finer aviator alive."

The fairies nodded, keen minds flying ahead, addressing the chal-lenge. This is no kits' play, it's a Class Three intervention.

"Tonight, Strobe will be flying alone, bringing the FerrJet back to Medford from the Air Expo in Los Angeles. More than one kit's decided to become a pilot, meeting Strobe at an airshow."

A paw raised.

"Bailey?" said the chief fairy.

"All due respect, sir. But no way they're going to meet . . ."

". . . because the FerrJet's up at altitude and Stormy's flying low?"

"Yes, sir."

It was an obvious question. "We have had one bit of luck. Tech Angel Gnat's started a chain."

The ferret fairies turned to each other, pleased with the news.

"First link," said Marcus. "Gnat found metal fatigue, a weak spring in the FerrJet's cabin-pressure system. He bent it a little, and just after takeoff, the spring's going to fail. That's going to drive the cabin-pressure outlet valve full open."

"Well done," the fairies murmured. "Good job, Gnat . . ."

"Our second link is Strobe himself. There was so much demand for oxygen by the other jets at the show that he stood back, let the other pilots have it instead of refilling his own supply. With cabin pressure, who needs oxygen?"

The fairies smiled.

"Without cabin pressure, though, and without oxygen," their chief continued, "Captain Strobe Ferret . . ."

". . . will have to fly at low altitude," said the fairies together.

Marcus nodded.

A question from the back of the room: "The weather?"

"Unfortunately," said Marcus, "the weather's fine."

Baxter raised his paw. "Excuse me . . ."

The leader waited.

"This Stormy, sir. I've never seen her, but I know her face. It's hard to explain but I . . . do you follow me?"

The chief nodded. "Stormy's a Columbine."

The pilot looked blank.

"She's from Columbine Pod. Columbine Family," said Marcus. "Have you not been told about true families?"

"Why, yes, sir, I have."

"Stormy's a Columbine, same as, I believe . . . same as your grandkit, Willow."

The fairy's jaw dropped. Stormy's from Willow's family? Of course! The same flash in her eyes, that same learn-or-die look that had made Baxter shower the kit with toys and puzzles, such a short while ago. Now she grieved for her grampa; he couldn't get through to her that he was all right.

". . . part of the plan," the chief was saying. "If we make this happen, if Stormy meets Strobe, then later she'll meet Willow, when Willow's a Teacher. They're Columbines, it's rare, and the creative connection between them is going to . . ."

"My little Willow's going to be a *Teacher*?"

"Didn't you know?"

"And Stormy will change her life?"

Marcus shrugged. "Of course. Not just Willow's life, if Stormy meets Strobe, but thousands of other . . ."

Baxter rose to his paws as though he would take over the meeting. "Well, if the problem's the weather, can't we do something to change it?"

Marcus frowned. "Great souls share great ideas, Baxter. Perhaps you could take your seat?"

The leader turned back to the chart. "Do we agree? Redding airport is here, nearly on the airway, just south of the Siskiyou Mountains. If they both cancel their flight plans and divert to Redding at the same time, they're sure to meet."

The fairies shook their heads, doubting. Two determined mortal fliers cancel their instrument flight plans and divert to Redding? This was not going to be easy.

"If it were easy, their guardian angels wouldn't need us. We are professionals, gentlefairies. Coincidence is our business."

Marcus' reminder helped; the fluffy room filled with determination.

"Gnat, you've got a way with weather. Do you think you can generate enough turbulence aloft to make Stormy change her mind about flying straight through to Salinas tonight?"

"Over the Siskiyou? With energy from the Shasta Vortex? How do you want me to do it, sir, blindfolded or with four paws and my tail tied? Piece of cake!"

Gnat found this work delicious. He loved behind-the-scenes, the code words of his trade, his special skills with aeronautics, his influence upon the world of mortals.

Marcus did not smile. "Remember how she got her name," he said. "Once she's taken off, Stormy Ferret has never turned back because of rough weather. Never. She doesn't have passengers to worry about, it's just herself and her cargo."

"Siskiyou Mountains are easy for storms, sir. Bad storms."

"Thank you, Gnat. You'll remain Pinecone for this mission?"

"No, sir. Requesting code name Goosebeak."

By the time one becomes chief angel ferret fairy, one has infinite patience. "Thank you, Goosebeak." Marcus dropped the arrow of his pointer south on the chart. "Here's the hard part. We're going to need another storm, over Sacramento. A major storm. We need to catch these two ferrets between, so the only place they *can* divert is Redding."

"There's a May's Diner at Redding," said one of the fairies.

Marcus nodded. There was hardly an airport without a May's Diner for ferret aviators. "I need a team to generate the Sacramento storm."

Silence in the room.

"This will be difficult," said Marcus. "Not much help from nature. Fog is easy over Sacramento. Violent storm is not."

The fairies considered the challenge.

Baxter stood. "I'll do it, sir."

A hint of a smile from the chief angel ferret fairy. "Thank you for offering, Baxter. I'm glad you've got the desire, that's important. But you need the skill to bring this off, and you don't have that, yet."

Gnat raised his paw. "Suggestion, sir?"

"Go ahead, Goosebeak."

"I think I can do Sacramento, sir. I know I can. If I build a storm fast enough over the Sierra, the mountains will block it, force it to pile up west. The only place it can go is right down Victor Two-Three."

As he spoke, he convinced himself. "We can energize from the Tahoe Vortex or the one at Half Dome. Why don't you put Baxter in the Siskiyou, sir, instead of me? His grandkit's a Columbine, he'll know Stormy's mind before she does herself. Nimble and Prestor can help him cook up a terrifying storm, they can do it easy there. Baxter can tell them just how much is enough, without tearing her airplane to pieces."

Nimble hadn't been sure enough of his skills to volunteer for a Class Three intervention, but now he looked at his partner. Prestor nodded I can if you can.

"We'll do that," said Nimble.

Marcus switched off the light-pointer. "Thank you, gentlefairies. Stormy and Strobe will be in the intervention area two hours after midnight. This is our last chance, or these two will never meet. Esther, I'd like you to be the energy boss, your team can set an axis." He paused, considering. "No. Not an axis, Esther. Set a triangle. We'll use the Shasta Vortex, and Tahoe and Half Dome, in Yosemite."

Near the back of the room, a striking black-sable ferret stood. "All three vortices, sir? That's a good deal of energy . . ."

"We'll need it. We'll need two major storms. Anything less, Stormy's going to fly straight through. Probably Strobe will, too."

"Yes, sir."

"Any questions?" said Marcus.

Silence from the group, but all thought the same: power from Shasta and Tahoe, yes . . . *and Yosemite?*

"Very well. Their angels are counting on us. Start engines at your discretion, gentlefairies. Let's do it right!"

The berries were eaten, most of them, the basket nearly empty.

"The ferret's fading!"

Her mother watched. "Tabitha, honey, you're right!" The tall cloud twisted in slow motion, gradually became a swan, melting away.

"What is it now, Tab?"

"It's a cloud," said the kit, the snowy fur around her mouth turned the color of blueberries. "Does that mean the angel ferret fairies have gone away?"

3

T HE NIGHT, ON Victor 23, belongs to the air-cargo pilots.

Round midnight, out of May's Airport Diner, close on the loading docks at Seattle-Tacoma International Airport, the old propeller planes, the twin-engine turboprops and the four-engine cargo liners top off with high-octane and jet fuel.

Before they climb to their flight decks, the pilots, human and ferret alike, check their aircraft landing gear, ailerons and elevators and rudders, wing flaps and beacons and running lights.

Settled in their cockpits, pilots' hands and paws move fuel levers, ignition and starter switches—propeller blades and turbines spin to life in the sounds of flight beginning.

Machines with wings taxi through a maze of blue lights and finally, cleared for takeoff, howl up into the darkness toward Portland and Medford, Salt Lake and Paris, Anchorage and Honolulu and San Francisco and London and Hong Kong.

☁

Midnight-thirty on the dot. A Trans-World Cargo Express widebody jet, bound for Tokyo, released its brakes and pushed into the night, two hundred tons of fuel and steel and human crew accelerating into the dark, the runway trembling in the crackle and thunder of its engines.

Next in line for takeoff, four miniature radial engines cowled in aluminum, *Air Ferrets* painted crimson and yellow down its side, taxied an FDC-4 transport, wingspan 121 paws, twenty paws from the bottom of its wheels to the tip of its rudder. Its full gross weight was less than a single tire of the humans' monster jet, but in the air traffic system it was not an ounce less important than other aircraft.

On the flight deck within, Captain Janine Ferret reached a snowy paw and touched the flap control lever to *Takeoff*.

"Air Ferret Three-Five," called the tower operator, a specialist ferret working the late shift alongside human traffic controllers, "cleared into position and hold."

The captain pressed the microphone button on her control yoke. "Air Ferret Three-Five, position and hold."

Unimpressed with the size of the TWE transport, at home in the system, Janine Ferret had been flying air cargo for a long time, now. Her bright black eyes, her night-streaked silver fur, her flying scarf the color of gold and lace offered no hint of the skills she'd learned or the life she'd lived in the sky. Only her captain's hat, worn and creased under her headphones, gave a clue.

Under her right paw, engine throttles crept forward and the SkyFreighter taxied onto the runway, its nosewheel coming to a stop on a centerline hot from the fire of the wide-body's monster engines.

An easy run tonight, she thought. A little rain this side of Portland, then the weather report promised clear skies all the way to Salinas. Not that it mattered. The weather check was a formality, she'd fly her night missions no matter what the forecast called. It was not so much the cargo that mattered, she knew, but the idea of the cargo, her airline's principle: freight shipped on Air Ferrets will arrive on time.

Behind the flight deck of her transport, secure on pallets tied to the floor of the hold, were fifty containers of cargo—ferret food and bell-balls on their way south.

The tower operator peered at Stormy's airplane through binoculars, called as he watched from the high glass cab. "Air Ferret Three-Five, you're cleared for takeoff, caution wake turbulence from the departing aircraft."

"Ferret Three-Five's rolling."

She touched her flight timer and transponder switches, tightened her claws around the four throttles, thrust her paw smoothly forward and released the brakes. So long as she lifted off before the place on the runway where the wide-body became airborne, she'd have no trouble with the giant jet's wake.

Blue flame from the exhaust stacks, a whirling blast of propellers drove the transport down the runway, centerline moving, then blurring below, dropping away. Her airplane flew.

The ferret reached to her right, moved a wheel-shaped lever to the *Up* position, heard the whine and growl of landing gear retracting. Soon three up-and-locked lights glowed red on the instrument panel.

As she reached her paw to the flap-retraction handle, her machine was swallowed in cloud; rain cracked against the windshield, each drop swept away at once in the wind. Before the flaps were up, she had switched her attention to the flight instruments, mechanical windows into gyroscope skies, and relaxed into the routine of weather flying.

"Air Ferret Three-Five," called the tower, "contact Seattle Departure, have a good flight."

"Ferret Three-Five." Though she appreciated the kindness, Stormy wondered why those four extra words. Of course she'd have a good flight—she was in command of the aircraft! But those seconds on the same wish, over and over, add up to a lot of chatter, she thought, no purpose.

She turned a frequency selector and pressed her microphone button. "Hello, Seattle Departure," she said, her voice unhurried. "Ferret Three-Five is through one thousand two hundred paws for five thousand."

She touched the heading hold button on the autopilot, engaged the vertical speed and set the altitude hold to 5.

The rain snapped on her transport's windshield as it climbed through the weather, not the sound of water as much as a sound of gravel, hard and sharp against the angled glass.

Stormy Ferret loved her work, though it was not the stuff of glamour. She was aloft in the dark because there were ferrets sleeping tonight in Salinas depending on her for their food, kits depending on her for bell-balls in their play, though few would ever know it, few would ever see her aircraft or meet its captain.

"Ferret Three-Five is level at five thousand," she said presently. "Higher anytime."

Alone she flew, cleared through seven thousand and finally leveling at nine thousand paws, settled onto the airway called Victor 23 and into the routine of a long-haul air-cargo pilot.

The rain lashed her airplane. A lone animal high above the ground, her sleek features dim in the red glow of instrument lights, her paws touching this panel or that one, changing radio frequencies from Departure Control to Seattle Center southbound. The temperature outside hovered at freezing; on the windshield the rain clumped now into tiny ice-craters before the wind scoured them away.

So few of us, she thought, so few ferret air-cargo pilots. She sighed. Sometimes she almost wished she could be a normal ferret, snug in some soft hammock, asleep the night through.

"But who would feed us?" she said aloud on her flight deck. "Who would fly food for the ferrets, or bring hammocks and blankets, or toys for the kits?"

It's not an easy job, but I've been trusted with a mission. There is treasure behind me, fifty containers full. Rain or not, ice or not, it will get through, on time.

Seattle lost in the dark behind her, Portland lost in the dark ahead, her transport broke through the rain, rumbled between lofty canyons of cloud silvered in starlight.

The faithful old SkyFreighter, once so much complex metal and strange systems, had become more familiar than her own battered little automobile. She could no longer tell where her paws stopped and the aircraft began. She felt the wind as though it keened over her own fur. She no longer thought of what she had to do to make the airplane turn and climb, she thought *turn-and-climb* and it happened, metal wings and tail her body in the air.

Sky of ink, stars tiny beacons from heaven, warm breathing of engines . . . the beauty of it took her heart now as it had on her first night flight. An enchanted high land, the sky, a land of secret palaces only fliers could find.

A wall of mist directly ahead, Stormy took one last look at the stars before the SkyFreighter plunged again into the weather. Midnight clouds, wings and propellers and engines and instruments, headings and courses and altitudes in the wild pure arena of the air. She loved it.

From the time she was a kit, Janine Ferret had willed herself into the sky. Hiding in the tall grass not far from her home in Steep River, Idaho, her back against cool earth, she lost herself in the clouds turning overhead, saw herself playing among them.

Asleep in her hammock after bedtime, she dreamed of flying, of grassy hillsides down which she would run, faster and faster, then leap and spread her paws wide to soar upon the wind. So delicious, that melting of her soul into the sky; her dreams were sweet remembering what it is to be free of weight and body both.

It was magic she dreamed, for desires are magic indeed. A spirit that longs to soar, she knew, must by grace and the help of angels find a way to lift into that enchanted blue, and stay.

Her parents were artists, Glinda Ferret the potter and Denver the painter, the two in those days unknown beyond the town limits of Steep River. Stormy's kithood home was a gallery of easels and canvas and colors, clay and glaze and bowls and vases just out of her mother's kiln.

At Janine's room, the sky began. The kit had built models of ferret airplanes, dozens of them: biplanes and seaplanes and gliders and cargo planes, helicopters and trainers and racers, all in miniature. These hung by threads from her ceiling, stood upon her shelves by the books she read about flying.

Her parents would poke paint-spattered noses, clay-speckled whiskers into her doorway, see the newest models hanging, smile at their silver-fur daughter. They had helped her color her room noon-blue, fleecy white on walls and ceiling, luminous stars to shine overhead come dark. "Dear Janine!" they marveled. "Is it true you're going to *fly?*"

They were happy on the ground, they didn't hear the call of the sky, but they watched the young one listening. "Take your time to decide," they told their kit, "but once you know your highest right, run toward it and never look back!"

Stormy had lived that way ever since. Wherever her heart was bound, Mom and Dad would cheer the journey no matter how far it took her from home. How many times she had thanked them for honoring her choices, small ones first, then life-changing ones, till finally they blessed her and let her fly free, into her own destiny.

Each time a freight run took her near Coeur d'Alene, Stormy was off to the house at Steep River to share her adventures, to listen to theirs as the arts of Glinda and Denver Ferret became known, gradually, across the land.

Engulfed in cloud, Stormy pressed a switch labeled *Portside Ice-Light.* A beam of white shot out from the left fuselage, illuminating wing and engines. Through the beam raced a thousand comets, raindrops and snowflakes, trails of cold fire. The first snowflakes were beginning to freeze on the black-rubber de-ice boots along the wing's leading edge. She touched the switch again and the light went out.

Constantly the ferret rechecked her airplane's flight and engine instruments, while the autopilot held the controls. It would be nearly five hours until she'd fly her approach into Salinas, skating through the weather she knew would be waiting, down between the mountains funneling to the airport.

She reached to her flight bag, opened a small box of ferret food, nibbled absently, her black eyes scanning the instrument panel.

The only thing wrong with cargo flying, she thought, is that it's lonely. A copilot to talk with on the long hauls, that would be pleasant. But when Air Ferrets management had asked its captains if they believed a copilot was necessary for the safety of flight, Stormy had voted no.

Long hours away from home, it's not easy for a commercial pilot to find a mate, and Stormy had not done so. She could not imagine life with a ferret who did not love to fly, himself. So much of her time was aviation. Days off, she flew kits in her own seaplane, inspiring them as she had been inspired by others when she learned to fly. She loved to watch those faces on their first flight, just at liftoff.

No warning, a jolt of turbulence so sharp it took her breath, slammed her down in her seat, a clash and jangle of bell-balls from the cargo containers behind her. Yellow light glowed on the panel: *Autopilot Disconnect.*

She didn't notice, but at that moment Stormy Ferret had been joined in the dark by three tiny helicopters, the angel ferret fairies Prestor, Nimble and Baxter, the latter flying as close to her window as he dared, striving for a look at the pilot who could one day change his grandkit's life.

So much she didn't see. Far down the airway, a FerrJet aloft, heading north, the captain choosing to fly at a much lower altitude than usual for the failure of his airplane's cabin pressure. Had Stilton Ferret been aboard, Strobe would have returned at once for repair, but tonight he flew alone.

Also unseen, code name Goosebeak and a team of angel ferret fairies tampering with the earth's energy to boil storms for two.

"Stormy, hello!" said Baxter, his mind to hers. "It's important to everybody for you to divert tonight. We need you to land . . ."

"Oh-oh . . ." She saw the disconnect light, moved the autopilot switch to Off, then *On* again, pressed *Heading Hold*. Instead of engaging the flight controls and steering the airplane, the autopilot tugged at the control wheel, twisting to the right, and disconnected again.

Stormy Ferret sighed and took the wheel, holding the transport on heading and altitude by paw as it swept over Portland. The windows of her flight deck might as well have been painted black, the pilot alone in a tiny room suspended high midair, only her instruments to tell up from down, left from right, and those submerged in a pool of dim red cockpit light.

She pulled and reset the autopilot circuit breaker, adjusted trim wheels to be certain the machine was flying without pressures on the flight controls, then one more time tried the autopilot switch. One more time the airplane lurched to the right before the system shut itself off.

Ferret transports have backup communication and navigation radios, of course, and fuel cross-feed, should an engine fail. They do not have standby autopilots, however, and though her workload increases when the system fails, the captain is expected to control the airplane the old-fashioned way, by paw.

She shifted her seat forward a notch and continued her instrument scan, coaxing the transport left when it was thrown right by the rough air, lifting it up when it was pushed down, moving the controls with small pressures this way and that to keep the SkyFreighter on course.

A younger pilot would have wondered, Why this weather, when the forecast was clear from Portland south? But Stormy had learned early on . . . a pilot does not fly the forecast, she flies the weather that's in the sky, makes no difference it's not supposed to be there, makes no difference there's no warning of a change.

For a split moment she considered diverting from her plan, landing to repair the autopilot. In a flash of horror at the idea, though, she pushed the suggestion from her mind. She was flying to deliver her cargo to Salinas, and it would arrive at Salinas, on time, before dawn. I'll land if all four engines are on fire, she thought, or if they all quit. Otherwise, there's a mission to fly.

Outside her window, Baxter looked to heaven. His job was not going to be easy.

As she flew, Stormy Ferret considered what may have failed in the autopilot system. A tension bar broken by the shock of that hard bump, perhaps. That would make the electronics veer the plane in the opposite direction, when the failproofs would shut it down. It was a loss she could not correct from the cockpit.

Slowly fell the needle of her outside air temperature gauge. When the pilot touched the ice-light switch once more, snowflakes rocketed past the wings as ever, but raindrops struck the metal and froze at once. The SkyFreighter's airspeed had dropped already, for the weight of the ice and the effect it had, dragging on the wings. Nothing about ice in the air is a friend to aviators.

She did not notice that the sudden flare of the ice-light had blinded poor Baxter, sending his helicopter spinning away, out of control.

"*Stormy!*" he cried. "*Think* before you hit the ice-light, please! Think *time for the ice-light*, please? A little warning?"

In a few seconds he could see again, and forgiving her because she did not know he was there, the angel ferret fairy closed once more on the mortal's transport.

High in the night alongside the Air Ferrets transport, Baxter thought of Willow, grieving the death of her grampa. What gift could he send, to let her know he loved her, that he wasn't dead? How could he help her understand that life does not end?

There was not enough ice, Stormy decided, that she needed to inflate the de-icing boots. She was cautious about them. On one flight she had let the ice build, and when she activated the boots, only half the system inflated. Ice on one wing and not the other. She had made it to Modesto, cargo arrived on time, but the strain of flying an unbalanced freighter had made that a flight she did not want to repeat.

"Seattle Center," she called, "Ferret Three-Five requesting seven thousand, if that's convenient."

Two thousand paws lower would increase outside air temperature by four degrees. For the time being, it would solve the icing problem, put it off till later.

"Roger, Ferret Three-Five, you can expect lower in two minutes."

"We'll expect it in two."

Once she had wondered why pilots say *we* on the radio, even when they fly alone. Me and the airplane, she had answered herself, me and my airplane is *we*.

"Stormy Ferret! It's me, Baxter, I'll be your angel ferret fairy tonight. You'll need to follow my suggestions . . ."

How pleasant it would be, she thought, if the copilot seat were not empty. Another pilot aboard to ease the burden, every half hour or so, share the task of flying by paw. And melt the loneliness. Is there no special ferret I'm destined to meet? Would that be asking too much?

"Interesting that you would mention that," said Baxter to her in his mind. *"As a matter of fact, if you divert to Redding, you'll meet a flier by the name of Strobe . . ."*

But there is no copilot, she told herself sternly, special ferret or otherwise, and whatever must be done to get this cargo to Salinas, I shall do by myself.

Knot my tail! thought Baxter. Why can't she listen? A little practice, they had told him, it's easy to talk to mortals who pay attention. What about when you haven't practiced and she doesn't care?

"Ferret Three-Five," called the Center, "you're cleared to seven thousand paws, pilot's discretion."

"Ferret Three-Five, out of nine for seven thousand."

Stormy reset the failed autopilot altitude display to 7, pressed the control yoke forward and trimmed it to stay. The freighter sank through the night, a thousand paws per minute, swallowed in darkness.

Frightening at first, isolated in a machine that flies, becomes deep easy pleasure with practice. Why do I love it so, she wondered, why is this fascinating? I take off into the weather, sit alone in the sky for hours, no moon, no stars sometimes, I glide down, break out of the clouds, there's the runway ahead, I land. Why does this mean so much to me?

The only others to share her peculiar loves and skills were the ferrets who fly, distinguished more by their silence in the face of visions aloft than their descriptions of what it means, to have wings. Pilots, she had noticed, rarely show their love for the calling in words.

For Stormy, flying was a mystical waterfall, a rippling enchanted mirror through which she passed every day to a different land beyond. One moment a ground creature, surveying her aircraft from a distance, the next she bound her spirit to the spirit of her airplane, the two a different being than either had been before.

"*Attention, Stormy Ferret, attention, Stormy Ferret!*" called Baxter. "*The next suggestion you will hear will be authorized by your guardian angel: You must land at Redding airport. You must change your destination to Redding airport! Over.*"

She could not believe that other ferrets had different loves, and convinced that could only happen because the poor dears hadn't been properly introduced to the air, she resolved to make the introductions herself.

Dawns and sunsets of most every day off, she lifted young ferrets into the cabin of her own polished seaplane. She showed them how she started the engine, how to taxi from shore into the silver-blue lake by her modest home; she let them push the throttle forward, pull the control wheel back and slant them away into the sky.

"*If you hear me, touch your nose,*" called Baxter.

The pilot flew on, paws on the control wheel.

It was as though, unable to hold the beauty of flight within her, Stormy Ferret had to give it away to love it best; unable to see flying's joy mirrored in her own eyes, it pleasured her to watch it in the eyes of others.

Such were her thoughts, as she flew. Part of her mind disciplined, intent on the business of professional flying, another part the dreamer, reliving the sparkle and flash that yesterday's seaplane flight had ignited in little Estrella Luisa Ferret, her first time in the air.

"Time for the ice-light," she thought.

Outside her window, the tiny helicopter leaped aside an instant before the beam lashed out.

"*Thank you,*" said Baxter. "*Please confirm that you can hear me. I'm your angel ferret fairy, and I'm here with you in the night. You may not believe this, but I'm here to help . . .*"

Pilot and aircraft approached the Medford, Oregon, radio beacon, Stormy Ferret holding her SkyFreighter on course, at altitude. Beneath the clouds the foothills of the Siskiyou Mountains reached to the sky, driving moist air aloft where it would freeze at once on any moving surface. At this point, she knew, she would have to climb again, to the minimum airway altitude over the high country.

Desolate land below, she thought, and glanced at the aircraft clock. It was two-fifteen in the morning. "You can do anything with an airplane in perfect safety," her instructor had told her long ago, "until you hit the ground."

Stormy had never hit the ground except for gently, wheels first, on a runway. She was not interested in trying any other way.

A different channel, thought Baxter. She won't take my help, but perhaps she'll help me. "*What gift can I bring to my Willow?*" he called. "*She thinks I've left her. She thinks I'm dead!*"

A flash of old memory, then all at once came to Stormy's mind the helmet and goggles her father had given her when she was a sky-struck kit. He wouldn't take his first airplane ride until he flew with his daughter when she got her Ferret Cub, but one day, no reason except that he loved her, he had brought home a flying helmet and goggles for her, bought for pennies at a used-thing store.

How she had treasured them! Her father's love had transfigured the gift. Helmet and goggles, she had worn them on her first solo flight, kept them still, cherished them now more than ever.

Seattle Center called, breaking the dream. "Ferret Three-Five, you're cleared to one-one thousand, eleven thousand paws crossing the Rogue Valley VOR."

"Ferret Three-Five," she replied, "out of seven thousand for one-one thousand, eleven thousand."

The awkward official wording came when a pilot cleared to descend to one-one thousand paws misunderstood, began descending instead to one thousand, saw mountaintop where he expected sky. Every rule of the air, they say, was born in somebody's mistake.

Now the hard part begins, she thought, now I shall earn my keep. She advanced all throttles for her climb. At that instant the number four engine misfired, its smooth drone broken into irregular trembling. Stormy felt it through the control yoke in her paw, pushed the engine's fuel-mixture lever forward till it smoothed.

"That's not right," she said.

"Hello, Nimble," Baxter called ahead on the fairy communication frequency. "Are we failing her number four engine? I thought we were doing the weather, just the weather. It's a little dangerous, isn't it, to fail her engine up here?"

On the airway south, Nimble and Prestor had done a fine job with the storm. The energy of the Shasta Vortex exploded warm air aloft as from an invisible volcano. When they uncapped the energy of the Tahoe Vortex and turned it north, it was fuel to a fire— lightning-forks everywhere, searing branches ripped and split through a towering electric forest.

"Of course we're not failing her engine, Baxter," Nimble called over the thunders. "And don't you do it. She's going to need all the power she can get!"

Esther, the energy boss, gave a cool warning from her helicopter high over the Sierra as the Yosemite Vortex broke loose. "Attention all angel ferret personnel, we have a force ten burst heading three-five-five, locked on the force eight aloft. All units remain clear until impact." Then, seeing the cloud-fires boiling from the horizon: "*Here she comes, gentlefairies! Half Dome's coming at you!*"

Nimble saw it streaking toward him from the south, an avalanche of tortured air from sea level to nearly eighty thousand paws, twisting rolls of cumulus rimmed in blue fire, tumbling up the airway at the speed of heat. When that force met the storm they had already cooked, over the Siskiyou . . .

He rolled and dived to the north, eyes like dinner plates. "Let's get out of here, Prestor!"

His partner agreed, the two golden machines darting full throttle up the airway toward Stormy's airplane, surfing the shock wave of the monster they had created.

"Baxter!" called Nimble as they flew. "We may have overdone the storm. It's got a long way to go but it's coming awfully fast . . ."

Stormy glanced at the number four fuel-pressure gage. Wavering, just a little. At the number four oil pressure. Was it trembling as well, ever so slightly? She looked to her right, across the flight deck and out the window toward engine number four. No sparks, no fires, nothing out there but darkness.

Airplane crashes never happen by themselves, she knew, they always end a chain of events, and every takeoff of every flight is the beginning of a chain. These were the links that she had accepted:

She had taken off,

she was flying alone,

on instruments,

at night,

with a failed autopilot,

climbing into known icing,

over rugged terrain,

toward uncertain weather.

The next link, she thought:

with an engine that could fail at any time.

It didn't take imagination to finish the accident report: *The pilot was unable to feather the propeller of her failed engine. The aircraft, with a heavy load of ice, lost altitude until it contacted mountainous terrain.*

She double-checked the propeller anti-ice switches *On,* hoped the electrics were warming the heavy blades against the cold ahead.

Everyone knows it's a pilot's job to break chains before crashes can happen, she thought. Yet a professional knows as well that it's her job to fly her cargo south, to get it there by dawn.

Stormy frowned, pulled the control yoke back, the slightest of pressures, and the SkyFreighter began to climb. This leg is the worst. It'll be a while before we're out of the mountains.

It took a minute longer to climb than she had planned, and by the time she leveled, ice was building steadily on the wings. The airspeed was down considerably. When she snapped on the light, she knew what she would see: ice a blanket over the curve of the metal surface, dazzling as angels' wings, a brilliant glare in the night.

The number four engine choked, recovered.

Stormy was a busy ferret in the cockpit, too busy to be frightened. She increased the carburetor heat to all engines and ran it full hot to number four. The engine gasped again and smoothed.

"*Stormy,*" called Baxter. "*Try to hear me. In two minutes . . . well, we're sorry but in two minutes it's going to be a little rough up here. All of us hope you could divert to Redding airport . . .*"

Time to blow the boots, she thought, and pressed the switch to inflate the wing de-ice system. At once, ice like sheets of plate glass exploded from the transport's wings, shattering behind her into the night, dark silver knives spinning away.

If he hadn't already crossed the Rainbow Bridge, the eruption of razor edges through his helicopter would have taken Baxter there in the twitch of a tail. As it was, he dodged by reflex, never quite knowing whether he had missed the explosion or if the glowing daggers had passed harmlessly through the helicopter and his own body.

Everything's okay, he thought, everything's going according to plan. One minute to go.

"Come on, Stormy," the cargo pilot said aloud, "let's settle down. Everything's okay, it's just another flight. This is just one more flight."

Had she been watching with a different sense, she would have seen the rendezvous: her transport lumbering ahead, two angel ferret fairies fleeing backward from their own storm, a runaway freight train the size of Sicily.

Nimble and Prestor turned to join the transport, flew ahead of it by a hundred paws. They would meet the chaos an instant before the SkyFreighter.

Baxter closed on the cockpit, peered through the glass at Stormy Ferret.

She's going to share my Willow's destiny, he thought.

While she watched her flight instruments, he watched her dark eyes, felt her thoughts, the connection between them slowly opening.

"Tell her to hang on," Nimble panted. "We had to do it. What's coming at us, if I say so myself, pretty soon she'll change her mind . . ."

"It's her destiny," said Prestor, his best apology. "She's got to meet Strobe!"

Gently as he could, Baxter flew yet closer to the cockpit, reached for Stormy's mind with his own: Everything's going to be all right. But you must land, you must land at Redding!

Nimble's voice: "Here we go!"

"*Stormy!*" shouted Baxter to the mortal in the cockpit. "*You've got to land!*"

It was like nothing she had ever struck in the air. Stormy flew her SkyFreighter head-on into air torn to tumbling blocks by the updrafts, into Niagaras by the downdrafts, copper lightning forking swords and spears around her, her wings struck once and again, holes melted through metal.

Almost never does a pilot hear thunder in the cockpit; it crashed in now, time and again. So ferociously was her transport shaken by the tempest that the instrument panel shivered to an unrelenting blur.

Had she looked out her window that moment with serene and loving spirit, Stormy would have seen a tiny helicopter yanked upward by the violent air, would have seen it reappear for an instant by her window as the pilot fought for control, then disappear, yanked downward out of sight.

Not expecting angel ferret fairies beside her window, however, she did not turn to look. She gripped the control wheel tightly in her paws, hauling what she could see of the artificial horizon back to what she hoped might be level flight.

The windshield ahead had long since frozen over; she did nothing to clear it, halfway expecting the shaking to crack the ice, the other half expecting the windshield itself to disappear.

She pressed the microphone button on her control yoke, fought to hold it down. Her message sounded like a voice from a paint-shaker: "Seattle Center, Ferret Three-Five. We're picking up a little ice and a bit of a rough ride. Be advised we'd like a lower altitude, soon as that might be convenient for you."

Baxter appeared again by her window, gesturing, pointing. "*Down!*" Then he was hurled away.

Far below, a controller ferret watched his radar screen, responded to her call. "Ferret Three-Five, this is Seattle Center. The best we can give you is one-zero thousand, ten thousand paws, if that would help."

"It would."

"Tell him to warn her!" called Baxter. "Nimble, tell the controller to warn her!"

"Ferret Three-Five," said Seattle Center, "you are cleared pilot's discretion to one-zero thousand, ten thousand paws."

Ten thousand paws was still above the freezing level, the ice building as fast as ever in the storm. With every cycle of the boots, it was as though the SkyFreighter had flown through some vast show window aloft, great shards and fragments shearing away, glittering, falling.

Ten thousand paws was a joke. Stormy could no more hold an altitude in the hurricane than she could read the jackhammer instrument panel.

"Sorry our radar isn't much good for weather, Air Ferret," said the Center, "but it looks something fierce from your position all the way down Victor Two-Three."

She didn't reply. Captain Janine Ferret fought to hold her aircraft on course, ice erupting now and then from her wings, Baxter striving to stay up with her transport, to change the pilot's mind, Nimble and Prestor in their own little helicopters beyond the SkyFreighter's wingtips, hanging on.

Bell-balls a crazed melody, as though the cargo plane had become some mad sleigh bounding out of control on snow boulders ten thousand paws high.

On the transport's unprotected surfaces—the nose cone, the propeller domes, the radio antennas, the tips of the elevators and rudders—ice built unceasingly.

Gradually the tempest gained the upper paw. Stormy gave up her fight to maintain altitude, set herself simply to hold her freighter right-side up, letting the gale hammer-toss her where it would.

She clenched her teeth, one second her body squashed flat, the next, jammed hard against her safety belt, the pilot ignoring part within her that knew she'd had enough, tonight. Had-enough makes no difference. One can't give up. One must fly the aircraft.

Shaken in the skyquake, she thought of her seaplane, safe in the hangar at home; in a few days' time she'd be flying kits again on their first rides. In spite of the battering, as she burst the ice away from her wings yet again, she smiled at that.

Stormy thought for a long moment before calling the Center. It was her habit to understate reports of turbulence and ice, but she couldn't allow another pilot to fly this route unwarned. Any lesser machine than a Ferret SkyFreighter would be torn asunder.

Deciding to call, her paw was jerked from the microphone button. No! Gripping the wheel firmly in both paws, she braced for the updraft that was sure to follow. It did, snapping her head down as it blew the transport straight up.

"Seattle . . ."

For three seconds the sky went flare-white around her, not a bolt of lightning but a sheet of it, blinding. She flew the airplane by feel, waiting for sight to return.

Over the roar of engines and storm, the ferret captain heard a crash in the cargo bay behind her, a freight pallet breaking loose inside the containers. Not good. If a container itself failed in this weather, it would be thrown through the fuselage, and that would be the end.

Mountains slid below, heavy and slow as solid rock. With great difficulty, her paw continually jerked from the selector panel, Stormy changed to the Oakland Center radio frequency, desperate for a warmer, smoother lower altitude.

The radio antennas did not have de-icing boots. She was reminded of this by a call from Center.

"Ferret Three-Five, this is Oakland Center. Be advised there's a new SigMet Alpha One for convec—"

She finished the warning in her mind, guessing that the sudden silence was not a Center radio failure but an iced antenna torn away from her airplane. The radio was dead, not a sound save for a roll of static, white noise matching the wild blizzard outside.

She didn't need a warning to tell her of the SIGnificant

METeorological conditions, as air-talk so delicately put it, for she had no hope of escape. The shortest way out of difficult weather is straight ahead.

The SkyFreighter plowed the whirling air like a tramp steamer through a typhoon at sea, pitching, thudding, rolling in the dark. The pilot switched to the number two radio, unsure how long its antenna would survive the ice.

"Hi, Center, Ferret Three-Five."

"Ferret Three-Five, acknowledge the SigMet."

"We're in the SigMet!" she said, suddenly cross. "We've lost our primary radio antenna; be advised that if we lose the number two, we will proceed as filed to Salinas."

It was standard procedure, but she wanted it on the record. She carried a battery-powered backup radio in her flight bag and thought tonight may be the night that she would need it.

"Roger Three-Five. Salinas weather is wind calm, measured five hundred paws, overcast, light rain, fog . . ."

She nodded. Of course, she thought. Center was hinting that Salinas weather was worse than forecast, that she might divert to an easier landing place.

"*Yes!*" cried Baxter. "*Divert! This will not look good on the accident report, that you continued . . .*"

Even my mind is playing tricks tonight. She clung to the control wheel. Everybody wants me to quit. A grim smile. Not likely.

She chose not to quit, aware that she was adding one more link to her chain: *Pilot declined opportunity of precautionary landing after storm damaged her aircraft.*

The cargo plane skidded and shuddered through a sky blacker and rougher than any Stormy had known, her charts and clipboard thrown across the flight deck, strewn back again. Her course was memorized, but as far as she knew, there was no one else over the Siskiyou tonight, no one so crazy to be here.

Not so, she thought, tightening her shoulder harness as hard as it could go. She gripped the wheel for the next careening blow. Not crazy. Determined.

"Nimble! Prestor!" called Baxter, his voice jagged in the storm.

"She's set her mind, she's going to take it through! *Rougher! More turbulence!*"

Prestor called back, "We're full-out, Baxter! We can't make it any worse!"

Minutes were months. The SkyFreighter flew as if it were a truck run away on great square wheels, off the road, down a mountainside. Stormy's jaw ached from clenching shut, she barely remembered what an altimeter looked like that wasn't blurred just this side of invisible.

In the midst, her artificial-horizon indicator tumbled, the gyro thrown beyond its limits, screaming that the SkyFreighter was upside down and spinning. "No, you don't," said the pilot. She pulled its reset knob; the swirling instrument recovered.

In the cargo compartment, a second pallet failed, and a third. But the pilot was locked on her mission. If she lost the rudder itself, she would still fly her transport straight ahead, she'd steer with the engines, if she had to.

The calm voice of the controller, down in his calm radar room: "Ferret Three-Five, you are cleared to nine thousand paws reaching Shasta Intersection. Say the nature of your weather, please."

"Oakland Center, Ferret Three-Five," she replied, out of breath. "We've got heavy mixed rime and clear icing. And severe to extreme turbulence . . ."

Shasta Intersection was still long minutes to the south, hard granite patiently below, waiting.

In the midst of her struggle, the ferret watched the number four engine gages, blinked quickly to freeze an image of the shuddering dials. Oil pressure was down, all right. Above minimum pressure, it was, but down a needle-width on the instrument. A needle-width low on the oil pressure, that's a whisper to a pilot that something unpleasant is about to happen. A whisper lost. Stormy refused to believe that an engine would fail when so much else was tearing loose.

Almost to Shasta Intersection, Stormy told herself, though it wasn't true.

She groped for the de-ice switch once more, pressed it, and instead of sheets of ice flying away, the de-ice circuit breaker failed.

Fang, she thought, hanging on to the control wheel against the avalanche outside. This is not what we need.

It took a long time to reset the circuit breaker, her paw missing it again and again for the SkyFreighter's bucking and rolling. Then she pressed the de-ice switch, nodded briefly at the welcome shower of ice from the wings. After a few seconds, though, the breaker failed again. Add that to your chain: *de-icing equipment failed.*

"Almost to Shasta," she said aloud.

Ice building, her airplane slowed. The number four engine is ready to fail, she knew, the autopilot's gone, main radio antenna's gone, standby radio is ready to fail, ice-protection system is telling me good-bye. Not many links left, before the crash.

With a minute to go, she pulled the number four throttle back by a quarter.

"Oakland Center," she called. "Ferret Three-Five is Shasta Intersection, out of ten thousand for nine."

There was no answer from Center. Nor did she hear any word from them, second after second.

"Oakland, this is Ferret Three-Five, radio check."

Not a sound.

The number two antenna had failed. She shrugged. No matter. I am out of this to nine thousand.

It was easy to lose the altitude, the frozen transport not much willing to fly.

I should have climbed, she thought. First thing, I saw ice, I should have climbed as high as I could go. Get that outside air temperature colder than twenty below, I could have flown above the ice. She blinked. Wouldn't have worked. Updrafts carry the cold water higher, the icing would have been worse, would have forced me down.

Considering this, down she came, Stormy Ferret in the thundering silence of her transport.

Outside her window, Baxter watched it all slip away. The pilot had made it through the worst the AFF Task Force could throw, she was almost in the clear.

"*Stormy!*" shouted the angel ferret fairy. Then, desperate: "*Janine! For Willow's sake! Land now!*"

She heard the sound of it in her mind, a clear, strange voice. Then she tossed her head, shook the words away.

All at once, as she descended, pandemonium ceased, her square-wheel truck vaulted off its boulder-field mountainside to skate on tilted glass. Ghost-blue light fluttered on the frozen windshield. Gentle, soft. Static-electric fingers pressing the skin of the freighter.

Her snowy face turned cobalt in the light, reflecting the eerie glow through half a paw of ice on the windshield. Any other animal would have burst into tears, grateful for the calm. Stormy sighed happily. What a wonder, she thought, an instrument panel I can see!

Most of the instrument lights had failed, broken glass on the floor of the flight deck. She flew by the dome light, overhead.

The outside air temperature was up to two degrees centigrade. She would not have to climb into the ice again, all the way to Salinas. Reckless, she pressed the wing de-ice switch. Nothing happened but the silent pop of the circuit breaker. The system was lost.

She reached to the floor behind her, where her flight bag had been thrown by the violence. From a zippered pocket, just under the crystal-covered propeller of her first model airplane, she took her pawheld radio, attached its antenna, pressed its tiny speaker under her headphones.

"Hello, Oakland Center, how do you hear Ferret Three-Five?"

"Ferret Three-Five, Oakland Center, we read you four-by-four. Go ahead."

The animal relaxed, letting go tensions she had not known she was holding. "Oakland, Ferret Three-Five is level at nine thousand paws, requesting eight."

As if there had been no problem, as indeed there had not been in the quiet radar rooms of Oakland Center, the voice, affable, was happy to help. "Ferret Three-Five, cleared pilot's discretion to eight thousand paws, Red Bluff altimeter two-nine-five-two."

The captain acknowledged this, eased her transport down into the warmer air. At eight thousand paws, the first sheet of ice ripped away from the wings, its grip melting away. Then, windshield ice broke and disappeared, first a tiny patch, then instantly the whole surface was clear, rain once more spraying the glass.

In the beam of her ice-light, the snow was gone, just raindrops streaking through the dark. She did not notice small helicopters.

"We've failed," said Baxter. "We couldn't stop her. She's going through!"

"Can't win 'em all," said Prestor. "I've seen it before. Sometimes they get so stubborn there's nothing we can do, nothing their guardian angels can do. They're not asking guidance, not their highest right, even. Stormy's decided her destiny is to get her cargo through. Not to meet Strobe, not to change the world."

"We only suggest," said Nimble. "She's the mortal. She decides."

"But my Willow . . ."

"Your grandkit will be all right," said Prestor softly, as though he knew something that Baxter didn't.

Stormy held the number four engine at low cruise. If it could keep running, she'd prefer to have it with her, in case she missed the instrument approach at Salinas.

A new voice on the radio:

"Oakland Center, MusTel Two-Zero. We're abeam Redding, out of seven thousand paws for one-two thousand, twelve thousand, Medford next. And you might advise your southbound aircraft of severe weather through Sacramento."

Stormy blinked, unbelieving. Medford next? This pilot is going to fly through the same sky that shredded my SkyFreighter?

The angel ferret fairies heard the call.

"It's him!" said Baxter. "It's Strobe!"

Stormy waited for the Center to advise MusTel 20 that an Air Ferrets SkyFreighter had reported severe to extreme turbulence, heavy icing, on the route ahead.

They did not. She waited. Had the shift changed at Center, the new controller unaware of her report?

She pressed her microphone button. "Oakland Center, Air Ferret Three-Five with a message for MusTel Two-Zero, if he can read my transmitter."

"MusTel Two-Zero, do you read Air Ferret Three-Five?" said the Center controller. "She's got a message for you."

The voice came back, broken as though the pilot's paw had been pulled from the microphone button. "I read you four square, Air—Air Ferret. Go ahead."

Stormy made it short: "MusTel, Air Ferret's a SkyFreighter southbound on Victor Two-Three. If you intend airway Victor Two-Three to Medford, be advised there's extreme weather on that route. I got heavy ice at one-one thousand, turbulence broke the cargo loose, unable to maintain altitude in the shear."

"Roger, Air Ferret. If you're southbound on Victor Two-Three, you've got a prob—"

Then silence. Had MusTel lost an antenna, too?

Then the same voice, on a different transmitter. Something had happened to his primary radio. "Oakland Center, MusTel Two-Zero's requesting vectors to the back course at Redding. We'll divert to Redding."

"Roger, MusTel. Confirm you're canceling your destination Medford."

"That is affirmative. We are canceling destination Medford, diverting to Redding. We'll let the storm have Victor Two-Three for a while."

"Roger. MusTel Two-Zero, turn right heading one-seven-five, expect the Redding Localizer/DME Back Course Runway One-Six approach, maintain seven thousand paws, expect lower shortly."

The MusTel pilot read back the clearance, a voice remarkably calm, Stormy thought, for somebody turning about in the storm that had just torn pieces off her airplane.

Then he called again. "Center, this is MusTel Two-Zero. You might advise Air Ferret she's got a bit of bad weather down Victor Two-Three southbound. We left a little paint on the hail, back there. I know it's Sacramento, but there's hooks all over my radar, it's a pretty wild ride."

Together the three angel ferret fairies screamed to the pilot, "*Divert, Stormy Ferret! DIVERT NOW!*"

She sighed, listened to the faintest voice of her highest right. To fight through one runaway cold front was noble under the circumstances, she thought. To survive one and immediately take on another, that would not look good on the accident report.

All at once, she was exhausted.

"Hi, Oakland," she called. Words she had never spoken before: "Air Ferret Three-Five, we'll divert. We're canceling our destination Salinas, requesting direct Redding for the Back Course One-Six and a full stop Redding."

"Roger, Three-Five, we have your cancellation Salinas. You're cleared present position direct the Redding VOR, expect the Redding Localizer/DME Back Course Runway One-Six approach, maintain eight thousand paws, lower shortly."

"Three-Five," said Stormy, "present position direct the VOR and the loke-demi Back Course One-Six, maintaining eight."

The fairies were wild with joy, looping and rolling their helicopters around the SkyFreighter, sparkling trails of fairy dust behind, barely missing the spinning propellers.

"Mission accomplished," said Nimble. *"Mission accomplished!"*

Likewise had Gnat's despair been turned to triumph. Flying close formation with Strobe, Goosebeak had failed, had been unable to force the pilot to divert any more than Baxter could convince Stormy. The fairy breathed a prayer of thanks and rightness. The only force that could change these minds was the power of the other mortal's suggestion.

Stormy turned her SkyFreighter toward the Redding Omnirange, found the approach plate, LOC/DME BC RWY 16, the instrument procedure for weather landings, clipped it to her control wheel, gave it a quick study, reading aloud.

"Fly outbound on the zero-four-four degree radial to the Itmor intersection, thence maintain six thousand paws out the three-five-seven degree radial of Red Bluff to the Garsa intersection, thence a descending arc on the Redding beacon to intercept the localizer, thence cross Milar at forty-two hundred paws, cross Entar at two thousand, descend to the missed approach point at nine-two-zero paws to land."

She nodded, remembering. She had flown it before—not the easiest approach in the world, not the most difficult.

Miles ahead of her, the whisper of jet engines behind his flight deck, Strobe Ferret studied the same diagram. At the touch of a button his global positioning system showed the path to follow, outlined headings and altitudes in glowing color on the panel before him. He touched a lighted square on his panel and the autopilot turned the FerrJet to fly the approach on its own.

Soon he was slanting down past Garsa intersection, the Center handing him off: "MusTel Two-Zero, contact Redding Tower intercepting the localizer. Have a good morning."

Strobe wondered, every time a controller spoke them, why the four extra words? Everyone's in charge of their own morning, why would we have a bad one? But those seconds spent on the same words, over and over, they add up. It's a long wait to sunrise, he concluded. The controller's lonely.

The FerrJet sighing down through the arc of the approach, Strobe relaxed in his scarf of midnight and gold stripes, monitoring the autopilot as it intercepted the final approach course. He thought of the weekend ahead, four kits eager to ride in the biplane. Of course they'll need to wash it first, and they'll need to learn the names of all its parts.

In a sudden blink of a world returning, MusTel 20 broke out of the base of the clouds, twin rows of runway lights directly ahead.

With the touch of a paw on the control wheel, Strobe disconnected the autopilot, tilted the jet's nose upward ever so slightly as it descended, let the main wheels chirp on the rain-slick runway, gentled the nosewheel down a few seconds later, pulled the thrust levers into reverse.

"MusTel Two-Zero, turn right at the next intersection," said the ferret controller in the tower. "Say your destination on the airport."

"Transient parking. I'll just be an hour."

"Roger, Two-Zero. Taxi to transient parking, remain this frequency."

"Two-Zero, roger," said Strobe. "May's Diner open?"

"Twenty-four hours, Captain."

Stopped on the parking ramp, MusTelCo's chief pilot pulled the FerrJet's thrust levers back to *Off*, listening to the music of its engines whispering into silence.

He finished shutting down his airplane to the drum of rain on the windshield and fuselage, filled out squares in the aircraft log. Then, removing his headset and midnight-gold scarf, he rose and set a cap of tattered red corduroy upon his head, pulled the earflaps down against the rain outside.

Pressing the *Door-open* switch by the exit, the pilot padded down the stairs, turned as soon as his paws touched the ground and moved the *Door-close* lever up.

He did not notice the golden helicopter hovering at his shoulder as he walked to May's Diner. Nor did he hear Gnat's soft call on the AFF frequency as he entered the restaurant: "*Goosebeak is in the Birdcage, Goosebeak is in the Birdcage . . .*"

At that moment, the nose of the Air Ferrets SkyFreighter broke through the bottom of the clouds, the same patient runway lights stretching ahead.

Stormy double-checked three green lights, landing gear down and locked. What a flight, she thought. Good decision. Bella will be working at the hangar, this hour, she can replace the antenna and take a look at the number four engine. Secure the cargo, a snack at May's, and off to Salinas. I'll be late, but still before dawn.

A second later the tires of the SkyFreighter whispered against the glistening runway, a puff of steam, then spray flying as they touched.

Stormy eased the nosewheel down, moved the flap lever up, and as her airplane slowed, tapped the brakes. Slowing with her, the three angel ferret fairies air-taxied alongside.

"Air Ferret Three-Five, turn right at the next intersection," came the voice from the tower. "You can taxi to transient parking, remain this frequency." A pause, then: "Is that you, Stormy?"

The pilot smiled, considered that at this hour she did not have to stick so close to rules. She pressed the microphone button. "Hi, Bart. I'll taxi to the Air Ferrets hangar, if I can. A little wild weather for you tonight?"

"You're cleared to the Air Ferrets hangar, Stormy," he said. "A little wild? Oh, yes! Without our shields we'd have lost the glass!"

4

T HE THREE ANGEL ferret fairies hovered near the Sky-Freighter's wingtip, resting in the air while Stormy found Bella, mentioned her problems with the transport.

How difficult that was, Baxter thought. The truth is that there's nothing we did to stop her from flying south, past the one who will be the love of her life. Why do mortals so resist their own beautiful destinies? Why couldn't I have whispered, instead of screaming at her? Why couldn't she *listen*?

He wasn't expecting an answer, so new an angel ferret fairy that he had forgotten that life was different on this level. Here, every question asked is answered.

"We can only suggest to our mortals," he heard the voice of his own mind, drawing from a deeper well of knowing. "Sometimes they're distracted by the seems-to-be. Sometimes they forget what good can happen when they listen within."

I used to be distracted, too, Baxter thought. So easy it is to mistake task for purpose.

"All of you working together," the voice went on, "all your powers together, you couldn't force them to choose. But you caught her attention tonight, and Gnat caught Strobe's. They decided on their own."

Baxter's helicopter trembled in the air. How do I know this? Is it you? My own guardian angel still with me, though I'm an angel now, myself?

"With you, and always will be." Baxter listened, filled with delight at what he heard. "The most powerful souls accept the most humble places. You're an angel ferret fairy, you and your flying friends. You're more, as well, you're infinitely more. Keep following your own right, Bax, no matter what, and watch how lovely it is, your life unfolding before you!"

"You'll never leave?"

"You can tune me out. You're always free not to listen. But never can the bond to our highest self be broken."

For the first time, Baxter understood what he had not asked. Even you! he thought, even you have your own guardian angel!

He sensed that the voice was smiling. "Even me."

And your guardian angel?

"She has her guides, too. We all do. We're all guides, one to another, on a thousand different levels. As we are led, so do we lead our own dear others."

But . . .

"Bax. Listen." There was a long moment of quiet, the fairy eager to hear. *"As I am to you, so are you to little Willow."*

Baxter caught his breath and understood. *I'm Willow's guardian angel!* He imagined his own guardian-angel ferret, a creature of glory, eyes of love, fur of pure spun light, sitting alongside him in the helicopter.

You're . . . beautiful!

"So are you, dear Baxter! Have your forgotten? We don't become beautiful as we grow. We realize that we've been beautiful all along."

He blinked, and when he looked again, the angel was gone.

"I'm not gone," said the voice within.

5

Mᴀꜱᴋʟᴇꜱꜱ, ᴇʏᴇꜱ the color of coals, fur white as fine linen, Bella Ferret lifted a new radio antenna in her paw, moved a wheeled scaffold to the SkyFreighter.

"Say, Captain," she called to the pilot in the cargo bay, where Stormy worked to secure a container that had been ripped from its tie-downs, "what does an albino ferret say when you blow in her ear?"

Stormy stopped and leaned out the cargo door, smiling down at her friend. "I don't know, Bella. What does an albino ferret say when you blow in her ear?"

"Thanks for the refill!"

Stormy laughed. "Oh, Bella! Will you ever run out of dumb-albino jokes?"

"I'd doubt that, Cap. I didn't used to could spell *albino*, and now I *are* one!"

Cargo secured, Bella working to replace the antenna, Stormy climbed down the ladder and set off in cap and scarf through the rain toward May's, trailing three tiny helicopters in her wake.

Between the hangar and the diner was parked a sleek FerrJet, royal blues and whites sparkling in the ramp lights, golden *MusTelCo* on the vertical stabilizer. The paint on the leading edge of the wings and tail had been peeled as though sandblasted. A mechanic was inside, nose and whiskers disappeared in the space behind the aft cabin.

That will cost a bit, repainting, she thought, and smiled. What a life Stilton Ferret must lead!

Yet she was just as happy tonight not to be the world's richest ferret. So much happier she was, battling weather and schedules in her airplane than ever she would be, some helpless magnate blown by winds of business and privilege.

She wondered where the pilot had gone, the one who had taken her advice not to continue. Whose advice not to continue she had taken, as well.

"Not here," whispered Baxter, eager to whisk her along. Then he relaxed. I can only suggest.

Off in the limousine to his suite, she guessed.

Not admitting fatigue even to herself, for her flight was not finished, Stormy climbed the three steps to May's, her fur beaded with rain, sparkling like diamonds.

The place was empty, save for May herself at the last booth, a fluffy ball of champagne fur, talking with a shabby-looking ferret in a rag hat.

The owner glanced up when the bell chimed over the door.

"Bless my burrow!" she called. "If it isn't Miss Stormy Ferret herself!"

She didn't notice three golden rotorcraft at the edge of a shared dimension, whirling through the door after Stormy, spiraling down one after another to land by Gnat's helicopter on the tabletop.

Stormy smiled to see her, hugged her old friend. "May! What are you doing here before dawn? Fine restaurants at every airport, she can't afford to sleep?"

The round ferret laughed. "I knew you'd be at Redding tonight, kit, so I rushed on down to fix your breakfast!"

"Oh, May. I didn't know I'd be here myself till Mr. Stilton Ferret out there suggested I'd save some paint if I landed for a bit. Can you imagine a storm like that, a wild storm over *Sacramento*? This is the first time I've ever landed for weather. First time!"

Stormy nodded to the animal in the booth. In front of him was a cup of hot chocolate, a plate of toast and pickles. He nodded back.

It wasn't the ferret that was scruffy, she noticed, it was his hat. Ragged earflaps askew, stitched together in patches, rain-soaked. The creature himself, dark fur touched with silver, was not unattractive.

She smiled. "Nice hat," she said.

"My goodness," said May. "Stormy, don't you know this ferret? Stormy, this is Strobe; Strobe, meet Stormy. Can't believe you haven't met!" She wiped her paws on her apron. "What can I get for you, kit? The usual?"

So his name is Strobe. "Thank you, May," she said. "I'll just be a bit, then I'm off again when the weather moves through."

The proprietress bustled away, a hidden smile, determined to take her time with the order. Bless my burrow. Who would have thought these two had never met?

The other ferret rose. "Would you care to join me, Miss Stormy?"

"Janine's my real name. I don't have the sense to come in out of the rain, so they call me Stormy. Tell me about your hat."

"It would be my pleasure." Is it the raindrop diamonds, Strobe thought, or her dramatic entrance from the night . . . what is it about her? Confidence? Knowing? There's a serenity here. Then he gave up descriptions and accepted that here was the most beautiful animal he had ever seen.

He recovered, not wanting to stare. Thinking fast under pressure was second nature. He glanced at the table-side music box, jotted something on a napkin, turned it over. He dropped a coin in the machine. "You choose," he said.

"Why, thank you, sir." She didn't have to turn the index cards to find her favorite. She pressed button *F* and button *7*. "I love this song."

In the moment before the music began, Strobe turned the napkin. On it was written *F-7*.

Stormy looked up, caught her breath.

The ferret dropped his jaw in a look of wonder, he couldn't believe his own amazing powers. "Why, it's Zsa-Zsa and the Show Ferrets!" he said. "'If I Could Fly.'" Then he smiled, suddenly shy, gave away the secret. "What else would you pick?"

Stormy, charmed, didn't know what to say. It was a lovely ballad, Chloe Ferret's voice a low, haunting chime, Zsa-Zsa and Misty echoing the notes behind. "'Feathers for fur,'" she hummed along, "'wings grown from my shoulders . . .'" He must love it, too.

Strobe considered telling her that his friend Boa, of the Ferret Rescue Service, knew Chloe, that he knew her quite well. Next he thought he might ask if Stormy had heard that humans choose ferret musicians to play backup on fully 80 percent of the music they record in studios. But he remained silent before this radiant new acquaintance, watching her eyes.

"Your hat's been with you for a while," she prompted.

"Oh!" He was caught off balance by her words. He removed it, examined it as though for the first time, set it on the seat beside him. "It's my second hat, actually. I had to retire the first one. It was getting a few too many hours on it."

She raised her eyebrows, interested. Only pilots talk of hours on things.

"You fly, do you?"

He nodded. "Some. I guess you do, too."

"SkyFreighters. For Air Ferrets."

"So you're the freight dog!" he said, one of the few times in his life he spoke before he thought. It's a term of respect, he chafed at himself, she knows that's how I mean it. "There's work for the adventurous. I used to have the courage for that. Long ago."

She liked his manner. "Where did you fly?"

"East Coast, mostly. Rochester–Albany–New Haven. Allentown–Pittsburgh–Chicago . . ."

". . . Cleveland–Erie–Rochester?" she asked.

"Pretty well."

Some of the worst weather in the world. "My hat's off to you, Mr. Strobe."

"Why, thank you. I could use one."

They laughed together.

Unstrapped from their machines, watching now from the table-top, the four angel ferret fairies nudged each other happily.

May brought Stormy's order, warm ferret food and mountain-snow water. "Here you go, darlin'. You enjoy that."

The water glass came down perilously close to Baxter's helicopter, and he pushed his rotorcraft farther down-table, out of the way. The other fairies watched and smiled. Old habits die hard.

Stormy looked up at her friend. "Thanks, May."

"You're a healthy one, I'd guess," said Strobe.

"I wish I could guess the same for you. That's not much nutrition, is it, toast and pickles?"

He touched his plate toward her. "Care for a bite?"

"No thanks. Behind the bell-balls, I've got thirty cases of ferret food aboard for Salinas." She smiled at him. "I believe in my cargo."

The angel ferret fairies looked at each other. "Operation Midnight Snack, mission accomplished," said Gnat. "They're going to love each other." He yawned and stretched. "Congratulations, Nimble. Great work, Prestor. You did a good job, too, Baxter, your first time out. Very good job."

"How about pears?" asked Strobe. There had to be some way to see her again.

"Pears?"

"Ever tasted a Sultana pear?" I could talk with her forever, if only she weren't mid-rush, ready to fly away.

"No, as a matter of fact, I haven't. What's a Sultana pear?"

"Friend of mine has orchards, not far from Medford. Sultanas . . . well, I can't quite describe them. They taste . . . they're firm, sweet, juicy clouds."

She looked at him, startled, pleased at the language. How nice it would be to know this one, she thought, if he weren't waiting on the storm, ready to fly away. "And?" she asked.

"Why, nutritious, of course! Stormy, they tell me that one Sultana has more vitamins than a dozen oranges!"

"They do sound good," she said. "I'd like to try one of those, someday. A firm, sweet, juicy cloud . . ."

"Well," said Gnat. "Very nice. Goosebeak is returning to base."

Nimble and Prestor agreed. The three climbed behind the controls of their helicopters, rotors began to whirl.

"I'll stay awhile," said Baxter. "Stormy might need some help."

Prestor smiled. "She's had all the help she can refuse, tonight. She's flying south, he's flying north, Baxter, but those two are going to be lost in each other all the way home. Stormy's not likely to be an eager listener."

"No matter," said the newest fairy. "I'll fly along with her, anyway."

Stormy glanced out the rain-streaked window into dark. The weather has moved through Redding, soon it will be off the airway, too. She'd give it another few minutes.

"So what do you fly now, Strobe?"

He shrugged. "Gliders. And I've got a little biplane."

At once he became more attractive to her. Gliders? He flies for fun! She widened her eyes, watched him closely. "Oh? And what sort of a biplane?"

The three angel ferret fairies lifted into the air. Baxter remained on the tabletop in front of his machine, watching Stormy, listening to the conversation.

"It's an Ag-Kit," said Strobe.

"You're an ag-pilot, are you? Seeds and plant food, flying under the telephone wires?"

"No. That's like freight-dogging. I did my share of that, down South, till I ran out of courage. Again." He took a sip of chocolate. "I found an old Ag-Kit and converted it to a two-seater. I fly youngsters in it, as much as I can. Their first rides. You can't imagine the sight of those little faces . . . they don't know you're watching them, from the rear cockpit. They look around in the air like they've all of a sudden gone to heaven." At once he thought he had said too much, rearranged his cup and plate. "I enjoy it."

"Let me get this straight," said Stormy. "You removed the seed hopper and you installed a front cockpit in an Ag-Kit biplane, and you take kits up for rides? That's what makes you happy?"

"Don't knock it till you try it, ma'am." How can she not like taking kits for rides? "Some of them, you change their lives! They go on, a few, they learn to fly . . ."

She reached her paw toward his, did not touch. "Strobe, I do the same thing in my seaplane. We're a boat for a while, taxiing on the water, then I let the kits push the throttle forward and away we go into the sky! That's a thrill, they like that."

He cleared his throat. "Well, what do you know . . ." Can it be? She flies because she loves flying, she shares flight with kits, and on top of it all she's so . . . incredibly . . . beautiful?

"I'm pleased to meet you, Strobe."

The way she said that, a hidden door opened to him, swept every possible reply from his mind.

Stormy changed her tone, yet left that inner door open. "And what brings you to Redding at this hour? You're not flying the Ag-Kit in the dark?"

"No," he said, recovering. Her paw had nearly touched his own. "I'm flying a different airplane tonight."

"Oh?"

He pointed out the window.

Gleaming under the ramp lights stood the FerrJet. It was the only aircraft in sight.

"Oh, my," she said. There fell a silence. "You're MusTel Two-Zero."

Stormy wanted to sink through the floor. How could she have been such a fool? You fly, do you? she had asked, of a corporate jet pilot who had more logbooks, probably, than she had hours in the air.

He nodded. "Thanks for the warning about the weather, Stormy."

"*'You fly, do you?'*" she said. "I'm so sorry, Strobe . . ."

"For nothing. The hat is not one that Stilton Ferret recommends for his pilots."

"But the FerrJet . . . you fly over the weather! What were you doing down with us freighters in the storm?"

He shrugged. "Strange thing. I had to fly low. Los Angeles to Medford, the cabin pressure failed just after takeoff. It's the outflow valve stuck open, I'm sure, an easy fix. But the oxygen tank was nearly empty, and without the pressure, of course . . ."

"You couldn't go high." She looked at him, bemused by events. We wouldn't have met.

He smiled at her. "Isn't that odd? If it weren't for an outflow valve and a Sacramento storm hotter than West Pittsburgh, you wouldn't be buying my pickles!"

She lifted her snow water, a toast to him. "If it weren't for your storm, and a bump or two over the Siskiyou, you wouldn't be treating me to breakfast. How I love coincidence. Healthy ferret food at no cost to myself!"

A bump or two? thought Baxter. *A bump or two?*

Strobe didn't raise his voice. "May?" he said. "You wouldn't have a Sultana pear for us, would you?"

She replied from the kitchen pass-through, her nose and whiskers appearing where they were not seen before. "They'll be on the menu when I go upscale, Captain Strobe. May's Airport Diners are for your starving pilots, they're for your good, wholesome airport food without the frills."

"Don't you deserve a frill, May? If I could arrange a box of Sultanas . . . ?"

"You just got your vittles free, kit! And your guest's, as well."

"Thanks, May," he said.

"Thank you, May," said Stormy, and then softly, "Thank you, Strobe."

He could barely speak. "My pleasure," he managed after a while. "So . . . how did you start to fly, Stormy?" He needed to know.

She watched him, considered the lightest of answers—I was unsafe on the ground—decided no.

"I had dreams when I was a kit," she told him. "I stood at the top of a big grassy hillside, then I'd run fast as I could, put my paws into the wind and I flew. It was beautiful, Strobe, looking down at the meadows below, the flowers."

He closed his eyes. "When you learned to fly, you were disappointed, weren't you? Wished you didn't need the airplane because the cockpit was so . . . mechanical . . ."

"Yes! Until after a thousand hours, the mechanical, it . . ." She reached for words. How can I tell him?

"It melts away."

She looked up at him. "It melts away."

"And there you are in the air."

"You dreamed it, too, didn't you? When you were a kit. The hill-side?"

He nodded. He had never told anyone. "I've been looking for it ever since. I'd run down the slope . . ."

She turned away, looked out the window. ". . . and you'd fly . . ."

Then it was quiet, a silence gone as deep and comfortable as though all at once they were old friends.

She spoke at last. "I'm glad we met, Strobe."

He nodded.

Outside, the rain had stopped.

Stormy caught her breath. The time!

"I'd better run." She reached for her scarf and cap. "I need to file a flight plan, be on my way. You know the weather at Salinas— fog by sunrise."

"The ferret food," said Strobe.

She smiled, rising. "It's good for you."

"Bell-balls in heavy weather. Sounds like Santa Ferret's on his way?"

She looked down to him, amused. "Now how would you know that?"

"Allentown to Pittsburgh."

She laughed, wanted to hug her new friend, hold him fast, tell him he was the only one she had ever met . . . She offered her paw instead. "A pleasure to meet you, Captain Strobe. I hope we meet again."

"In better weather." He stood, took her paw in his own, held it longer than ferret custom required.

The two thanked May once again, called good-byes to her, walked together from the diner, Baxter's helicopter darting out the door an instant before it shut. Overhead, the clouds parted, stars peeking down.

May's voice from behind them: "Captain Strobe! Your hat!"

He turned back, retrieved the rag and set it on his head, not bothering to smooth the earflaps into place. They walked in silence, stopped at the FerrJet. "Do you have a minute?" he asked. "Take a look at the flight deck?"

"I'd love to see it sometime. I need to run, now."

"Good-bye, Stormy."

She set off to the Air Ferrets hangar, turned to him, walking backward, laughing. "Captain Strobe, your hat! Unforgettable!"

He smoothed the ragged flaps down over his ears, knew that wouldn't help. "Then don't forget, Janine! Have a good flight . . ."

She waved her paw, disappeared toward the hangar. He watched well after she was gone.

She takes kits for rides. In her seaplane.

He stood in the cold dark.

Whom, have I, just met?

6

THE ANTENNA WAS replaced, the spark plugs changed on the number four engine.

"It ground-checks okay," Bella told the pilot, "but with your permission, Captain, I'd like to look at the magnetos. Could be something worse, you know. Could be a cam ring . . ."

"Gotta get my wheels up, Bella. I'm sure it'll run fine."

"Well, you've got three other big fans out there to keep you cool," the mechanic replied cheerfully. "Oh, Stormy. Speaking of . . . What's the difference between an albino ferret and a ceiling fan?"

On takeoff, not a hundred paws in the air, the number four engine backfired, once, a shower of sparks streaming into the night. Stormy shot a glance to her right, checked the temperatures and pressures shortly before the SkyFreighter was swallowed into the weather.

Refreshed from her stop at Redding, though, she agreed with the mechanic. If she had to shut an engine down, there were three others to fly on. And it was not so far to Salinas.

A ceiling fan turns clockwise. She smiled, in such a glad place of heart that she would have seen Baxter flying at her wingtip, had she turned to look.

⌒

Before dawn she was almost to Salinas, tired as a badger, refreshment worn away, flying by paw through the last of the storm.

"Air Ferret Three-Five, this is Monterey Approach Control, we have you in radar contact. Fly heading two-six-zero for vectors to the Salinas one-zero-seven degree radial. Confirm you have Information Bravo."

The recorded weather still echoed in her headset. "Salinas Airport Information Bravo for ferret aircraft: wind calm, indefinite ceiling overcast at two hundred paws, altimeter two-nine-zero-five, Runway Three-One visual range one thousand eight hundred paws."

This ought to be interesting, thought Baxter, flying close enough now to watch the pilot through her flight deck window. I've never seen an approach to minimums.

"We have Bravo," said Stormy. "We're through eight thousand for five."

"Ferret Three-Five, you're cleared for the Salinas ILS Runway Three-One approach, maintain five thousand paws, present heading to the Salinas one-zero-seven degree radial, heading one-nine-seven degrees to intercept the localizer, contact Salinas tower at the marker."

Stormy suspected that Monterey Approach was betting she'd call again soon, flying her missed approach, diverting to an alternate airport.

That will not happen. The image flashed through her mind: an innocent kit reaching for toast and pickles, instead of proper ferret food this morning. If Salinas has bare minimum visibility, she vowed, we *will* be landing. Then she smiled. Toast and pickles.

At that moment the number four engine coughed, and again. Then it blew up.

As the pilot turned, startled, sparks burst to flame pouring from the cowling, a giant torch directly upon the wing, a fraction of a paw from the SkyFreighter's fuel tank. The fourth fire-suppression handle overhead illuminated, flashing white and red, alarm bell raucous on the flight deck.

With neither word nor change of expression, Stormy Ferret pulled the number four engine fuel selector to *Off*, its propeller lever to *Feather*, tugged its fire-suppression handle, slapped its mixture lever to *Idle-Cutoff*, its magneto switch *Off*.

Flames disappeared in a dense cloud of scarlet powders from the fire bottle, the exploding sounds fell away into the smooth drone of cruise flight, quieter than before, the number four propeller blades slowing, stopping at last, edges to the wind, stark and still in the glare of the right-side ice-light. Black oil streamed from the number four cowling, blown in the wind.

Airspeed sighed away, and the pilot increased the power on the remaining engines to keep her transport in the sky.

Stormy shook her head. Almost made it, she thought, not quite. She took no notice that she was trembling. No time for fear in the air when action's required, she had learned, no need for fear when the action's over.

Outside, Baxter's helicopter darted to the failed engine. Connecting rods had broken inside, he couldn't tell how many, pushing pistons through the top of cylinders, nearly through the engine cowling.

He was spun in dismay. Why was this happening? He had ordered no such failure. Stormy had met her destiny, she had diverted to Redding and found Strobe when otherwise they would have missed. She did not need another test before sunrise.

Stormy turned the SkyFreighter to the new heading, wheeled into a soft right bank as her transport found the final approach course. Then she cleared her mind and forgot all goals but one: tonight she must fly the perfect instrument approach.

Soon she watched the glide-slope needle ease down from the top of the navigation display to the center, held the centerline smoothly. Not long after, blue light flashed on the panel: the Salinas outer marker. She touched her approach timer to Start, checked her altitude against the number on the approach plate, set the flap handle to one-third down, moved the landing gear handle down.

Nothing happened, an empty click from the handle. Of course, she thought. The number four engine drove the aircraft hydraulic pump. No engine, no hydraulic pressure. She would have to pump the wheels down by paw, on the standby system.

The first approach had better be the good one, she told herself. Once lowered by the emergency system, the wheels could not be retracted.

She moved the landing gear hydraulic selector to *Standby*, extended the emergency hydraulic handle and pumped it swiftly with her right paw, holding course and altitude down on the instrument landing system with her left.

After seventy pumps the uplocks released and the landing gear swung down. Swift air rumbled below, whirlwinds pouring around the gear doors as they opened, wheels lowering ponderously, one after another, thumping to lock in place.

"Salinas Tower," she panted, "Ferret Three-Five is the marker inbound on the ILS."

Three green lights glowed to her right. Landing gear is down and locked, she thought, too exhausted to say it aloud.

The captain knew that she should declare an emergency. If she did, the control tower would launch the fire engines, rush special handling for an Air Ferrets airplane.

I do not require special handling, she declared, I can take care of myself.

It was a mistake that she did not tell the tower her airplane was in trouble. If she failed the approach, if she crashed now, she would crash alone in the dark.

With a full load of cargo on board, flying on three engines, landing gear down, flaps down, the SkyFreighter was unable to climb. There would be no missed approach. Stormy's flight hung by the last link of its chain.

"Air Ferret Three-Five, this is Salinas Tower, you are cleared to land. Runway visual range is down to nine hundred paws."

Nine hundred paws was minimum legal visibility for ferret aircraft.

Stormy clicked her microphone button to acknowledge, advanced the power on three engines to hold her descent at five hundred paws per minute. The glide path fell away beneath her, faster than she had expected. She thought of the terrain in the fog below, mountains crowding both sides of her approach.

Stay on that glide path, Stormy, stay on the centerline!

She pulled the throttles back, farther than necessary with a failed engine, and the SkyFreighter sank down to meet the glide path. Power up to hold it.

Baxter was helpless, save to offer a blanket of confidence. "You're a professional pilot, Stormy. You've done this a thousand times before. You can shoot this approach. Piece of cake."

"Five hundred paws above minimums," she said aloud to her flight deck, feeling better without knowing why. "Wheels are down and locked."

Her life was in her paws, in her own skill, a perfect final approach. For the first time in her career, she had to land whether she could see the runway or not.

Landing lights on, a sheet of white, solid fog outside, a hundred paws above minimums.

Fifty paws.

"Good, Stormy," said Baxter. "You're doing fine. You chose this life, you practiced for it. You're a great airplane pilot."

Good Stormy, she told herself, holding the ILS needles nearly centered, nearly a perfect cross on her instrument panel. On centerline, just above glide path . . . She breathed evenly now, a little pressure forward on the wheel to center the needle of the glide slope. Though her heart was racing, her spirit was one with her airplane, smoothly together, easing down, reaching for the earth.

Baxter knew the instant it happened; he sensed it. The Salinas airport had gone to fog, ceiling zero visibility zero. Somehow, he had to open a tunnel in the cloud, let Stormy see to land. She has to see!

The world of mortals is a world of imagination, he had learned, and it changes by thought. He imagined the runway clear, bright moonlight, fog suddenly gone.

Stormy glanced at the altimeter. A white light flashed dit-dit-dit-dit on her instrument panel—the middle marker, her minimum legal altitude, 279 paws above the ground. No runway in sight, said the rules, you must go around and try again or divert to a different airport. Her eyes left the instruments for an instant, quick glance to the windshield. Solid fog. No runway.

Good Stormy, she thought, fly it smooth, fly it so smooth . . .

On centerline, a little high on glide path . . . She eased the throttles back, visualized her wheels gentling down.

That instant, a hundred paws in the air, there came a sudden flicker in the mist, a flash of green threshold lights, black runway and giant white numbers, *31*, thrown against the dark and gone, glare from her landing lights in fog.

"Moonlight, moonlight," Baxter muttered. "No fog. Bright, clear air . . ." Nothing happened.

The ferret brought her three throttles gently back while she sat tall in her seat, looking out the windshield, hoping for a single runway stripe to flash toward her from the fog as the nose of the freighter rose, tires just a few paws above what she hoped was pavement.

So glad I didn't declare the emergency, she thought, for the chance I'd hit a fire truck, in the fog. The glass might as well have been snow, and her eyes flew back to the instrument panel.

"Heading-heading-heading!" she scolded. "Hold that compass straight on, Captain, dead-on, no matter what! Heading, heading!"

Came the chirp of rubber touching pavement, the transport wreathed in mist, runway invisible. The second her nosewheel touched down, the pilot pulled propellers two and three into reverse pitch, steered her heading not a single degree left or right, pressed hard on the SkyFreighter's brake pedals.

Stormy was all tense agony, waiting for the rumble and crash as her plane rolled high-speed off the runway into whatever waited in the dark.

The crash never came. In one long breath, the transport slowed to stop on the Salinas runway, she had not a clue where. From her cockpit, window slid open, engines idling, she could not see the ground.

His helicopter a few paws from Stormy's window, Baxter's eyes were nearly closed, concentrating. "Clear skies, clear tunnel of air opening before us . . ."

It happened. From ground to the top of the rudder, the fog disappeared. Stormy saw wet runway shining under her landing lights, a taxiway not a hundred paws ahead. She pressed the throttles of her inboard engines forward, and the SkyFreighter began to move.

"Ferret Three-Five's clear the runway," she called, "taxi Air Ferrets terminal."

The tower controller could not have seen her landing in the fog. If no one said anything about arriving below minimums, it would all be legal and forgotten.

"Ferret Three-Five, remain this frequency, taxi to the terminal. Did you notice the ceiling when you broke out?"

"Three-Five, sorry I didn't," she said. "How are you doing this morning?"

"We were in solid fog till a second ago. Patchy stuff. It must be better on the runway."

Baxter floated in triumph, hovering above the transport. He had cleared the fog!

The next second, however, the cloud fell as though its strings had been cut. In fluffy darkness, the pilot struggled to hold the secret blue glow from the nearest taxiway marker.

Safe on the ground, the ferret captain went limp with fatigue, caught herself at once.

"Hang on, Stormy," she said aloud. "This flight is not over until you are parked at the terminal. Just a little more, and it's easy . . ."

Taxiing through night fog from one isolated blue light to another, trusting experience to stay on an invisible taxiway is not so easy as her confident words, but no longer did her cargo and her life hang in the balance.

Finally, groping through the dark, the mist thinned and she recognized a vague outline, the Air Ferrets terminal.

The ground-crew ferret saw her, waved two lighted wands, guiding the SkyFreighter that loomed from the cloud to its place by the loading dock.

Hi, Travis, she thought. Earnest and hardworking, the young animal had told her about his flight lessons, promised that one day he would be a cargo pilot, too.

At last he crossed the wands overhead in his paws, X for "stop." Then, happy for Stormy's arrival, he saluted her smartly.

The pilot smiled, set the brakes, touched the bill of her cap in response.

She finished her after-landing checklist, brought the mixture levers of the three remaining engines to *Idle-Cutoff*, thanking them for the power they had given, listened to their low thunder suddenly vanish into the silence of a predawn airport. Cool air washed from the side window onto the flight deck.

"On time!" Travis called up to her.

"Almost," she replied, the word sounding harsh and strange in the quiet.

As she shut down radios and master switch, she heard the ground crew clattering a stairway to the side of the transport, the whine of the main entrance door sliding upward.

"Thank you, all my guardian angels tonight," she said aloud. "I needed you."

Hovering over the ruined engine, Baxter did not catch her comment.

Now Stormy returned her charts and approach plates to her flight bag, reached for the aircraft maintenance log.

Autopilot tugs to right on engaging, then circuit breaker fails system, she wrote in neat, clear letters. *De-icing system overloads with continued use, then circuit breaker fails system when power applied. Multiple lightning strikes. Numerous instrument lights broken in turbulence. Number four engine severe vibration, flame from cowling. Fire suppression activated, engine shut down in flight. Landing gear extended by emergency system.*

She wrote this without distress. Most often the Air Ferrets SkyFreighters were trouble-free. Once in a while, of course, every pilot has her tests.

Loadmaster Max Ferret was first through the entrance door. He turned aft, opened the side cargo doors for the unloading crew, then came forward to stand in the space behind the center console on the flight deck, gave the pilot a long look.

"We had a problem with our number four engine?"

Stormy nodded. "Hi, Max. Just a little." She listened to the whine of a forklift, hoisting the first of the ferret-food containers from the hold. "We may need a new cylinder out there."

"May need," said Max. "May need several. You had to pump the wheels down, I guess?"

She nodded again.

"Weather's a bit low," he said. "We were surprised you made it."

She nodded a third time. "Piece of cake," she added, then smiled. "Too much cake, though, is not good for ferrets."

Finishing her logbook entry, she looked up at him. "Three of the containers broke loose, Max. I tied them back the best I could. Is the cargo safe?"

He touched her shoulder, kidded her gently. "The ferrets in Salinas, Stormy, every one, shall have their proper food this week."

"Not toast and pickles?" she said, a tired smile for her friend.

He looked out the right side-window at the number four engine, blackened from the fire, dripping oil. "Nice job, Captain. Nice job of flying."

She shrugged. "Cargo for Seattle?"

"Portland–Seattle–Coeur d'Alene. Tomorrow midnight."

"Airway Victor Two-Three," she said. "I'll fly it."

She unstrapped her shoulder harness, rose from her seat, stretched luxuriously, then lifted her flight bag and walked to the entrance-door stairway, dawn fog swirling into the airplane.

At the foot of the stairs, waiting patiently, stood a distinguished-looking ferret in a devastated corduroy hat. In his paw a scarlet box, tied with ribbons.

"Hi, Stormy."

"Strobe!"

"Have a good flight?"

She ran down the steps to him, fatigue vanished. "Strobe! How did you . . . ?"

He said nothing.

She looked about, saw the FerrJet parked in the mist near the Air Ferrets terminal.

"Oh. You beat me here. How was your approach?"

"Easy," he said. "Ceiling was five hundred paws when I landed."

"Good."

Strobe watched her. "It was lower for you."

"A bit." She looked up at him, her silver fur and dark eyes the picture of adventures past and yet to come.

"I'd like to hear about that," he said, offering the scarlet box.

She sniffed the wrappings. "Could this be a firm, sweet, juicy cloud?"

"Let's find out."

They walked together toward the terminal.

"Did you say you take *kits* up in your seaplane?" he asked. "All those little paws touching the controls? Why would you do a thing like that?"

The two disappeared toward the terminal, lost in each other, leaving Baxter to hover in the dawn.

Helmet and goggles, Stormy had told him. He couldn't send Willow any but spiritual gifts, yet somehow, there had to be a way to let her know . . .

The ferret fairy tilted his helicopter forward, accelerating, climbing like a homesick angel, high into the sky.

7

THE CLOUD WAS a giant cavern in the air, lit within, a maintenance bay for angel ferret fairy helicopters parked in rows, each to its own numbered spot.

Baxter landed on 35, stepped out to the sound of mechanics' air drills, rivet guns, socket wrenches turning.

The old-timers here knew none of it was necessary, that the helicopters could be maintained by thought alone, that fairies can fly without machines if they wish, yet pilots and mechanics so loved messing with aircraft, as they had when they were mortals, that no one questioned the custom.

"Welcome back," said Geoffrey, the helicopter mechanic, his nose smudged with engine oil. "You're way overdue."

"Sorry."

"No need for that. We haven't worried here for so long I'm afraid we've forgotten how to do it." He looked at the pilot carefully. "Tired?"

Baxter smiled at the joke. "I can be tired if I want to be, Geoff. It hasn't been that long, for me." He yawned, as much for nostalgia's sake as for demonstrating his words.

The mechanic climbed to the rotor hub, happily running the post-flight inspection. "You've lost a safety wire here," he said. "You didn't let your rotor overspeed, did you?"

"I'm not sure. It was a rough flight. There was a lot happening."

"You took your rotor overspeed."

Geoffrey noted it so calmly that Baxter asked, "What's the harm?"

"None. Machines can't be hurt here any more than we can. But I'll replace the rotor."

"If there's no harm . . ."

The mechanic paused his inspection, whiskers askew against the rotor mast, glanced at the angel ferret fairy. "Do you like flying?"

"Of course I like flying. I love flying!"

"Loves don't leave us when we graduate from earth," Geoffrey said. He climbed down from the machine, lifted a pair of diagonal pliers, a socket wrench and a spanner from his toolbox. "You love flying helicopters, we love working on 'em."

They talked for a while as Geoffrey rested the golden blades carefully on rotor stands, clipped safety wire from the attach fittings, removed bolts and laid them carefully on the stand. "She's got a grand transmission," he said, and then in wonder to himself, "the clutch, inside, it's liquid ferret-metal . . ."

After a while Baxter made his way out of the hangar, toward the angel ferret fairy base exchange, thinking of Willow and Daphne.

Dying did not end Baxter's relationship with his mate. In time the two had learned, as had many ferret couples, that death is a doorway, not a wall. Each of them lifting above appearances, mortal and graduate both kept imagination open to messages from the other, trusting that what they imagined was true.

At first it had felt to Daphne as though she were inventing Baxter's voice, making up his messages in her mind. With practice, and with information she couldn't have imagined, she put doubts away.

Ungrieving, then, Daphne had been nearly as excited as Baxter by his choice to become an angel ferret fairy. Already she knew of his mission aloft with Stormy and Strobe; she yearned to hear the outcome.

Sitting relaxed, she found, eyes closed, fur unruffled, she could link her heart with Baxter's. In time it was easy.

She had told him that their eldest grandkit, Budgeron, successful now as a waiter in Manhattan, had begun writing stories. In return she marveled at Baxter's news that Willow, their youngest, would one day become a Teacher.

Little Willow, however, was not so immune as Daphne from distress at her grampa's dying.

The two had been inseparable, his grandkit riding on Baxter's lap while he flew his gyrocopter every sunny day from the field behind her home.

Death is not a wall, Baxter had learned, but grief is. He had been unable to get a single message through to the heartbroken little ferret except in dreams, now and then. Dreams forgotten. How he missed the touch of her bright spirit!

Down the corridors of the base exchange he walked, looking for toys that Willow might treasure. He lingered over a small box of spiritual understanding, decided it might be too grown-up a gift for her, just now.

A stand of colored bottles caught his eye: increased psychic powers. She already has all the psychic powers she needs, he thought. Too many bottles of psychic without that box of understanding, it's a curse, not a blessing.

As he was about to leave, he saw on a counter directly in front of him, a jar of simple cream, clear as air: the ability to see what already exists.

A thrill went through him. Perfect! He caught it up, bought it at once, rushed back to the quarters he had built from thought, a small thatched house on a hill above the river.

Baxter loved the sky, but he loved his little house, too. The view down the deep-grass slope to the meadows below, and the river, one might as well be flying.

He threw himself upon the hammock, closed his eyes, brought a picture of Daphne before his mind. Delicious. All heaven about him, yet to be with his mate as well!

"I knew it was you," she said in her imagination. "I was just about to call."

They talked for a while about the affairs of both worlds. He shared his adventure in the storms, every detail, his lesson from Geoffrey as well, the way our loves remain, one life to the next. In turn she told him of their kits and grandkits, said she was giving special attention to Willow, grieving for her grampa.

"I found a little gift for her," Baxter said, told Daphne of the jar and cream, the way it might let Willow see what was already there, might be a way to cheer her.

The spiritual gift could get through to Daphne easily enough, they decided, wrapped in love. "But how," he asked, "can we get it from you to Willow?"

There was a silence, each of them light as clouds, touching hearts. "It's a cream?"

"Sort of a cream. Like soft, smooth air."

After a moment of reflection: "Why, Bax, that's simple! I'll spread it over something of yours, rub it in, then just hand it to her, let her play!"

"Something of mine?"

"One of your old scarves, she'd love that, or a hat, there's plenty of those . . ."

In a flash, he knew. "Not a hat, Daph. My helmet and goggles! They're on the peg by the door in the garage. Give her my fluffy old flying helmet and goggles!"

"It's got airplane oil on it. Remember the day you were changing the oil in the gyrocopter and Willow asked, 'Grampa, why are you wearing your helmet and goggles to change the oil?'"

He laughed. "All the better! To remember that day, it'll help set her free. Through the goggles, she'll see what's real. Happiness for sorrow, joy for grief. Maybe even her grampa in his helicopter, right there in front of her. I'm tired of her looking through me when I'm with her, Daph, when I'm practically landing on her nose!"

Thus the mystical jar was passed from Baxter to his mate across the border of life in one form and life in another, the two conspiring that it should be soaked and rubbed by paw into the flier's old helmet and goggles and presented to his youngest grandkit.

The gift to see what already exists.

8

T HE SKY ROLLED beneath her. From the front seat of the open-cockpit Ag-Kit, Stormy turned to look back, caught Strobe's eyes watching hers.

Soft-fabric helmets and goggles they wore, and silken scarves whipping in the wind. When she rolled the little biplane inverted once again, she laughed and released the control stick, pressed the interphone button.

"You've got it, Strobe!"

Her joke to him, and a test. Would the owner roll his aircraft back to straight and level or pull the control stick back, split-S down and away? The first would lose no altitude, the second would lose a lot.

"Why, thank you, Stormy!" He spent less than a second to be startled that she would give him the controls while the 'Kit was upside down, held the pressures just as she had left them, added opposite rudder while the machine rolled, smoothly reversed it to bring them back to level flight.

Then Strobe pulled the nose to the noon sun. When the airspeed had fallen nearly to zero, he let go of the controls, Stormy's own medicine back to her. "It's all yours, beautiful!"

"What a mean ferret!" She laughed, taking the stick in her paws, touching it gently forward, pressing full rudder. The plane pivoted weightless, stopped in the air, its nose swiveling slowly to point from straight up to straight down.

Stormy pulled the throttle back, lifted the nose again when speed had returned and rolled the 'Kit once more. "I love your biplane, Captain!"

As they had shared an afternoon flying her seaplane from the sun-blue lake by her home, so they spent an afternoon here together, in the sky with his biplane.

"I have to go, Stormy," he told her after they had landed, the metal of the Ag-Kit's engine ticking softly as it cooled in the hangar.

"Whither bound?" she said, her feelings to herself.

"Florida. I need to take the F-Triple-Seven down there, fly Stilton from Orlando to Melbourne, then to St. Petersburg."

"He needs that huge airliner to fly Orlando–Melbourne–St. Pete? Strobe, he can do that in the helicopter. He can do it in his limousine!"

The pilot grinned. "Sorry," he said. "Stilton's flying from Orlando to Melbourne, Australia, then to St. Petersburg, Russia. The limo would be inconvenient."

Stormy ducked, laughing. "Well, excuse me!"

They were good friends now, Stormy and Strobe. They missed each other when they were apart.

9

SINCE HER GRANDFATHER had died, Willow had worn her wolf hat, as though somehow the fierce thing might protect her from an uncaring world. A snarling gray-flannel wolf head it was, black buttons for eyes, mouth agape. And there inside was little Willow, gazing out, sadly, from behind the wooden fangs.

When Daphne came to visit that Saturday, Willow brightened, a rare sparkle in her eyes.

"Gra'ma!" she called when her father opened the door. She held out her paws to be picked up.

Daphne touched hello to her son Raja, a gentle stroke at the side of his neck. She handed him a box to hold, its wrapping a cloud of helicopters, and swept beyond.

"There's my Willow-tree!"

She scooped her grandkit from the carpet, swung her through the air in a circle, their noses and whiskers nearly touching. Baxter had whirled her so, every visit, and the little one would squeal with glee.

When the turns were finished, Willow nestled on her grandmother's shoulder.

"Where's Grampa?"

"Grampa's with you."

"Grampa?" The kit looked for him, wolf hat turning left and right. She didn't find him, and the sparkle left her eyes.

What a bond, Daphne thought, between those two. She sensed the presence of her mate, felt his excitement at what was to come.

"Willow," she said. "Grampa sent you a present."

The wolf hat turned suddenly toward Daphne, as did Raja, and from the kitchen beyond, his mate, Skye.

"Raj . . ." said Daphne.

Willow's father brought the package, gay-ribboned, set it on the carpet in front of his kit. Her eyes looked to them both, and to her mother. Then she turned and looked behind. Grampa might be hiding.

For a moment she paused, almost as if she sensed the salt-and-pepper of her grandfather's mask, saw his wink to her: Go ahead, Willow, open it! She turned back to the gift.

Holding the box between her paws, she untied the bows, carefully unfolded the paper, raised the lid. Pulling aside the tissue within, she froze, looked to Daphne. Then, delicately, Willow reached inside and lifted the rich old fabric of Baxter's flying helmet, oil-stained, goggles dangling from their strap.

"Grampa . . ." So softly she whispered that no one heard.

She swept the wolf hat from her head, let it fall to the floor.

Refusing help, Willow slipped the helmet about her head and ears, set the goggles on her forehead at the same jaunty angle that Baxter once did, landing his gyrocopter in the meadow.

"Thank you, Gra'ma!"

Then Willow reached up and lowered the goggles over her eyes. Her jaw dropped. "Oh . . ."

At once her face wreathed in smiles. *"Dook-dook!"* she said. "Grampa! *Dook-dook-dook!"*

She leaped up, spread her paws like wings, dashed about the room light as a kitten chasing string. This way she darted, this way and that, dooking for all the world as though she had changed from ferret kit to baby helicopter.

Skye came to stand with Raja and his mother, astonished at what she saw. For so long Willow had been wasting away, drawing back, drawing back. All of a sudden, this.

For Willow, it was no miracle. Grampa couldn't leave her, he loved her too much to leave her, she knew he did. If only she called enough for him, inside, he'd come back.

When she lowered the goggles over her eyes, there he was. There his dear, funny face, merry eyes, mask and whiskers unchanged, Grampa sitting in a shining golden helicopter, rotors turning *dook-dook.*

"Willow!" he called, patting the seat beside him. *"Come fly, Willow!"*

She ran, sprang through the door, threw her arms around his neck. *"Grampa!* You're back!"

"Silly kit," he told her. "I was never gone! I was with you, I'm with you now!"

"I didn't see . . ."

He frowned playfully. "Oh, you didn't see. But what did your heart say?"

"Grampa loves me! He'd never leave!"

"Your heart knows, Willow, *your heart knows!"*

Then off the ground they lifted, bright rotors tilting forward, *dook-dook-dook*, zooming ahead, over the couch, blurring by the bookshelves, by the family picture, all the ferrets together, Willow on Grampa's knee.

Baxter climbed the bright machine straight up, hovered backward, flew sideways, stopped midair to watch Mom and Dad and Gra'ma, tears in their eyes for no reason.

"So much to learn, Willow-tree!"

"Of course, Grampa. I came to teach."

Baxter turned to stare at her, the helicopter nearly colliding with a floor lamp.

"You *know*?"

Watching her kit, Skye reached for Daphne, hugged her as though she would never let her go.

Raja stared at the scene. "Mom, how did you . . . ?"

"Your father thought it might be worth a try. He found it in the angels' store."

Watching Willow come to life, no one found that strange.

The kit slowed her mad flyings, hovered to a stop, staring through the goggles into empty air. Then she turned slowly, till her eyes came to rest upon the grown-ups, watching her. It was as though Willow saw lights of silver and gold about her elders, as though she understood, as though the impossible had become simple.

She lifted the goggles, same easy twist of her paw. "Thank you," she said. "Thank you, Dad and Mom, thank you, Gra'ma. Thank you, Grampa."

You're welcome, they mouthed silently.

Willow nodded. "I'm a Teacher," she said, that little voice. "Can I be a Teacher, Mom?"

There was silence in the room.

"Of course you can be a Teacher, my Willow," said Skye. "If you're chosen, if you love enough, and learn . . ."

"I'm a Teacher."

The kit set off for her room, goggles perched above her eyes. She left the wolf hat on the floor, and never did she wear it again.

10

FROM HIS OFFICE high above Manhattan, at the top of the MusTelCo building, the world's richest ferret tilted in his chair, swiveled it a slow half-turn to look out upon the city.

"You've never asked for anything," he said, a hidden smile for his friend. "As long as we've known each other, Strobe, you've never asked for anything."

The pilot sat opposite, watched the same view. He could see the tips of Stilton's ears over the back of the chair, turned away. "Not true. I ask all the time. I ask for the best airplanes, the best pilots, the best mechanics . . ."

"That's not asking, that's your job. Your life and mine, the life of every ferret who steps aboard a MusTelCo aircraft, we're in your paws. I expect the best."

Stilton turned again, swiveled slowly to face the flier.

Strobe held his gaze. "I'm asking now. The world needs pilots because it needs flight. Kits deserve perspective, and they get that when they fly. The deserve to learn how to command themselves! The biplanes are a long-term investment, Stilton."

"'*Kits for Kits.*" The chairman of the board and chief executive officer lifted a pen, jotted the line on a letterhead notepad. "You propose, all around the country, centers where kits can come, they rebuild old ag-planes, they learn to fly. You encourage other companies to support these centers. And this pays off for us . . . how?"

Strobe smiled. So many times he had heard the question.

"It's the second line, Stilton, that pays off for us: '*Kits for Kits— a MusTelCo Flight Center.* MusTelCo's investing in all those kits who love the sky, investing in the future of us all. MusTelCo's bringing the romance of flight to kits who otherwise . . . MusTelCo equals Romance, Stilton! MusTelCo equals Adventure!"

"And that'll make you happy?"

"No. I'm already happy." Strobe touched his scarf, midnight striped in gold. "I'm asking because it's my highest right, and because it's terrific for the company—not for us to say we're the spirit of the future, but for us to show it!"

Those dark eyes, that mask familiar to ferrets around the world, Stilton watched his friend. "Tell me what Stormy thinks about your plan."

The chief pilot grinned at his boss. "It's her idea. She'll never admit it. 'It's not the one who has the idea that matters—it's the one who makes it happen!'"

The chairman placed the pen softly back in its holder. For so long, they had been friends. Since college, when Strobe left school to begin his life in the air. All this time each had remained without a mate, Strobe for his here-and-gone flying schedule, Stilton isolated at the peak of the glass mountain that was MusTelCo.

Now Strobe has found a mate, thought Stilton. At last. He closed his eyes, glad once again for his friend. How I wish I could do the same. I try to see her, imagine her, but everything's misty.

"Then it's done," said the CEO. "Let's go for the first hundred Ag-Kits. You show me the company's become Adventure and Romance and we'll buy every old crate you can find out there, build 'em back to train your kits. And don't forget the scarf, Strobe, it's part of the program."

Strobe raised a paw to brush the side of his nose. "If I might suggest . . ."

"I agree. No MusTelCo there. Raw silk. Pure white. Every kit who learns to fly. They'll keep it forever, we don't need the logo."

That's how it began. Stormy and Strobe brought together by the thoughtful courtesy of a tempest on the airways; crafty Stilton won over to adventure and romance.

Before long the sound of bright-color biplanes had returned to the air, kits coming home to the high blue land of the sky, noses and whiskers chilled in the dawn, scarves flying. They learned courage and daring and self-reliance, how to navigate among the clouds as well as among the challenges and tests of their lifetimes. They graduated resolved to meet their highest right, to share what they had found, to give back to others the gifts they had themselves been given.

The world changed, by the love of two who loved the sky. By the love of more, counting angel ferret fairies on a dimension just out of sight, arranging coincidence for mortals as they have since beyond remembering.

Once Stormy found Strobe, of course, in time she found young Willow, a Columbine like herself, and a Teacher.

The tale of how they met, and how the world was changed once again, that's another story.